AF506013

Mass Housing in Europe

Mass Housing in Europe

Multiple Faces of Development, Change and Response

Edited by

Rob Rowlands
University of Birmingham, UK

Sako Musterd
University of Amsterdam, The Netherlands

and

Ronald van Kempen
Utrecht University, The Netherlands

palgrave
macmillan

First published 2009 by
PALGRAVE MACMILLAN

Palgrave Macmillan in the UK is an imprint of Macmillan Publishers Limited, registered in England, company number 785998, of Houndmills, Basingstoke, Hampshire RG21 6XS.

Palgrave Macmillan in the US is a division of St Martin's Press LLC, 175 Fifth Avenue, New York, NY 10010.

Palgrave Macmillan is the global academic imprint of the above companies and has companies and representatives throughout the world.

Palgrave® and Macmillan® are registered trademarks in the United States, the United Kingdom, Europe and other countries

ISBN-13: 978-0-230-00730-7   hardback

This book is printed on paper suitable for recycling and made from fully managed and sustained forest sources. Logging, pulping and manufacturing processes are expected to conform to the environmental regulations of the country of origin.

A catalogue record for this book is available from the British Library.

A catalog record for this book is available from the Library of Congress.

10   9   8   7   6   5   4   3   2   1
18   17   16   15   14   13   12   11   10   09

Printed and bound in Great Britain by
CPI Antony Rowe, Chippenham and Eastbourne

Contents

List of Tables

List of Figures

Notes on Contributors

Rob Rowlands is a lecturer at the Centre for Urban and Regional Studies, University of Birmingham. His research is based around housing, with a focus on the meaning and application of the notion of community and its application to public policy. In particular he has researched on public participation in policy development and is interested in the role of 'community' in the development and regeneration of residential areas.

Ronald van Kempen is Professor of Urban Geography at the Urban and Regional Research Centre, University of Utrecht. His current research activities are focused on housing for low-income groups, neighbourhood developments, urban policies and its effects on neighbourhood and their inhabitants, social exclusion, ethnic minorities and urban developments.

Sako Musterd is Professor of Social Geography at the University of Amsterdam, the Netherlands. His current research activities cover regionalisation of cities and spatial segregation and social exclusion in large metropolitan areas in Europe.

Manuel Aalbers is a post-doctoral researcher at the Amsterdam Institute for Metropolitan and International Development Studies.

Ellen van Beckhoven worked at the Faculty of Geosciences of Utrecht University, the Netherlands, within the RESTATE project on the Utrecht case. She now works at the Municipality of Utrecht.

Gideon Bolt is a lecturer at the Faculty of Geosciences of Utrecht University, the Netherlands.

Brechtje van Boxmeer worked for the RESTATE project and researched the Barcelona case.

Karien Dekker is an assistant professor in the Department of Sociology/ICS, Utrecht University.

Wouter P. C. van Gent is a researcher at Amsterdam Institute for Metropolitan and International Development Studies (AMIDSt), University of Amsterdam.

Alan Murie is Emeritus Professor of Urban and Regional Studies at the Centre for Urban and Regional Studies, University of Birmingham.

Richard Sendi is a senior researcher at the Urban Planning Institute of the Republic of Slovenia.

Marcele Trigueiro worked for the RESTATE project and researched the Lyon case.

Maša Filipovič works at the Institute of Social Sciences, University of Ljubljana, Slovenia.

Hanna Szemző works at the Metropolitan Research Institute, Budapest, Hungary.

Preface

Mass housing in Europe has been studied for a long period and the conclusions of this research, though varied, have tended to point to similar conclusions. The development of such housing has been at varying times an innovative solution to housing need, a problematic environment and increasingly areas of new opportunities. Yet while a rich picture of these estates has been established, the importance of patterns of differentiation between mass housing estates has not been sufficiently demonstrated before. This book takes as its core theme this differentiation. It is important to recognise such differentiation to understand the complexity of the problems faced and to develop responses which would harness the resources and opportunities they contain for future development.

We have selected the contributions to this book to provide a rich picture of the diversity of the contexts, problems and possibilities presented by these estates. Each of the chapters makes a unique contribution to the extant debate around pertinent issues. In some cases the contributions add to exisiting evidence and evaluations; in others, new issues and persepctives of mass housing estates are considered and adopted. We feel this book makes a critical and constructive contribution to the challenge of making the existing estates meet the needs of today's population. It also highlights potential challenges to the renewed densified development in Europe, North America and Asia.

The work arises out of a programme financed through the Fifth Framework Programme of the European Union (Cities of Tomorrow). The programme called RESTATE, which stands for Restructuring Large Housing Estates in European Cities, ran from November 2002 to November 2005. It involved ten European countries and the empirical research focused on 29 post-WWII large housing estates in 15 cities. Further information about the project is available from the following website: http://www.restate.geog.uu.nl/. We are grateful to the European Commission for their support in this project.

We extend our thanks to all of the researchers who participated in the RESTATE project. Without their input over the course of the project, this book would not have been possible.

Rob Rowlands
Sako Musterd
Ronald van Kempen

1
Mass Housing Estates on Different Tracks: An Introduction to the Book

Sako Musterd, Ronald van Kempen and Rob Rowlands

Introduction

Differentiation. This is the key concept for addressing issues related to post-WWII large housing estates[1], and therefore the 'red thread' in the chapters of this book. The reason for stating this from the start is that although there have been numerous research experiences about the problems of mass housing estates in Europe, few have sufficiently clarified the difference within and between them. The estates have different characteristics, different inhabitants, different positions in the housing markets, different functions, different judgements by their inhabitants and by 'outsiders'; they are differently located, have different histories and different contexts. All this has contributed to a wide variety of performances by post-WWII housing estates.

This book addresses the varying faces and experiences related to the post-WWII housing estates and aims at contributing to a better understanding of these estates. It is the result of outputs from an EU-financed project called RESTATE, which over a period of four years (2002–5) scrutinised 29 post-WWII housing estates on the basis of a common set of research questions. The story of differentiation begins at the outset of the research. Although these estates were initially selected in order to provide a focus on the presence of 'problems', our collective experience was that this sample was highly differentiated by origin and history, the recent trajectory and problems, their local contexts and their prospects for the future. Estates that were supposed to be some of the most problematic estates of a city did not turn out to be problematic everywhere, nor were they equally problematic when compared to each other. This therefore illustrates the complexity of dynamics within these neighbourhoods. For example, far from their all being neighbourhoods in which people do not want to live, many estates have residents who are highly satisfied with the areas and have no intention of moving out of the estate (Musterd and Van Kempen, 2005). Therefore this book focuses on a cross section of mass public estates in Europe, not just the most problematic but also those that are better functioning and more desirable. Through such an approach we reveal that, by focussing on differences and highlighting characteristics and processes hitherto overlooked or underemphasised in analyses, a better understanding of the functioning of post-WWII housing estates can be developed and so lead to improved responses.

In this edited volume we propose and present a more open view on the attributes of the estates, and of their functioning in a wider housing market context, and try to open existing and new perspectives on these built forms. Our proposition is that a more holistic consideration of the various attributes of these housing estates, both internally and externally focussed, provides a better basis from which to understand how problems may be addressed. To take a more open view on the functioning of housing markets in relation to these estates, their history and the future requires us to make a better connection with their functioning: as places where people live; the ways in which they are governed and managed; how they are used day-to-day; and how they are appreciated by those people who live there. As such, we pay significant attention to the differences that occur in estates that otherwise are assumed to be areas of greater similarity. We suggest that it is the differences in the factors outlined here, rather than physical conditions, location and position of these post-war housing estates alone, that are crucial to the understanding of their functioning.

The common discourse on the development of mass housing estates, especially regarding medium- or high-rise blocks, tends to be rather gloomy and pessimistic in tone, focussed on what has gone wrong rather than the benefits they have provided, and limited in scope of acknowledging the potential for improvement. It is typically focussed on the design and management of the estates, highlighting the physical forms, their large size, their uniformity of design, their construction methods and, increasingly, their mono-tenure (state/public/social renting) as a problem. However, it is an interesting exercise to think about what would have happened if early post-WWII estates had not been developed. Logically, other types of housing and environments would have been the destination of households with children searching for adequate accommodation. What would have happened within these alternative forms of accommodation? It may be assumed that other housing forms would have experienced similar problems, or, in other words, the building form or housing type is not necessarily the cause of an increasing number of problems. There is no scope in this book to explore this in detail, but highlighting it here helps maintain a more balanced perspective on the success and failures of these estates (see for example Forrest, 2009 or Feinstein et al., 2008 for a demonstration of this historical perspective in British council housing).

We should not conclude too rapidly that all estates experience problems or that they experience the same problems. The development of estates in Central and Eastern Europe as well as Southern Europe provides us with different starting points, different problems and challenges, together with the need for different approaches to the solution. Nor should we assume that today's problems stem from one source. Indications from previous research support our assertion that housing form alone is not a key variable in explaining issues such as the satisfaction of the inhabitants. Van Kempen and Musterd (1991) found that the housing market conditions and the initial inhabitants at the time of bringing the estates on the market, appear to have a major impact on the performance of estates; and that small time differences (and adjoining different economic climates, with adjoining different tensions in the housing market) seriously impact on the functioning of estates. They found that estates, which were similar in form and located at almost identical locations, performed very differently according to when they were put on the market.

In this chapter we introduce the critical questions addressed in the book. In the next section of this chapter we will introduce the problems of the mass housing estate: firstly, by critically reviewing the extant literature in the post-WWII housing estate debate; and secondly, reflecting on that literature to re-open the research agenda and policy debates by providing a showcase for alternative interpretations of what is going on in these areas.

Mass housing in European cities: The roots

The stimulus for the development of the need for mass housing estates was diverse. In short, five important processes, common across Europe, jointly impacted on the development of a fairly similar vision of housing in general, and the emergence of large housing estates in particular, throughout Europe in the first two decades after WWII (see also Turkington et al., 2004). These are:

- the deeper housing history, the legacy of the past and the changing supply-demand relationship;

- the need to address and relieve housing demand created through war damage, existing poor housing conditions and increasing population sizes;
- the state's increasing role in housing in many countries in general, and in the funding, ownership and management of many estates in particular;
- a common modernist architectural view on what was regarded as good architecture;
- the common political support for mass housing, in many places delivered by the state, but in some also by the private sector.

These are elaborated in more detail below.

It is the combination of these processes and motives that led to the adoption of one fairly common vision: citizens should be housed and helped to become 'modern' through the application of modern, prefabricated, high-rise housing construction in environments where the functions of life were clearly separated. Residential space was first and foremost regarded as social space, which was also expressed in common spaces in and outside the apartment blocks. Other functions were not allowed to interfere. Shopping should be concentrated in some places on the estate; places of work should be concentrated elsewhere (at the time these places were still often regarded as nuisances, bringing noise and pollution instead of positive implications like the short distance between home and work); and traffic should not hinder daily life and be as separate as possible, which in some cases even resulted in absolute separation of all modes of transport. In this section we will elaborate on the key forces that led to this similar vision.

Deeper historical legacies

The roots of the quantitative housing problems, which seemed so apparent after WWII, can in many parts of Europe be traced back as far as the industrialisation and modernisation of most European cities, mainly in the late nineteenth century. These processes triggered dynamics of rapid urbanisation similar to those that we now see in China's industrialisation and modernisation. A massive population shift, from rural areas to industrial towns and cities, resulted in a huge need for housing in these cities at the time. In most cities this shift was the greatest between 1850 and 1930, though in Southern Europe it gathered pace in the period immediately following WWII. The mainly privately organised housing markets had to respond to the dynamics, and private developers tried to profit from the new demand by building large volumes of housing in new expansions of existing cities.

However, much of the housing developed in the second half of the nineteenth and early decades of the twentieth centuries was not of good quality. As is often the case when processes are carried out at high speed, there were many failures in terms of quality of the dwellings and the neighbourhoods that had developed. Some researchers use concepts like 'revolution building' to express the type of change experienced. In any case, the sub-optimal private housing stock did at least offer shelter for those who went to the cities to find a new job in various manufacturing industries. It also offered moneymaking opportunities to the many private landlords, who were able to ask very high rents.

The quality of the stock that was built in the nineteenth and early twentieth centuries, and the prevailing privately rented tenure structures can be seen as two important factors that formed the basis for housing policies in later eras. Another factor, however, was related to increasing affluence, and population and household developments in the decades to come. Without going into the details of the various demographic processes and 'demographic transitions', improvements in the quality of drinking water and the large-scale implementation of sewage systems impacted greatly on life expectation in the cities in industrialised countries, and subsequently had implications for population growth. From the 1930s onwards, living in the nineteenth-century housing stock started to be regarded as sub-optimal. These conditions provided politicians with an opportunity to change their views on this housing stock, and demolition and slum-clearance entered the vocabulary of urban planning more and more. So, the new contours for a revolutionary intervention in the housing markets were being drawn before WWII.

Housing need

The most immediate problems faced in the post-WWII years were the housing shortages that resulted from a combination of wartime devastation and an unprecedented baby boom. The World War II had, to varying degrees, wreaked significant devastation on the housing stock of many European cities, leading to a large number of households looking for a home. At the same time, two demographic trends added to the pressure of housing need. Firstly, there was a natural increase in national populations. Europe experienced a baby boom, increasing the population at an unexpectedly fast rate. Birth rates in many European countries rose during the immediate post-WWII period, with population increases between 1950 and 1965 ranging from 7 per cent in the UK to 21 per cent in the Netherlands (Eurostat, 2008). In some

European countries, this process was complicated and compounded by new waves of international migration, for example immigration to the UK from the new Commonwealth countries such as India and Pakistan. This increase in population created a natural increase in demand for housing and provided a stimulus for the state to take action to increase supply.

Secondly, the trend towards urbanisation continued. In some countries this trend was at a similar or slower rate than during the war, but it continued to add to pressure on resources and the housing market in urban areas. In other countries, notably in Central and Eastern Europe and in Scandinavia, the process or urbanisation only gathered momentum in the post-WWII years. Whereas countries such as the UK, the Netherlands and Germany had witnessed this process as part of their industrialisation in the late nineteenth and early twentieth centuries, industrialisation was embraced with vigour much later in these other countries.

The increasing urban population was one of the most significant drivers for the development of more housing from the 1950s. Both processes: recovery from WWII and the demographic development created enormous demand for housing. Right after the war, housing shortages well over 10 per cent were not exceptional and many newly formed young couples had to live in their parents' or parents-in-law's house. In 1947 in the Netherlands, for example, 12 per cent of all households lived in the same dwelling as another household; in 1960 this figure had dropped to 7.5 per cent; and in 1970 it was 4.1 per cent (Statistics Netherlands, Census 1947, 1960, 1970).

Therefore the most immediate challenge was to replace the stock that had been lost and ensure a net additional provision which would deliver the necessary response to the increased demand. In order to achieve this, the state was seen as the best vehicle through which to deliver new housing quickly and in a planned, controlled way.

State intervention

Despite this recognised need, the rate of housing production remained very low in the first few years after 1945. While there was a clear consensus of opinion that residential needs should be addressed, two obstacles existed. Firstly, priority was given to the rebuilding of the economic and industrial infrastructure, which required resources and capacity. And secondly, there was concern about the market's ability to deliver the volume of housing required even without these constraints. The housing situation required rapid and co-ordinated intervention.

Scarcity in the housing market could easily result in market processes that could destabilise fragile economies: for example, because of scarcity, house prices might rise too much, resulting in a demand for higher wages from workers, which would raise prices of other goods and services, thus threatening the economic recovery process. This economic imperative was an important reason for state interference, but equally an important driver to search for cheaper ways of realising mass housing projects which underpinned the new vision.

There were also other motives for a more controlled intervention in the housing market to respond to the housing need. As explained earlier, in many countries, there was also a legacy of poor housing from before the war. Earlier attempts to provide public housing had often focussed on the better-off working classes and lower middle classes, and had failed to make a significant impact on the poor housing conditions in inner urban areas for the majority of the working class. A concerted effort to remove slums emerged among policy makers. New mechanics, which were being put in place to meet needs created by war-damage, also offered the opportunity to demolish ('slum clearance) or intensively refurbish ('renovation') large numbers of older dwellings of low housing-quality. A larger role of the state enabled a wider focus on all social groups and fitted into a much wider development of the so-called 'welfare state'. In fact, the post-WWII welfare state already had its roots at the turn of the nineteenth and twentieth centuries, and was further developed by the Beveridge and Marshall reports that appeared during and right after WWII (see Pierson, 1991). The wider state involvement facilitated later plans for huge state-led and subsidised housing programmes, which were, as mentioned, combined with quantity criteria and modernist views on what would be good for people (see also: Harloe, 1995; Balchin, 1996). Massive, publicly financed housing projects were filling urban landscapes at an unprecedented speed. This happened in the UK, France, Sweden, the Netherlands, Belgium, and many other countries. In Eastern European countries, the intensive construction of mass housing continued until the late 1980s (see Turkington et al., 2004; Hamilton et al., 2005) but the rationale for state intervention was somewhat different. Under the socialist systems, state intervention was necessary to implement a command economy. The construction of housing was an essential element of this, both to employ tradesmen in their construction and to house workers for newly developing factories and industries. The large estates also provided a means for the state to exercise control over the general populace (Tosics, 2005).

In Southern European countries, the involvement of the state was somewhat different, with the state acting as a facilitator of development but where the end result was always envisaged as private ownership of housing.

The architect's view: Modernist man

Prior to WWII, modernist architectural ideas were gathering support. Among these, most notable were the ideas of Le Corbusier together with the Bauhaus School in Germany, the Dutch *Nieuwe Bouwen,* and in part encapsulated in the Tudor Walters report in Britain. The challenges presented by the demographic changes and the blank canvases offered by the ravaged housing stock across Europe after 1945 allowed modernist architectural aspirations to be implemented as a widely acceptable solution.

The Charter of Athens prepared by Le Corbusier for the International Congress of Modern Architecture (CIAM) in 1933 set out a modernist view of planning and has since been adopted as the underpinning principles of post-WWII town planning. The Charter was a view of what the city could be and in essence was a response to the urbanisation of the early twentieth century, the needs of an urban population and to accommodate the latest technological advances. It was based on functionality and making the city work better. As stated above, central was the separation of functions: the purpose of residential areas was to provide accommodation for those working in the city but these areas should not be integrated with industry, as was the case in many mixed urban areas of the late nineteenth century. Above all the Charter promoted a technocratic solution to urban problems, focussed on design in solutions, innovation in products and industrial methods of delivery.

From this utopian ideal emerged a mutated form of the modernist vision. The high-rise principles were embraced wholeheartedly by architects, city builders and politicians as the new solution for housing problems in nearly all European countries.

Political support

The political expediency offered by this form of mass housing was one of the main drivers for its adoption across Europe. High-rise housing using prefabricated construction methods enabled a high volume of units to be built while achieving economies of scale, which were perceived as reducing some of the costs to the state of construction, at least in the short term. With this combination it was no surprise that governments supported the high-rise and large-scale solutions. Dunleavy has described this as housing's own technological short cut:

> solutions to a social problem which permit economies of scale to be made in resource allocation for managing the problem, or permit the problem to be tackled more directly.
>
> (Dunleavy, 1981, p. 100)

Governments in many countries were seduced by the lower-cost housing solutions because they helped to control price inflation and thus claims for higher wages, which could undermine export positions. So, state intervention was especially attractive for small countries with a smaller internal market and a greater reliance on exports. In general, it also meant extending the welfare state, in differing degrees, to provide affordable housing either through investment in the housing stock or through household subsidies. In Northern and Western Europe this initially led to greater emphasis being placed on the building of affordable housing, often in the form of social or public rented housing. In Central and Eastern Europe this was seen in the universal state provision of rental housing – the epitome of Nye Bevan's mixed community. In the south of Europe, more mixed housing was envisaged, though with less ongoing state intervention.

The evolution of housing development has been characterised by the same principles. Increasingly, during the inter-war period, housing was separated from other city functions. It was often 'zoned' on large areas of open land to allow the master planning of new settlements within cities. Demolition of existing housing stock was sometimes necessary to facilitate this, but was not the rule. The construction methods led to increases in the number of higher rise developments. In some places, initially the architecture remained surprisingly traditional, as exemplified by the walk-up flats developed in Northern Europe; later, when the elevator became a standard in newly built housing, the scale of the buildings increased substantially.

An early emerging new reality

This model of housing, though visionary and modern in realising a 'new world', continued to reflect the state-led, top-down, paternalistic strategy of provision. Yet at the same time, in many of the national and urban contexts in which the projects were realised, new ideas about good-quality living and about life in general were generated, particularly within local communities. In the aftermath of new waves of protest and political mobilisation, notably in the Prague Spring and later in the 1968 student revolt in Paris, many countries saw the development of population movements, which began to claim a bigger say in what should be done with 'their' neighbourhood and 'their' city. In Western Europe this initially resulted in clashes, both political and physical, between parts of the population, especially between the young and the authorities in power. With time these new movements attained a stronger position in the process, and had a significant impact on the trajectory of policy discourses and political philosophies. Thus social issues have slowly entered the policy arenas and, over the past three decades, have been present in the analysis of, and policy responses to, problems in the housing estates of many Western European cities. This change from authoritarian, top-down governance models to recognising mixed top-down and bottom-up models of development that require negotiation resulted in more demand-driven initiatives and much wider citizen participation. Again, differentiation is a key element of this change – residents' views of the estates and what was needed differed from those of central planners and policymakers. This has had important consequences for the relative position of post-WWII modernist housing in the larger housing markets and, as time has passed, the consequences have been felt more and more. This might also partly explain different experiences in later years.

In Central and Eastern Europe, processes of change after WWII were different from those in other parts of Europe, mainly because different economic paths were followed, or enforced, in these countries. Central and Eastern Europe governments still highly favoured manufacturing industry activities, thus the modernist principles of the new society were maintained and reflected in the production of housing. New estates were partly built to accommodate the workers in the industrial cities, but at the same time were seen as attractive alternatives to the existing housing by a broad range of households. Egalitarianism was a principal guideline in socialist countries (Enyedi, 1996). Partly as a consequence of this, segregation in Central and Eastern European countries before the 1990s was not as characteristic of cities as was the case in Western countries (Smith, 1996; Ruoppila, 2005). Therefore the large housing estates demonstrated a high level of social mix at the estate level, although segregation within the estates was also common (e.g., Dangschat, 1987; Gentile and Sjöberg, 2006). Nor was segregation absent across the city as a whole and a hierarchy of popularity of estates remained (see, e.g., Musil, 1987, Pichler-Milanović, 2001). The more attractive estates have become the concentration areas for high-income populations, creating new patterns of socio-economic segregation (e.g., Szelenyi, 1996; Kovacs, 1998).

The mass housing problematic: The tone of the debate

As a result of the processes sketched out above, many post-WWII housing areas are now characterised by high density housing layouts, often around high-rise structures. They were generally built for low to middle-income households. In the beginning many of the newly built estates were popular among the households who moved there: the dwellings were newer, more spacious and better equipped than their previous dwellings and the areas in which these estates were built were surrounded by large green spaces. They were the vision of the future, modern housing and part of the 'white heat' of progress.

Today these areas are the sustained focus of both policymakers and urban researchers. This attention is understandable in so far as the areas are characterised by a multitude of problems in different spheres, from economic problems of unemployment and inactivity to social problems such as racial tensions and environmental concerns about open spaces and building quality (see, e.g., Murie et al., 2003 and Dekker and Van Kempen, 2004; 2005 for an overview of problematic issues in the post-WWII housing estates; see Chapter 2 for a more elaborate account). However, the process of decline has not been homogeneous across all estates. Whereas some of the estates rapidly began suffering from physical problems due to bad construction, for example the concrete disease characteristic of some Spanish estates, most of the estates, were regarded to be of good quality, particularly those in countries such as France, Sweden and the Netherlands. In Central and Eastern Europe, the post-WWII large housing estates were not generally regarded as bad places to live in, both because they offered superior physical qualities compared to old inner-city housing, which often suffered from damp and lack of amenities, and inner-city neighbourhoods with their lack of space and green areas, and because to a significant extent they were allocated to those who had earned their better quality housing through political patronage.

Physical and design problems of a significant number of housing blocks and estates go hand in hand with a rapidly changing popula-tion, a process widely recognised in Western Europe as residualisation. But the population change is not only a consequence of deteriorat-ing housing stock in the post-WWII areas, but also the result of the increasing availability and accessibility of attractive housing elsewhere in and around the cities. So, for example, families who had first occu-pied the high-rise housing soon preferred single-family houses, espe-cially when raising children. Single and two-person households filled up the vacant dwellings, but not all of them were equally enthusiastic about living in the large-scale environments. Many of them were more interested in inner-city living or, often somewhat later in their life, in more suburban-like environments. High turnover rates resulted more and more in a situation where the vacancies were filled by those who were most in need. Consequently some estates rapidly developed concentrations of relatively poor, low-skilled households characterised by high non-activity rates, rising crime rates, antisocial behaviour, poor health and, in some Western European countries, minority ethnic families.

These problems, although mainly social, may sound familiar to many who were involved in studying and managing post-WWII housing estates and who actually contributed substantially to setting the tone in the debate (see, e.g., Dunleavy, 1981; Prak and Priemus 1984; 1985; Coleman, 1985; Page, 1993; Power, 1997; Evans, 1998). These authors mainly speak about 'problems in post-WWII housing estates' and tend to prefer uniform analyses and uniform policy interventions, while expressing a preference for physical and managerial policies.

For example, Prak and Priemus (1984) developed a model to predict decay in post-WWII high-rise estates. The trigger for this work was the rising level of vacancies within social housing complexes. The emerging model referred to three types of decline: social decline relating to the tenants, financial decline relating to financial management, technical/ physical decline relating to the complex. The suggestion was that these were the types one could think of and would be the starting points for intervention. Others have adopted the idea of a common spiral of decline affecting this generation of estates (e.g., Page, 1993; 1994; Power, 1997). In other accounts of neighbourhood development and decline, similar ideas of common causes and developments can be seen (see Chapter 3 of this volume).

However, while these and similar accounts broadly work with estates that are experiencing a cycle of decay and a large number of vacancies, such models do not tell us why some estates of a similar vintage experience these problems, while others that are almost identical do not (see, e.g., Van Kempen and Musterd, 1991). The housing-decline model does not explain why one complex gets caught up in a downward spiral, while another does not.

Moreover, we must recognise the gradual change and development of both the estates and the population. We should not forget that all over Europe many households still live very comfortably in these post-WWII housing estates (see above). In many cases they have lived there for many years, or even decades, and they remain satisfied with the quality of the dwellings, with the green areas surrounding the blocks of flats, their social contacts, the short distances to shops, the good connection with the city centre, the safety of the area and sometimes even their reputation. Others have lived there for a shorter period of time, and did not or do not plan to stay for a very long period of time; yet many of these households also appear satisfied because the affordable and spacious post-WWII housing estates offered them a good place to stay during a certain phase of their lives. Musterd and Van Kempen (2007) speak about 'springboards': households that start their housing career here but then move on to other housing situations. And similarly urban restructuring activities may already have improved the quality of the buildings and individual dwellings, sometimes very marginally (for example new double glazing), sometimes more radically (for example restructuring the whole floor plan), and sometimes not at all.

An eye for differentiation

It is first important to recognise the difference in the origin, model and development of these estates within Europe. In Western Europe, high-rise estates were built in a relatively short period of time after WWII. The era in which most of the estates were built was also characterised by a population explosion due to the post-WWII baby boom. That implies that initially households with young children found many of these estates an attractive place to live. Gradually, the children became older and these estates became the territory of youth, while the parents automatically also grew older. At the same time, a process of filtering started: many households, who could afford to, moved out; and vacant dwellings filled up with often lower-income households and, especially in Western Europe in the last two or three decades, minority ethnic groups. In the meantime, new and more attractive areas were constructed while existing early post-WWII areas gradually saw their position in the urban hierarchy decline. Problems became manifold: residualisation of the housing stock, vandalism, increasing concentrations of unemployed and welfare dependency, problematic public spaces. These are being tackled through a range and series of interventions over the past 30 years.

However, the origins are different within Europe and the focus of discussion has largely been around North-Western European interpretations of estates. The large housing estates built in Central and

Eastern Europe were constructed slightly later than those in the rest of Europe. They were constructed under state socialist governments which dominated in the post-WWII period up until the end of the 1980s. These governments initially invested in establishing the economy. Attention for the social infrastructure, including housing, tended to come at a slightly later stage. While especially in Western Europe, the construction of high-rise housing more or less stopped in the middle of the 1970s, new high-rise buildings in the Central and Eastern European countries were built until far into the 1990s (see Turkington et al., 2004). Estates in Central and Eastern Europe have very similar physical characteristics compared with Western European estates, although provision for parking space was more limited, green areas were less abundant and provision for communal activities was in some cases more extensive. Problems have only more recently been recognised, following the collapse of communism.

Southern European countries are characterised by estates of which many are in the owner-occupied sector. In general the estates are more luxurious and more popular than the estates found in Eastern Europe. The building of housing was in reaction to the post-war urbanisation and the increasing flow of people from rural areas looking for a place to work and live in expanding urban areas. The new housing estates were located at the periphery but in time these areas were absorbed by the urban sprawl of the main cities and are nowadays integrated in the built environment. Though the state took a lead in the development of this housing, the development was undertaken by private developers and was aimed at owner-occupiers from the outset. Therefore, from the outset, owner occupation was high in these estates, presenting challenges today for low-income homeowners and for the state in consolidating regeneration.

We regard an approach to the estates, which aims to understand the variety of functions performed both within and between the estates, to be potentially more fruitful. Housing is highly segmented and as such highly dependent on context factors, most notable of which are its location and position in the local and regional housing market. Therefore the same estate can perform a different role and meet the needs of a different client group based on its position within a very different housing market. For example, mass housing estates are generally less popular in lower-demand housing market areas but remain more popular in higher-stress housing market areas due to the constraints on the available choices. The outcomes for two such estates are likely to be significantly different, regardless of design or layout.

It is our assertion that some major current debates on post-WWII neighbourhoods suffer from placing too much attention on the built environment, and searching for too uniform solutions. Too frequently housing and the neighbourhood are blamed for the problems experienced. In our view, a closer look at the households themselves may reveal that, in many cases, the roots of the problems (which indeed very often exist because the social housing estates are most attainable and affordable to the households living there) have to be searched for in the sphere of the households operating in a specific geographical and housing context, and not particularly in the sphere of the dwelling or the neighbourhood. This implies that problems *in* estates or neighbourhoods should not always be addressed as problems *of* the estates or neighbourhoods.

In short, a deeper understanding of the development of post-WWII large housing estates is required than that available in the existing literature. This understanding requires the study of well-functioning estates as well as the not-so-well-functioning estates. An approach in which 'differentiation' is used as a central keyword for the description of these estates and the households living there may be more fruitful than an approach in which a 'problem-label' is put on them from the outset. Buildings and dwellings are different and differently located, but even when they look the same from the outside, they may house quite different populations. They may have a completely different function in the local and regional housing market in different countries, even in different cities within one country.

The wide variety of situations that are likely to be encountered in taking this approach presents a series of fundamental questions:

- Firstly, what are the variations between places and what are the changes over time?
- Secondly, as a result of these questions, how can we understand those differences and what are the factors that we need to look at if we want to understand the difference between good and poor functioning of large housing estates?

In order to answer these questions we must consider the real experiences of inhabitants and other important players in functioning post-WWII housing estates and consider the opportunities that are presented in these contexts. These are, by and large, the questions we try to answer in this book and in answering them we hope to provide an insight into more sustainable ways to solve the estate problems.

The research context of the book

The empirical base for this study is a series of studies carried out by a team of researchers in 29 estates in 10 countries[2] across Europe (e.g., Murie et al., 2003; Van Kempen et al., 2005). In the studies the functioning of the estates and the policy responses were the key issues. This research project, called RESTATE, an acronym for Restructuring Large Housing Estates in European Cities: Good Practices and New Visions for Sustainable Neighbourhoods and Cities, took place in the period 2002–5 and was funded by the EU within the Fifth Framework Programme.

This book sets out the various experiences of living in post-WWII large housing estates. This is not done through a list of experiences per individual estate or per city. The book offers chapters in which the different realities in various parts of Europe (West and North, Central and South) are central. All chapters have a central theme, which we consider relevant for the present state and future developments of large post-WWII housing estates. Within each chapter we focus where possible on differentiations between parts of Europe, between cities and even between individual estates. The chapters together form a picture of the essential aspects of large post-WWII housing estates and finally give a good basis for the general and more policy-oriented conclusions we draw in the final chapter of the book.

The structure of the book

The remainder of Part 1 (introduction and theory) of this book consists of two chapters. Chapter 2 is a short introduction in which some basic characteristics of the large post-WWII housing estates across Europe are presented. Chapter 3 focuses on existing theories that have been developed to understand changes in neighbourhoods and estates.

This is followed by Part 2 (key issues on large housing estates) in which five crucial issues are dealt with, in five different chapters. These issues are also central to the debates on post-WWII housing estates. In each of these chapters the differentiation between, and partly also within, the estates is dealt with. We address the satisfaction with the estates, physical aspects of the estates, and social aspects of the estates. An important question is whether we can detect crucial elements that explain different levels of satisfaction, both at the individual level (Chapter 4) and at the estate level (Chapter 5). Are there indications that indeed we should approach the estates with an idea that they are very different and thus require different approaches and interventions, if these are relevant?

In addition, we have to pay attention to the physical elements but in this book we intend to divert from dealing with medium- or high-rise housing as such.. In advanced debates about large housing estates, there is a growing attention to the public space related to the estates. Since this space conditions potential interactions and is highly relevant for feelings of safety, a focus on public space may shed new light on the estates. Good public space may be associated with well-functioning estates, whereas bad public space may be related to bad-functioning estates (Chapter 6). Although most attention by policymakers, housing associations and other owners of large housing estates seems to be on the physical characteristics of the housing stock proper, it is actually the social dimension that ought to be the centre of attention. We go into this dimension in two chapters, one addressing the inequalities and levels of segregation in the estates (Chapter 7); and one focusing on differences between levels of social cohesion and the conditions relevant to them (Chapter 8).

In Part 3 we deal with the policy and participation aspects related to large housing estates (Chapters 9, 10, 11). Chapter 9 addresses the policy interventions. Whereas most of the estates we are dealing with are less than 50 years old, many of them are characterised by major new policy initiatives. Since the dominant problem perception is often associated with a similar image of physical, social and financial problems, there is a tendency to think that similar policy initiatives are appropriate everywhere. This chapter suggests that there are very distinctive issues to be dealt with that require different interventions in different parts of Europe. In Chapter 10 the focus is on local participation. The authors show that the recent intensification of interventions in post-WWII housing estates requires the participation of various actors, such as housing associations and different sectors of local government, but also, crucially, the participation of residents. Increasingly, local participation is regarded as an important condition for successful urban redevelopment. However, the success of local participation partly depends on the organisation of this participation. Here the role of local and national governments appears to be crucial. This is set out in the chapter, which also highlights why participation at the neighbourhood level is organised so differently in the Netherlands, Spain, and Hungary. In Chapter 11 the attention is directed to the initiators, the planners and the developers. The roles of the private and public sector are brought to the fore, while special attention is paid to the interaction between private and public actors.

In Part 4 of the book we present some ideas about future (possible) developments with regard to large housing estates across Europe. We look at the question of whether a new way of looking at the post-WWII housing estates can provide room for a new discourse on that type of housing and whether and how it may impact upon policies and future developments.

Notes

1. We define a large housing estate as a group of buildings that is recognised as a distinct and discrete geographical area, planned by the state or with state support (Power, 1997). Large housing estates have at least 2000 housing units.
2. France, Germany, Hungary, Italy, the Netherlands, Poland, Slovenia, Spain, Sweden, United Kingdom,

References

Balchin, P. (Ed.) (1996) *Housing Policy in Europe*. London: Routledge.

Coleman, A. (1985) *Utopia on Trial: Vision and Reality in Planned Housing*. London: Kings College.

Dangschat, J. (1987) Sociospatial Disparities in a 'Socialist' City: The Case of Warsaw at the End of the 1970s. *International Journal of Urban and Regional Research*, 11 (1), pp. 37–59.

Dekker, K. and Van Kempen, R. (2004) Large Housing Estates in Europe: Current Situation and Developments. *Tijdschrift voor Economische en Sociale Geografie*, 95 (5), pp. 570–7.

Dekker, K. and Van Kempen, R. (2005) Large Housing Estates in Europe: A Contemporary Overview. In: R. Van Kempen, K. Dekker, S. Hall, and I. Tosics (Eds), *Restructuring Large Housing Estates in Europe*, pp 19–46. Bristol: The Policy Press.

Dunleavy, P. (1981) *The Politics of Mass Housing in Britain 1945–1975*. Oxford: Clarendon Press.

Enyedi, G. (1996) Urbanization under Socialism. In: G. Andrusz, M. Harloe and I. Szelenyi (Eds), *Cities after Socialism: Urban and Regional Change and Conflict in Post-Socialist Societies*, pp. 100–18. Oxford: Blackwell.

Eurostat (2008) Population Statistics http://epp.eurostat.ec.europa.eu/pls/portal/url/page/SHARED/PER_POPSOC

Evans, R. (1998) Tackling Deprivation on Social Housing Estates in England: An Assessment of the Housing Plus Approach. *Housing Studies*, 13 (5), pp. 713–726.

Feinstein, L., Lupton, R., Hammond, C., Mujtaba, T., Salter, E. and Sorhaindo, A. (2008) *The Public Value of Social Housing: A Longitudinal Analysis of the Relationship between Housing and Life Chances*. London: The Smith Institute.

Forrest, R (2009) A Privileged State? Council Housing as Social Escalator. In: P. Malpass, and R. Rowlands (Eds) *Housing, Markets and Policy*. London: Routledge.

Gentile, M. and Sjöberg, O. (2006) Intra-Urban Landscapes of Priority: The Soviet legacy. *Europe-Asia Studies*, 58 (5), pp. 701–29.

Hamilton, I., Dimitrovska Andrews, K. and Pichler-Milanović, N. (Eds) (2005) *Transformation of Cities in Central and Eastern Europe. Towards Globalisation*. New York: United Nations University Press.

Harloe, M. (1995) *The People's Home? Social Rented Housing in Europe and America.* Oxford: Blackwell.

Kovacs, Z. (1998) Ghettoization or Gentrification? Post-Socialist Scenarios for Budapest. *Netherlands Journal of Housing and the Built Environment,* 13, pp. 63–81.

Murie, A., Van Kempen, R. and Knorr-Siedow, T. (2003) *Large Housing Estates in Europe: General Developments and Theoretical Backgrounds.* Utrecht: Faculty of Geosciences, Utrecht University.

Musil, J. (1987) Housing Policy and the Social–Spatial Structure of Cities in a Socialist Country: The Example of Prague. *International Journal of Urban and Regional Research,* 11 (1), pp. 27–36.

Musterd, S. and Van Kempen, R. (2005) *Large-Scale Housing Estates in European Cities: Opinions and Prospects of Inhabitants.* Utrecht: Faculty of Geosciences, Utrecht University.

Musterd, S. and Van Kempen, R. (2007) Trapped or on the Springboard? Housing Careers in Large Housing Estates in European cities. *Journal of Urban Affairs,* 29 (3), pp. 311–29.

Page, D. (1993) *Building for Communities.* York: Joseph Rowntree Foundation.

Page, D. (1994) *Developing Communities.* Sutton: Hastoe Housing Association.

Pichler-Milanović, N. (2001) Urban Housing Markets in Central and Eastern Europe: Convergence, Divergence or Policy 'Collapse'. *European Journal of Housing Policy,* 1 (2), pp. 145–87.

Pierson, C. (1991) *Beyond the Welfare State.* Cambridge: Polity Press.

Power A. (1997) *Estates on the Edge: The Social Consequences of Mass Housing in Europe.* London: Macmillan.

Prak, N. L. and Priemus, H. (1984) *Post-War Public Housing in Trouble.* Delft: Delftse Universitaire Pers.

Prak, N. L. and Priemus, H. (1985) A Model for the Analysis of the Decline of Postwar Housing. *The International Journal of Urban and Regional Research,* 10, pp. 1–7.

Ruoppila, S. (2005) Housing Policy and Residential Differentiation in Post-Socialist Tallinn. *European Journal of Housing Policy,* 3 (3), pp. 279–300.

Smith, D. M. (1996) The Socialist City. In: G. Andrusz, M. Harloe and I. Szelenyi (Eds), *Cities after Socialism: Urban and Regional Change and Conflict in Post-Socialist Societies,* pp. 70–99. Oxford: Blackwell.

Statistics Netherlands, *Census 1947, 1960, 1970.*

Szelenyi, I. (1996) Cities under Socialism – and After. In: G. Andrusz, M. Harloe and I. Szelenyi (Eds), *Cities after Socialism: Urban and Regional Change and Conflict in Post-Socialist Societies,* pp. 286–317. Oxford: Blackwell.

Tosics, I (2005) Large Housing Estates in the West and in the East: What can We Learn? Keynote presentation at the RESTATE Conference in Ljubljana, 21 May 2005.

Turkington, R., Van Kempen, R. and Wassenberg, F. (Eds) (2004) *High-Rise Housing in Europe. Current Trends and Future Prospects.* Delft: Delftse Universitaire Pers.

Van Kempen, E. T. and Musterd, S. (1991) High-Rise Housing Reconsidered: Some Research and Policy Implications. *Housing Studies,* 6, pp. 83–95.

Van Kempen, R., Dekker, K., Hall, S. and Tosics, I. (Eds) (2005) *Restructuring Large Housing Estates in Europe.* Bristol: The Policy Press.

2
Theories of Neighbourhood Change and Decline: Their Significance for Post-WWII Large Housing Estates in European Cities

Ellen van Beckhoven, Gideon Bolt and Ronald van Kempen

Introduction

Only since the beginning of the 1990s has research attention for post-WWII large housing areas started systematically. On the one hand, this has to do with the fact that in the 1970s and 1980s the older (pre-war) neighbourhoods in European cities were subject to processes of regeneration and gentrification, which resulted in physical, social and economic improvement of many of these areas. On the other hand, because of the declining physical quality, and because of massive population changes in the post-WWII areas (low-income and often migrant households were forced to migrate to these areas, because the older areas were renovated or gentrified and had become too expensive for them), these parts of the cities underwent radical changes. They very quickly, and sometimes unexpectedly, became the most important housing areas for low-income households in a large number of European cities.

Estates that were built in the first decades after WWII distinguish themselves from areas built in earlier periods, in several ways. First, they are in many cases characterised by a concentration of affordable (social rented) dwellings in multi-family apartment blocks. Second, these blocks are in most cases situated in open and green living environments. Third, they are often more remote from the city centre than the older areas. An important question is whether the specific characteristics of post-WWII large housing estates are related to the occurrence of problems in these neighbourhoods.

In the last two decades, some authors have already focused specifically on the problems and developments of the post-WWII large housing estates (see, e.g. Coleman, 1985; Power, 1997). Many more authors have formulated more general ideas and theories on neighbourhood change and decline in the course of the years. The main aim of this chapter is to find out if and how a number of these existing ideas and theories of neighbourhood change and decline can be used to explain the current changes in post-WWII housing estates in European cities. We will give a critical account of those ideas that are currently still used in explaining neighbourhood change and try to make clear if and how they might be relevant for the post-WWII housing estates. Throughout this chapter we use the definition of neighbourhood change, as used by Temkin and Rohe (1996: 159): 'neighbourhood change encompasses a variety of objectively measurable changes to a neighbourhood's physical and social environment'.

It is not our aim to review *every* model or theory of neighbourhood change. For several reasons some ideas have been left out. There is, for example, no elaborate review of the work of the Chicago School, because this has been done elsewhere (Van Kempen, 2002); only some elements of the human ecologists that are regarded as very central to the developments of post-WWII neighbourhoods are dealt with. Furthermore, processes of gentrification are not dealt with, because they are more typical for older and more central urban neighbourhoods with private ownership and are not so common for post-WWII areas (Hamnett, 2003).

The structure of this chapter is as follows. First, we focus on the literature in which neighbourhood decline is strongly linked to physical processes. This is followed by a section on filtering and neighbourhood life cycle theories. Then we will discuss the literature in which social processes and external factors are brought to the fore as the main explanations of neighbourhood decline. After this we will focus on a model which was specifically designed to explain social rented housing. Subsequently, we will go into the positive and negative aspects of the behavioural approach. In this approach the social fabric is considered to be of influence on whether or not a neighbourhood is confronted with decline. The relevance of the institutional and managerial approach will be discussed in the section just before the conclusions.

Physical processes to explain neighbourhood change and decline

In many explanations of neighbourhood change and decline, physical decay is considered to precede social downgrading. The quality of the housing stock or the design of an estate are seen as explanatory factors for the deterioration of a neighbourhood. Oscar Newman (1972) was among the first to criticise the design of post-WWII high-rise housing estates. He argues that the physical design of these estates discourages collective community actions and therefore makes these neighbourhoods susceptible to crime. He concludes: 'For low-income families with children (…) the high-rise apartment building is to be strictly avoided. Instead, these families should be housed in walk-up buildings no higher than three stories. Entries and vertical and horizontal circulation corridors should be designed so that as few families as possible share a common lobby. This puts a density limit of about fifty units per acre on a housing project composed solely of this housing type' (Newman 1972: 193). The view that density has a negative effect on the social fabric of the neighbourhood was, of course, not new and already formulated by Wirth (1938).

The environmental deterministic position of Newman has also been adopted in Europe. Alice Coleman, for instance, argues in her book *Utopia on Trial* (1985) that the design of high-rise public housing estates is responsible for antisocial behaviour (many of the post-WWII housing estates in Europe contain relatively large numbers of high-rise structures; see Turkington et al., 2004). The work of Anne Power (1997) is less one-sided, but she also stresses the role of physical conditions in fuelling social problems. She describes the problems of post-WWII large housing estates as a vicious circle of design, lettings and social difficulties. The circle starts with signs of physical decay that may cause difficulties with letting. In order to avoid vacancies, this can lead to the acceptance by housing officers of more vulnerable households, which in turn may even worsen the image. A concentration of these kinds of households may make social problems more complex. This is related among others to the interaction of communal design and social conditions of large housing estates. Power illustrates this with the difficulties with which lone parents can be confronted. A mother with a young child in a high-rise flat on an unpopular estate can have great difficulty in creating a secure social environment; the design of the areas, with many common anonymous places may cause a decrease in social control and may result in a situation in which the social and physical environments decay. Simultaneously, a poorly maintained public space is expected to affect their level of pride in the estate. As a result, the mother and her child may reject the social as well as the physical environment, and may withdraw or move. This withdrawal strengthens the process of physical decay, which completes the circle (Power, 1997: 101–2). As already implied, the question is whether the importance Power gives to physical issues is legitimate. In our opinion social aspects are much more relevant. We will come back to this later in this chapter.

Filtering and neighbourhood life cycle

The focus on physical processes that characterises most accounts of post-WWII housing estates is also apparent in more general theories about neighbourhood dynamics. In many of these theories, the concept of filtering has a central place. The general idea is that as dwelling units grow old, they tend to depreciate. This is not only due to physical deterioration or obsolescence, but also to relative depreciation. Even if neighbourhoods remain in good condition, they will have more and more trouble over time competing with new neighbourhoods that are usually added to the market at the top of the quality and price hierarchy and more geared to contemporary housing preferences. Therefore, according to this theory, dwellings and neighbourhoods inevitably filter from higher-status to lower-status populations. The construction of new homes starts a chain of residential moves. This creates the filtering of households up the housing scale and consequently the filtering of dwellings (i.e. estates) down the social scale (Myers, 1990).

The concept of filtering dates back to the work of Hoyt (1939), one of the proponents of the Chicago School and is also central in life cycle theories that developed later. The notion of a neighbourhood life cycle implies that the development of a neighbourhood follows a fixed path of stages. Hoover and Vernon (1959), for instance, distinguish between five different stages: subdivision and build-up, transition into intensive land use, conversion and downgrading, thinning out, and finally renewal and gentrification (see, e.g., Birch, 1971; Bourne, 1981).

The neighbourhood life cycle theories can be criticised for several reasons. First of all, neighbourhoods do not all follow the same trajectory automatically. Even estates that are very similar to each other in terms of design and management may perform very differently in the course of years (Goetze, 1979). With respect to post-WWII housing, for example, not every estate is subject to the same level of decay (Kennett and Forrest, 2003). This is illustrated in the research of Van Kempen and Musterd (1991) who compared several ill-functioning *and* well-functioning post-WWII housing estates in the Netherlands. The differences between these estates could not be attributed to physical and management characteristics. Instead, the population composition seemed to be crucial for the performance of the high-rise blocks. This suggests that social processes play a more important role in the decay of these estates than physical processes. In more general terms, many post-WWII estates in European cities have been functioning very well on the housing market for decades. In most cases, problems have started to occur only in the past 15 years.

This can definitely not be attributed to a physical process of downgrading, but should be seen in the context of a change, sometimes radical, in population, which in its turn caused a number of processes related to social downgrading, such as less social control, less social cohesion and more vandalism and criminality (see also Murie et al., 2003).

Another critical comment on neighbourhood life cycle theories is that it is not always the case that new housing estates are by definition better than old housing estates. In fact, some post-WWII housing estates were already problematic from the outset. The initial quality of the housing stock can be a forceful determinant of its later situation, physically as well as socially (Prak and Priemus, 1986). No matter what you do, if the initial quality is low, deterioration may start quickly and continue rapidly. Post-WWII housing estates have not always been built to very high standards. This is related to the fact that building in large quantities was more important than building high-quality dwellings, especially in the early post-WWII period, when housing shortages were high. An example where the result of bad construction became sadly visible was at Ronan Point in London; a block of flats that was built in 1968, which partly collapsed in the same year due to a gas explosion (see, e.g., Woolley, 1985). The problematic start of some housing estates was in several cases not only due to the bad quality and design of the building, but also to the fact that they were perceived as housing 'undeserving poor' from slum neighbourhoods (Murie et al., 2003). This is again a clear indication that social processes are more important than physical issues.

Once a bad reputation of a neighbourhood is fixed rather early in the course of its history, it is very hard to get rid of that stigma (Hastings and Dean, 2002). An example of a neighbourhood with a spoiled reputation from the beginning is the Gorbals in Glasgow. This originally was a high-rise neighbourhood that was built in the late 1950s at the site where a disreputable slum was cleared. Due to its location and the composition of the population (many former slum inhabitants) the Gorbals could not get rid of its stigma. Combined with the bad quality of the design (from the beginning there were problems with dampness and draughts) some flats were demolished just 30 years after they were built (McArthur, 2000). However, the example of the Gorbals also shows that the course of a stigmatised neighbourhood is not fully determined by its history. Recent urban renewal seems to have turned around the process of decay. Gradually the area has been converted from a high-rise neighbourhood to one with much more mixed housing and a much more mixed population.

A third objection to neighbourhood life cycle models has to do with the concept of life cycle itself. Myers (1990) has stated that *life cycle effects* are often confused with *cohort differences*. Life cycle effects involve changes occurring to dwellings as they age (such as physical deterioration, relative depreciation, or ownership transition). Cohort differences, however, describe 'differences in the rates at which different vintage dwellings are filtering' (Myers, 1990: 281). For example, how much have the 1950s houses changed with respect to their population in their first 30 years (1950–80) compared with 1960s houses in their first 30 years (1960–90)? Cohort effects play an important role in the field of housing as each era is characterised by a different volume and style of construction. For instance, large housing estates built in the 1960s are, much more than neighbourhoods built in other periods, characterised by a strict separation of functions and a high proportion of high-rise blocks. Because of these characteristics, their condition after, say, 50 years will be different than the condition of the areas built in the 1950s after 50 years.

Despite these critical comments, we do believe that filtering and life cycle theories have a number of useful elements for the explanation of developments in post-WWII estates. It turns out, for example, that in many post-WWII large housing estates high-income households are indeed replaced by lower-income households. People often leave because of attractive (newly built) dwellings elsewhere (filtering). Although many large housing estates were built in the 1960s, and the housing stock is therefore not yet that old, competition from new building areas is considered to be a problem for many of these estates. In the case of the Bijlmermeer estate in Amsterdam, problems with vacancies were present from the beginning. Unpopularity of multi-family dwellings combined with the supply of other dwellings elsewhere (i.e. single-family dwellings), did not make the area an attractive place to live (see Aalbers et al., 2003). A neighbourhood's position on the local housing market, and changes within this position, can therefore influence the situation within a particular neighbourhood (see, e.g., Brama and Andersson, 2005).

Several points of criticisms with regard to the theories that are dealt with hitherto are encountered in the model of Grigsby and colleagues (1987). They focus more on social processes rather than relying solely on physical aspects to explain neighbourhood decline and, moreover, they do not believe in a fixed linear development of neighbourhoods. Furthermore, and unlike many others, they are not blind to exogenous factors (or, when changes in external factors in the course of time are considered, 'period effects' in the terminology of Myers) that have an influence on neighbourhood decline. In the next section we will focus on these external factors, as well as on the social processes that explain neighbourhood decline.

Social processes and external factors explaining neighbourhood change and decline

William Grigsby and his colleagues have criticised the widely held belief that the ageing of the housing stock is the primary cause of neighbourhood decline. One of their starting points is that the lifespan of dwellings and neighbourhoods does not have a fixed period: houses and neighbourhoods can be almost endlessly renewed (Grigsby et al., 1987; see also Megbolugbe et al., 1996). Furthermore, they assume that succession is a constant factor in urban growth and likewise in neighbourhood change. Like filtering, the concepts of invasion and succession were also adopted from the human ecologists in Chicago (Burgess, 1925; Park, 1925). Succession is very much related to the filtering concept of Hoyt (1939), but the difference is that Hoyt is more focussed on the supply side of the housing market, arguing that new housing developments bring about the filtering-down of dwellings, while Burgess (1925) focuses more on the demand side. To him, invasion is the mechanism that leads to filtering-down.

Grigsby and his co-authors (1987) define neighbourhood succession as: 'a shift in the income profile of occupants of a geographically defined neighbourhood of dwelling units' (Grigsby et al., 1987: 27). Related to this, they see physical deterioration as a consequence rather than a cause of population succession. In their view, 'given the existence of needy households who are spatially concentrated, physically deteriorating neighbourhoods are inevitable' (Grigsby et al., 1987: 58).

To demonstrate how this works, they have aimed to capture the process of neighbourhood change in an all-embracing model in which several variables involved in neighbourhood succession are linked. They depart from the thought that an urban housing market consists of sub-markets in which social and economic features are differently influenced by factors that are exogenous as well as endogenous to the neighbourhood. According to the model, neighbourhood change starts with *changes in social and economic variables*, such as the number and composition of households, the relative cost of housing, and public-sector policies. These macro-factors cause households, who act directly or indirectly through *a system of housing suppliers and market intermediaries* (such as owners, developers, builders and lenders), to make *different maintenance and moving decisions*, which alters the *characteristics of dwellings as well as neighbourhoods*. These alterations may in turn cause a second-round perturbation as they may feed back to changes in social and economic variables, or to changes in the system of housing suppliers and market intermediaries, or to maintenance and moving decisions (Grigsby et al., 1987: 33).

Probably the most significant contribution of the model is the idea that neighbourhood change is approached from a broad view. While the tendency in most literature about neighbourhood decay is to look for explanations within the dynamics of a neighbourhood (Murie, 2005), Grigsby and colleagues put emphasis on external factors, such as demographic changes, economic changes, governmental interventions and the site or location, that have an effect on neighbourhoods. Also, there is an increasing attention paid to the importance of external factors on the national and even international level. One of the most prominent for explaining developments on a macro-scale is the process of globalisation. Globalisation has many features, such as the global integration of economic activities, the global movement of capital, international migration of people, and the changing values and norms that spread among various parts of the world (Marcuse and Van Kempen, 2000). Numerous studies have implied that the process (or at least aspects) of globalisation has seriously affected urban development, including processes of neighbourhood change and decline (see: Castells, 2000; Murie et al., 2003 for an overview). At the same time it should be noted that globalisation is just one major explanatory factor on the macro-scale. Processes of demographic change (e.g. the increasing number of small households and the declining number of family households), processes of racism and discrimination (impeding minority ethnic groups from living in some neighbourhoods) and the changing role of the public sector – in Western European welfare states as well as in Central and Eastern European former socialist countries – are a few crucial developments that influence neighbourhood change (see, e.g., Marcuse and Van Kempen, 2000; Murie et al., 2003). The same holds for some more specific institutional issues; these are dealt with later in this chapter.

The basic idea then is that in order to explain changes on the neighbourhood level (e.g. population change in a post-WWII estate), structures and developments (with respect to the economy, demography, housing market, politics, socio-cultural trends) on other spatial levels should be incorporated. For instance, high pressure on the local housing market makes it less likely that a neighbourhood is subject to decline than in a situation of low pressure (Van Kempen and Musterd, 1991).

This does not mean that Grigsby and colleagues see endogenous developments as insignificant: these developments may reinforce the direction of change generated by the operation of exogenous forces.

The change of income profile (succession) is the endogenous factor that gets most attention in the work of Grigsby et al. (1987). Like Burgess, Grigsby and colleagues emphasise the role of the concentration of poverty in the decline of neighbourhoods (see also e.g., Evans, 1998; Lupton, 2004). This is relevant for the situation in post-WWII housing estates, particularly in Western Europe. Many of these areas have been increasingly confronted with problems that are associated with a population more and more characterised by the unemployed, people on workmen's benefit, lone-parent households, mentally ill, drug addicts and people who exhibit asocial behaviour (see, e.g., Aalbers et al., 2003; Andersson et al., 2003). Such a concentration of poverty may lead to an unravelling of social fabric in a neighbourhood and to a destruction of the residential, educational, and employment environment (Downs, 1973; cited in Grigsby et al., 1987). There is an abundance of literature about the negative effects of poverty concentrations (see, e.g., Galster, 2005; Atkinson and Kintrea, 2000), but within this literature few authors pay attention to the implications for neighbourhood decline.

Related to this discussion is the possible importance of a social mix or the effect of spatial concentrations on developments in neighbourhoods in general and social mobility more specifically. The question often is: do spatial concentrations of poverty or of minority ethnic groups negatively influence social outcomes? Especially in European contexts, the answer to this question is, maybe surprisingly, that spatial concentrations have some importance, but not much. Earnings of adults, for example, can be explained more by personal variables (such as education) than by neighbourhood characteristics (see, e.g., Anderson et al., 2007; Musterd et al., 2008; Galster et al., 2008).

Also Massey and Denton (1993) focus on the possible effects of segregation and concentration. In their book *American Apartheid*, they describe the deleterious effect of residential segregation. In a poor neighbourhood, it is likely that some owners and landlords cut back on their maintenance expenditure. The presence of even a small number of dilapidated dwellings is taken by other property owners as a sign that the neighbourhood is deteriorating, which implies that they have little incentive to invest in maintenance and improvement. The pattern may become self-reinforcing (see, e.g., Galster, 2000). According to the 'broken windows' theory of urban decay (Wilson and Kelling, 1982), minor forms of public disorder (graffiti, garbage, broken windows) attract criminal offenders, which leads to a downward spiral of decay.

Interestingly, Sampson and Raudenbush found that the perception of disorder is much less influenced by actual observed disorder than by the population composition in terms of socio-economic status and, especially, ethnicity (Sampson and Raudenbush, 2004: 319). This association between the perception of disorder and population composition is also found in a research in post-WWII housing estates. Dekker and Bolt (2005) carried out a survey in two Dutch post-WWII neighbourhoods (one in The Hague, the other in Utrecht; both areas constructed mainly in the 1950s). They found that many respondents complained that their neighbourhood was deteriorating and that this appeared to be highly related to the (perceived) increase of the number of ethnic minorities, in this case mainly Turks and Moroccans (Dekker and Bolt, 2005). Population change thus seems again a crucial issue.

Other studies of post-WWII housing estates have looked at the relation between objective indicators of decline and population composition. For example the Märkisches Viertel estate in Berlin (constructed between 1960 and 1975) seems to follow the classical *invasion* and *succession* trajectory. Like in many other post-WWII housing estates, lower-income households have indeed replaced high-income households. Due to technical deficiencies and an influx of households that faced economic difficulties as well as families with a Turkish background, the image of the estate decreased. This negative image caused many households who could afford to do so to move out (Knorr-Siedow and Droste, 2003: 77).

From this brief overview it may be concluded that the central role that Grigsby et al. attribute to changes in population composition, and especially to the concentrations of poor households, is also supported by other research into neighbourhood decay. However, while Grigsby and colleagues (1987) mainly focus on changes in the income profile of neighbourhoods, there are numerous indications that changes in the ethnic composition of a neighbourhood play a very significant role in neighbourhood decay. At the same time, it should also be noted that the moving away of white families definitely does not always have to do with ethnic or racial change; in some cases they simply translate social mobility into geographical mobility (Molotch, 1972; see also Varady, 1979).

Although the work of Grigsby and colleagues addresses some of the shortcomings of the more traditional life cycle models, their model does not suffice to explain the neighbourhood changes in post-WWII housing estates. We focus on two points of critique.

The first point of critique is related to the fact that the powers behind neighbourhood change are seen as impersonal. Although, for future developments of metropolitan areas, they consider the influence of residents' attitudes towards fellow residents, they mention this social variable without taking into account its ability to influence the situation in a neighbourhood; they do not consider residents' potential to develop successful strategies in order to continue stability within their neighbourhood or to resist changes (e.g. by formal collective action or by informal social behaviour). Apparently, Grigsby and colleagues consider that residents react to particular developments without being able to influence these developments. The behavioural approach, on the contrary, does focus on collective efforts to maintain stability. This approach is the subject of a later section of this chapter.

The relevance of the model by Grigsby et al. for the developments on European post-WWII housing estates can also be questioned on the fact that it refers, like the ecological and neighbourhood life cycle models, to neighbourhoods that are predominantly private sector. The American context, on which the work by Grigsby and colleagues is based, is entirely different from the context of Western European (and in the past also Eastern European) post-WWII housing estates, where the share of social and public rented dwellings is still much higher. That implies that maintenance of dwellings in Western Europe is less dependent on the decisions of individual households, as municipalities and/or housing associations are to a large extent responsible for the management of the housing estates. At the same time, however, it should be mentioned that, especially in many post-WWII estates, a more market-oriented approach is becoming more pronounced. Especially in Central and Southern Europe many dwellings have been converted from rental to owner-occupied units, while in Western Europe owner-occupied stock is on the rise too, because of selling off part of the social/public rented stock, partly because that stock is demolished and replaced by more expensive alternatives (owner-occupied dwellings and units with a relatively high rent; see, e.g., Belmessous et al., 2005). Because of these developments, the work of Grigsby et al. may become more and more relevant for the European situation.

A specific model explaining the decline of social housing

Niels Prak and Hugo Priemus can be seen as the first researchers who focussed specifically on the situation in post-WWII *social* housing estates in Europe. In 1986, they developed a model, which was based on the idea that the decay of such neighbourhoods was the result of three fortifying spirals of decline: social decline, economic decline, and technical decline. A few years later, some adaptations were made to the model (Onderzoeksinstituut OTB, 1989). Again in 1993, Heeger – at the time a PhD student of Priemus – renewed their model. Among others, he added aspects of urban design (e.g. location, living environment, level of services), and reputation/image.

The first spiral of decline, *social decline*, concerns the tenants and, more specifically, changes that take place within the tenant population (left part of the model). When the attraction of an estate decreases and mobility increases, the number of low-income households in these particular areas will rise. In some cases this may lead to the departure of more and more high-income households. As a result social control may diminish, vandalism and crime get the chance to expand and the attractiveness of the area may decrease further.

The increasing mobility of residents causes faster turnover rates, which in turn can lead to vacancies, vandalism, pollution and low tenant participation. These developments may result in *technical decline*. A declining housing quality can again lead to further mobility. The point of departure of the housing stock (i.e. the initial quality) is of importance as well; sometimes it seems difficult to maintain a particular housing block because of its bad general quality. In this case, decay is the result of higher powers instead of unwillingness of owners to invest in their properties.

Both social and technical decay have an impact on the operational costs of the landlords; income from rent decreases because of increasing mobility and the influx of more and more low-income households. At the same time, higher turnover rates, problems with tenants, increasing maintenance, and for example landlords' attempts to ensure that the complex remains competitive, result in higher running costs. In the model this is described as the third spiral of decline: *economic decline*. Landlords may react to this unfavourable situation by loosening the allocation rules for their properties. Also, they can decide to invest less in maintenance. In the first case, an increasing influx of socio-economic weak households may be the result, while the second 'solution' may cause further decrease in the quality of the housing stock.

As Prak and Priemus focused on the situation in post-WWII social housing estates in Europe and in the Netherlands in particular, it is no surprise that their model can very well be applied to the developments within these areas. Some specific points are stressed in their model.

First, it has become clear that the *initial quality of the housing stock* can be a forceful determinant of its later situation, physically as well as socially. No matter what you do, if the initial quality is low, deterioration will in general start quickly and continue rapidly. It is a well-known fact that post-WWII housing estates were not always built to very high standards. This is related to the fact that building in large quantities was more important than building high-quality dwellings, especially in the early post-WWII period, when housing shortages were high (Murie et al., 2003).

Furthermore, Prak and Priemus were one of the first who focussed particularly on estates with an over representation of social rented dwellings. Such a situation, often the case in post-WWII large housing estates, was expected to be an influence on the social situation as well as on the level of maintenance in such areas. Many other housing researchers have elaborated on this idea. They have time and again asserted that owner-occupiers are in general more inclined to invest in their dwellings and neighbourhood, financially as well as socially. The fear of declining house values can be seen as an important determinant of this tendency (see, e.g., Forrest and Kearns, 2001; Atkinson and Kintrea, 2000).

Despite these positive aspects of the model, some problems can also be raised. First, it is not very clear from the model where exactly the starting points for the decline of housing and neighbourhoods can be found. The idea of a spiral more or less automatically assumes that all developments logically follow each other and there is no clear idea which development is the most important one. Secondly, the model has a clear negative connotation. Everything seems to lead to decline. There is no clear idea how to stop decline or reverse a spiral. Finally, although it is clear that inhabitants do play a role in the decline of these neighbourhoods, it is not quite clear what exactly motivates people to act. This is a much more central issue in the behavioural approach (see next section).

A behavioural approach to neighbourhood change and decline

The behavioural approach is a reaction to the ecological models of neighbourhood change. Followers of this approach criticised several assumptions of the human ecologists, for example, the economic determinism of these models. Firey (1947) argues that the main motives of households to move from or to a neighbourhood may not be purely economic; the place where one lives can evoke sentimental and symbolic ties that bind an individual to a neighbourhood. Also, Ahlbrandt and Brophy (1975) are much more aware of the complex nature of neighbourhood change than are most human ecologists. Although they also identify several 'traditional' economic, social and demographic variables that affect the housing demand in a neighbourhood, they also state that social and attitudinal indicators are necessary to explain neighbourhood change and decline.

According to researchers within the behavioural approach, neighbourhoods do not follow the same trajectory through time and are therefore not doomed to deteriorate. Researchers such as Temkin and Rohe (1996; 1998) concentrate on the inhabitants' ability to influence the situation in their neighbourhood. Basically, inhabitants that are confronted with neighbourhood decline face a trade-off between actively changing the situation, for example in the form of locally based (political) activism, and relocation (Cox, 1983). Researchers in the behavioural tradition suppose that residents' attachment to their neighbourhood has a negative effect on the propensity to relocate and a positive effect on the will to work on the improvement of the neighbourhood (Ahlbrandt and Cunningham, 1979). Indeed, there is evidence that attachment to the neighbourhood and the level of social networking have a positive effect on the civic participation. Next to that, social cohesion is found to be a strong determinant of neighbourhood confidence (Varady, 1986), which in its turn plays a key role in explaining mobility decisions (Goetze, 1979). A less mobile population in many cases means more attachment to the neighbourhood. Indeed, when attachment reinforces the will of the inhabitants to improve the area, a negative spiral may be stopped.

This is not to deny that changes in social and economic variables are crucial in the explanation of neighbourhood change. However, the authors who focus on aspects such as attachment and the will among residents to counter negative developments in their neighbourhood or estate do have an important point. Estates with a strong social fabric are able to resist (negative) changes better than areas with a weak social fabric. An active residents' organisation (i.e. an element of the social fabric in an estate) can react to processes of decline (such as dirt on the streets, graffiti) and can try to take action in more positive directions (they might even have the power to keep problematic households out of the area). In the view of Temkin and Rohe (1996, 1998), neighbourhood stability requires a dedicated group of residents who successfully express their feelings to the actors in control (i.e. the ones who are responsible for changes or stability in an area). It can then even happen that a restructuring plan for a neighbourhood can be completely disapproved by the inhabitants of that area and finally be replaced by a new plan, that is approved by the inhabitants or even (partially) produced by them. This happened for example in the post-WWII estate of Bouwlust in The Hague in the Netherlands (Van Marissing et al., 2006).

On the one hand, the strength of the social fabric is influenced by the level of power residents have. In the UK, for example, involving residents in plans that concern their estate is considered more important than in Hungary or Spain (see Van Beckhoven et al., 2005). On the other hand, however, residents need to be willing to react to changes. In certain neighbourhoods residents have indeed been able to enforce changes and improvements better than in others. Due to demographic changes that have taken place in various post-WWII large housing estates, the social fabric has been affected negatively and has in some cases even disappeared. When an estate is increasingly characterised by many different groups (young and old, high- and low-income households with different lifestyles and interests, different kinds of minority ethnic groups) a lack of interest and mutual respect can cause a situation in which residents are not very willing to cooperate. As a result, there is little chance that action is undertaken against aspects of neighbourhood decline. Van Beckhoven et al. (2005) describe this for the post-WWII housing estates of Kanaleneiland-Noord in the Dutch city of Utrecht.

Thus, according to the behavioural approach, a breakdown of social relationships can be seen as a basic cause of neighbourhood decline. However, two critical comments have to be made here. Firstly, the question is whether the social fabric is really an independent factor in neighbourhood stability, or merely the resultant of population composition, a factor that is very central in the model of Grigsby (see also Chapter 4 of this book, in which Van Gent makes clear that social cohesion seems to be more important in explaining dissatisfaction than in explaining satisfaction with the neighbourhood; see also Musterd, 2008). Some findings seem to support the latter assertion. Varady (1986), for example, found that neighbourhood confidence is primarily a function of population shifts and, more recently, Dekker and Bolt (2005) showed that attachment to the neighbourhood can (partly) be attributed to the satisfaction with the population composition.

Secondly, the idea that residents have an influence on neighbourhood change is challenged, especially by political economists. In the political economy approach it is stated that urban areas are used by powerful elites to facilitate capital accumulation. In this framework, Molotch (1976) focuses on the influence of so-called growth machines: coalitions of urban elites who seek to capture and retain economic power primarily by promoting real estate and population growth. According to political economists urban development, and likewise neighbourhood change or stability, is driven by actions of these urban elites instead of by an ecological process or the activities of neighbourhood residents (Palm, 1985; Squires and Velez, 1987). Institutions working in real estate (banks or realtors) are often considered to be responsible for steering certain people to certain neighbourhoods – especially along racial lines – in order to meet the interests of the growth machine. In this context, Swyngedouw (2000) talks about the mythical reality of the local. Although literature focusing on these aspects is almost exclusively from the United States, there is no reason to believe that this is not applicable to Europe. The role of institutions is also central in the institutional approach. This approach is the subject of the next section, where its significance for large housing estates is discussed.

The institutional and the managerial approach

Rex and Moore's *Race, Community and Conflict* (1967) marked the beginning of the institutional approach in housing and neighbourhood development research. They stated that (desirable) housing is a scarce resource and different groups are differently placed with regard to access to these dwellings ('housing classes'). Due to the role of state intervention, access to housing is not (solely) determined by a household's income. The accessibility of housing is not always the same for people with an identical socio-economic status. The competition on the housing market does, in other words, not only take place through the price mechanism, but also through the position in the distribution system. Due to the role of public and private institutions on the housing market, the association between income and housing quality is weakened.

Within the *institutional approach*, the role of the central state is seen as one of the major factors in determining the distribution of housing. The retreat, or changing character of the welfare state is a major topic for many housing and urban researchers in this respect (see, e.g., Musterd and Ostendorf, 1998). Changing priorities within a welfare state (e.g. a development from a social towards a more entrepreneurial state with much more focus on economic development and much less on supporting the poor), can result in declining incomes of those who do not work (elderly, handicapped people, unemployed, people on welfare). As a result, these state-dependent, low-income households run the risk of ending up in those areas where dwellings have a (very) low rent, such as the post-WWII housing estates. The dependency of welfare state arrangements becomes increasingly important when macro-developments lead to more state-dependent households. Global economic restructuring has led to huge losses of industrial jobs in European cities. The increasing number of unemployed in post-WWII areas is a result of this process, as has been indicated by studies in for example the UK and the Netherlands (Lee and Murie, 2002; Van Kempen, 2002).

Another consequence of a welfare state in which priorities change is the impact on the quantity, quality, location, and allocation of the housing stock itself. Austerity programmes may lead to lower subsidies for housing. A deliberate choice for a more market-oriented approach may lead to more and more expensive owner-occupied dwellings, while at the same time affordable dwellings are demolished to make place for these more expensive alternatives. As a consequence, low-income households are increasingly forced to find shelter in a constantly declining public or social rented housing market. Especially in the welfare states of Western and Northern Europe this combination of an increasing focus on building in more expensive segments, a decreasing affordable segment of the housing stock and, consequently, an increasing concentration of low-income households in neighbourhoods that are not yet changed by processes of urban restructuring (Slob et al., 2005), has occurred in the last decade. In those countries the large post-WWII housing estates, with their large segment of affordable dwellings, are now important for a growing number of low-income households. Developments of those estates in large parts of Europe can therefore not be seen as separate from welfare state developments and those developments are not recognised in the works we have mentioned before. A deliberate choice for area-based policies, which implies a focus on some areas and not others, will further diversify the developments of different estates. When local government decides (in some countries, such as the Netherlands and the UK, often together with housing associations and private partners) to start a process of urban restructuring in a post-WWII estate, leading to the demolition of affordable housing, households with low incomes often have to move elsewhere to find a suitable home, because in general the affordable housing is being replaced by more expensive alternatives. Again, it is now becoming increasingly clear that post-WWII areas have become major invasion areas for these displaced households (Slob et al., 2005).

As a consequence of this combination of demolition, rebuilding more expensive dwellings and displacement of poor households, a process of residualisation is becoming common for post-WWII housing estates. Residualisation refers to the narrowing social profile of the social rented sector: a growing number of low-income households can increasingly be found in the less expensive segments of the housing market. Because the least expensive segments are in many cases also the segments with the lowest quality, this concentration of low-income households takes place almost automatically in housing with a low quality. In most cases these dwellings are spatially concentrated in a small number of areas of the city, notably the post-WWII estates. Residualisation can be observed in several Western European countries, but the developments seem to be more dramatic in some countries (e.g. Britain and Germany) than in others (e.g. Denmark and the Netherlands) (See Forrest and Murie, 1983; 1988; Meusen and Van Kempen, 1994; Harloe, 1995).

Allocation rules

Within the institutional approach, there is much attention paid to allocation rules and procedures, which have been subject to change. In the immediate post-WWII period, tests of ability to pay and appropriate social behaviour were applied. According to Kennett and Forrest (2003: 51) it was in part 'this active exclusion of the poorest or those deemed to be less deserving which gave the social housing of the early post-war period its social status'. However, in the course of time, middle and higher incomes were excluded more and more from social rented housing. Only applicants with a relatively low income were eligible for social housing. This has led to an increasingly homogeneous socio-economic profile of the population in many post-WWII large neighbourhoods in countries such as the Netherlands (Musterd et al., 2003; Van Kempen, 2000) and Britain (Goodchild and Cole, 2001). In the popular imagination, large housing estates are nowadays seen as concentrated enclaves of poor people (Kennett and Forrest, 2003).

Currently, allocation rules are also applied in order to avoid or cope with a concentration of low-income households. This is the case in some large housing estates across Europe. In the post-WWII estate of Husby (Stockholm), for example, housing managers introduced allocation rules ('Järva Rules') to create a mixed neighbourhood population (i.e. with respect to socio-economic background). According to these rules, potential residents with a particular income-level or particular profession, such as teachers and policemen, got priority. This rule has been abolished however, as it was considered politically incorrect; freedom of choice to settle wherever you want to is considered important in Sweden (Andersson et al., 2003).

In the UK, some housing associations also try to increase the social mix in pot-WWII estates through changing allocation rules, which is – disguisedly – termed as 'community' or 'flexible' letting. The paradox in this policy is that housing managers exclude certain types of tenants in the name of combating social exclusion (Goodchild and Cole, 2001). Also in the Netherlands, part of them post-WWII estates, there is a discussion about these kinds of interventions (see Bolt and Van Kempen, 2007). In the city of Rotterdam, some areas have been allocated where people who depend on welfare (except for retired people and students) are not allowed to get hold of a social rented dwelling.

It should be noted that in none of these examples is it explicitly stated that minority ethnic groups are refused in certain neighbourhoods. This would not only be politically incorrect, but even discriminatory. But at the same time it is clear that by putting up barriers for low-income households, minority ethnic groups are also affected and maybe even more than native households (because in most Western countries minority ethnic groups disproportionately belong to the lower-income categories; see, e.g., Van Kempen, 2002).

Formal rules are important for deciding who will be the next inhabitant of a vacant dwelling. However, the allocators themselves may have an important say, as is stressed in the managerial approach, which can be seen as a specific form of the institutional approach. Henderson and Karn (1984) have stated that it is essential to look beyond the level of formal policies and turn our attention to the informal and semi-formal, decision-making processes within organisations. The crucial role of 'managers' (also referred to as 'gatekeepers') in these organisations is also elaborated in the work of, for example, Pahl (1975, 1977) and Lipsky (1980). They pay attention to the fact that managers within local government or housing associations have the power to decide to allocate a dwelling to a certain household in one neighbourhood rather than in another. The so-called managerial approach strongly adheres to the idea that normal individuals or households do not have a decisive power. This means that neighbourhood change is not something that emerges from the ideas and acts of inhabitants, but originates in concrete actions by those in power.

Of course, gatekeepers are not only found in the (semi-)public sector, but also in the private sector. We can for example think of mortgage providers (Galster, 1999; Wyly, 2002; Aalbers, 2005) and real estate agents (Philips and Karn, 1992, Yinger, 1999; Galster and Godfrey, 2005). Sometimes, the strategies of gatekeepers are aimed at stabilising the neighbourhood by preventing certain groups from entering, such as persons with criminal records. In other cases, gatekeepers act to engender a high turnover rate. Research in the United States on the effects of the HOPE VI programme showed that managers in suburbs sometimes refuse to build homes for those who leave the public rented dwellings in cities (see Crump's (2002) study of Minneapolis). The private sector indeed also refuses people with criminal records who are in the HOPE VI programme (Popkin et al., 2004).

The discourse on the importance of managers has recently focused on a new phenomenon: the strong leader (Judd and Parkinson, 1990; Purdue, 2001) Strong leaders are increasingly seen as important actors in urban development in general, and in the restructuring process of neighbourhoods in particular. The direction of neighbourhood change may increasingly be determined by such a strong leader. The positive side of this is that an intricate process of urban change may be speeded up. The negative side might be that the process of urban restructuring is becoming less democratic.

This brings us back to the possible influence of inhabitants of the area on the future of their neighbourhood. From recent research into post-WWII neighbourhoods it has become clear that inhabitants sometimes do have an important say when it comes to future developments. In various ways residents are involved in diverse stages of a restructuring process. They take part in so-called soundboard groups, they make themselves strong to keep services in the area and sometimes succeed, budgets and targets are discussed with inhabitants, etc. (see Van Kempen et al., 2006, for a more complete overview of all kinds of practical arrangements in post-WWII areas in which inhabitants are involved).

Having a say in the neighbourhood is no longer important when inhabitants have made the decision that they want to leave the neighbourhood, for example because they cannot stand the negative developments in the area. Recent research has indicated, however, that only a small percentage in post-WWII housing estates wants to move out of the estate, because of very negative developments (Musterd and Van Kempen, 2007). In fact, many residents in many estates are quite, or even very, satisfied in their dwelling and with their neighbourhood (see also Chapter 3 in this book). Those who want to move out of the neighbourhood definitely do not always point to negative developments in the area. They do mention housing market reasons, such as the wish to move to a larger dwelling, to a single-family house or to an owner-occupied dwelling. When these types of dwellings are not available in the present neighbourhood, they have to look elsewhere. This also indicates that large post-WWII housing estates may be important areas for households at certain stages of their life.

Conclusions

The changes and decline of post-WWII housing estates in European cities can partly be explained by some of the older theories and theoretical notions that are probably applicable for developments in any other kind of neighbourhood. However, those theories go beyond the specific internal and contextual characteristics of the post-WWII estates. Therefore, it is also useful to examine the studies that refer to one or more individual post-WWII housing estates, in which the design and the physical quality are considered as important explanations for neighbourhood decline.

The shortcoming of these neighbourhood-focused studies, however, is that they are not very suitable for explaining why estates with identical characteristics often develop in different ways. That is because they mainly look for explanations within the dynamics of a neighbourhood, and take no notice of the external factors that have an influence on neighbourhood decline.

This does not mean that internal developments are unimportant. Probably one of the most powerful explanations of the negative developments in the estates is their initial situation. The design of the areas was more or less revolutionary at the time they were built, especially with respect to the combination of large green areas, open blocks of flats, sometimes with over ten floors, and separated traffic streams. In the beginning of their existence, most housing estates attracted a lot of people with reasonable incomes who migrated from homes in older areas in the city or started their housing career there. Housing in the new estates was relatively cheap, but generally not as cheap as in many of the older neighbourhoods of the city.

But the initial situation did not last forever. While inexpensive housing in older neighbourhoods gradually disappeared through the processes of urban renewal, demolition, and gentrification, newer, more attractive areas started to emerge on the outskirts of the cities, in suburban locations and in many cases also in the more inner city parts. The rented multi-family dwellings in the post-WWII estates started to become less attractive compared to the newly built, in many cases single-family dwellings, elsewhere. At the same time, the housing supply in these post-WWII housing estates started to belong to the least expensive housing segments of many urban housing markets, and signs of physical decay began to appear. This caused a filtering process: households who could afford to move left the estates and moved to more attractive housing and areas (either to more central or to more spacious, suburban environments). Households that did not have any alternative on the local housing markets started to migrate to the post-WWII estates, which gradually, and sometimes even rather quickly, became the most important concentration areas for low-income households in European cities. Grigsby and colleagues (1987) were at least partly right in indicating the significance of increasing poverty for negative developments in neighbourhoods. More poverty means less money for maintenance and less expenditure in shops. Moreover, when people have to settle in dwellings and areas which they have not really chosen, the responsibility for the dwelling and environment may be expected not to be very high, leading to negative developments, such as increased dirt on the streets, on squares and on public playgrounds. We do believe in the existence of negative spirals of decline (see also Prak and Priemus, 1986) in which intricate combinations of developments explain the downgrading processes of urban areas. At the same time, however, it is important to warn against automatic reasoning: each estate is different in itself, differently located in the city and differently placed in the subjective hierarchy in each local and regional housing market. This means that developments in one area may have very different effects compared to developments in another area. It means for example that the influx of poor households may lead to negative reactions of the existing population in one area (resulting in negative attitudes or even moving away), but that in another area the in-migration of these poor households is seen as a normal urban phenomenon and does not cause any problems.

There are many studies that show that the presence of ethnic minorities may add another dimension to the social problems in a neighbourhood, as contacts between original inhabitants and newcomers are not always found to be very good. Stereotyping, discrimination and avoidance lead to disrupted relations within a neighbourhood with, as a result, a further decline of the area. More difficult to determine is the effect of the concentration of minority ethnic groups itself. Does an estate with a concentration of minority ethnic groups always fare worse than an estate with only native inhabitants? In some examples this is definitely the case, although it should immediately be said that other variables can be more important than the ethnic one. When estates with a majority of natives show more positive developments than areas with ethnic minorities, this can in many cases be attributed to the fact that the natives have lived in the area for a long time, even decades. It is the area where they have spent a large part of their lives. Newcomers, including minority ethnic groups, do not (yet) have such ties with the area, which results in less interest in the area. In this case, it is thus not ethnicity that counts, but duration of living in the area. Other factors that influence the differential developments of areas include: household type, age, income and education which often differ between ethnic groups. Definitely more research, explicitly focusing on controlling these possible intervening variables, is needed here.

It should already be clear from the previous paragraph that residents matter. The way they act in and with respect to their housing estate is crucial for the development of these estates. This is recognised in the behavioural approach. Stimulating local participation of residents of the area may be a successful strategy for improving the area. Participation is not only a way to ensure that residents have a say in the (regeneration) plans for their neighbourhood, but it may also strengthen the social cohesion in the neighbourhood (Dekker, 2006), which in turn engenders more stability. The problematic issue of involving participation by all relevant groups in an area should however not be overlooked. This seems to be the most problematic issue of resident participation in the whole of Europe (see also Chapter 9 in this book; and see Van Beckhoven and Van Boxmeer, 2006).

Furthermore, the role of institutions should not be underestimated. National or local government attention for developments of decline in urban neighbourhoods is crucial for the path that will eventually be followed by the estates. Areas that are excluded from governmental attention are most in danger. This may sound trivial, but under the label of area-based policies, politicians do include and exclude areas from policy attention, with two logical results: (1) problematic areas become better areas because of the policy attention, but (2) less problematic areas become more problematic because they lack policy attention and because they can be seen as the reception areas of the problems of the targeted areas (displacement of problematic households, criminal activities, etc.).

Policy attention, especially in combination with financial assets, can change the trajectory of an estate immensely. At the same time however, attention is needed for the role of urban governance. In all parts of Europe, (local) government has traditionally been the main actor in urban and estate-based projects and this is still the case in many urban restructuring projects in Europe, as shown in a recent study by Wassenberg et al. (2007). At the same time, urban government has encountered a movement leading towards more differentiated forms of governance. More sectors, such as the private sector, the voluntary and community sectors, are becoming involved in governing activities and decision-making, and public matters are definitely no longer the exclusive responsibility of the state. At neighbourhood level, many new ways to be creative, to build strengths and to access and utilise resources, for example developing social capital to resolve local problems, are currently put into effect. The concept of collaborative planning is important here: the agenda for city planning should be inclusive, all stakeholders should have the right to a voice in the decision-making process (see, e.g., Healey et al., 1995; Healey, 1997). Related to the work discussed in this chapter, it points out that the concept of governance can be seen as a way to diminish the influence of managers, gatekeepers and strong leaders. As pointed out, among others in the work of Temkin and Rohe, the significance of the interaction between residents and institutions should increase. The dialogue between different actors that are involved in a neighbourhood can therefore be considered an important aspect in neighbourhood change, particularly neighbourhood regeneration.

In this chapter we gave some attention to the importance of physical issues on social processes in large housing estates. We do believe that the social and institutional aspects, as well as the position of an estate in the local and regional housing market are more important than physical characteristics per se. Even when blocks of flats look unattractive from the outside and to outsiders, there is a big chance that a large part of the inhabitants are satisfied with just living there (see also Chapters 3 and 4). We should therefore be careful not to pay too much attention to physical issues.

References

Aalbers, M. B. (2005) Who's Afraid of Red, Yellow and Green? Redlining in Rotterdam. *Geoforum*, 36, pp. 562–80.

Aalbers, M., Van Beckhoven, E., Van Kempen, R., Musterd, S. and Ostendorf, W. (2003) *Large Housing Estates in the Netherlands, Overview of Developments and Problems in Amsterdam and Utrecht*. Utrecht: Faculty of Geosciences, Utrecht University.

Ahlbrandt, R. and Brophy, P. (1975) *Neighbourhood Revitalization*. Lexington: D. C. Heath and Company.

Ahlbrandt, R. S. and Cunningham, J. V. (1979) *A New Public Policy for Neighbourhood Preservation*. New York: Praeger.

Andersson, R., Molina, I., Öresjö, E., Petterson, L. and Siwertsson, C. (2003) *Large Housing Estates in Sweden. Overview of Developments and Problems in Jönköping and Stockholm*. Utrecht: Faculty of Geosciences, Utrecht University.

Andersson, R., Musterd, S., Galster, G. and Kauppinen, T. (2007) Wat Mix Matters? Exploring the Relationships Between Individual's Incomes and

Different Measures of their Neighbourhood Context. *Housing Studies*, 22 (5), pp. 637–60.

Andersson, R. and Palander, C. (2001) National and City Contexts, Urban Development Programmes and Neighbourhood Selection. The Swedish Background Report. In: J. Vranken, P. De Decker and I. Van Nieuwenhuyze (Eds), *Urban Governance, Social Inclusion and Sustainability: National Context Reports*, pp. 1–85. Antwerp: Garant.

Atkinson, R. and Kintrea, K. (2000) Owner-Occupation, Social Mix and Neighbourhood Impacts. *Policy and Politics*, 28 (1), pp. 93–108.

Belmessous, F., Chignier-Riboulon, F., Commerçon, N. and Zepf, M. (2005) Demolition of Large Housing Estates: An Overview. In: R. Van Kempen, S. Hall, I. Tosics and K. Dekker (Eds) *Restructuring Large Housing Estates in Europe*, pp. 193–210. Bristol: The Policy Press.

Birch, D. (1971) Towards s Stage Theory of Urban Growth. *Journal of the American Institute of Planners*, 37, pp. 78–87.

Bolt, G. and Van Kempen, R. (2007) Allocation Policy as a Solution to Urban Problems. The Case of Rotterdam. Paper presented at the ENHR-Conference on Sustainable Urban Areas, Rotterdam, 25–28 June 2007.

Botman, S. and Van Kempen, R. (2001) *Spatial Dimensions of Urban Social Exclusion and Integration. The Case of Rotterdam, the Netherlands*. Amsterdam: Amsterdam Study Centre for the Metropolitan Environment.

Bourne, L. S. (1981) *The Geography of Housing*. London: Edward Arnold.

Bråmå, A. and Andersson, R. (2005) Who Stays and Who Moves? A Longitudinal Analysis of Stayers and Migrants in Sweden's Large Housing Estates. In: R. Van Kempen, K. Dekker, S. Hall and I. Tosics (Eds), *Restructuring Large Housing Estates in European Cities*, pp. 169–92. Bristol: The Policy Press.

Burgess, E. W. (1925) The Growth of the City: An Introduction to a Research Project. In: R. E. Park, E. W. Burgess and R. D. Mckenzie (Eds), *The City*, pp. 47–62. Chicago/London: University of Chicago Press.

Bierzyñski, A. (2005) *Large Housing Estates in Poland Success and Fail Factors of Policies*. Available on Internet: <www.restate.geo.uu.nl/results/sf/sfpolanddoc>

Blokland-Potters, T. (1998) *Wat Stadsbewoners Bindt: Sociale Relaties In Een Achterstandswijk* [Ties between Urban Dwellers: Social Relations in a Problematic Neighbourhood]. Kampen: Kok Agora.

Castells, M. (2000) *The Information Age: Economy, Society and Culture, Volume I: The Rise of the Network Society (Second Edition)*. Oxford: Blackwell.

Černič Mali, B., Sendi, R., Boškić, R., Filipović, M., Goršič, N. and Zaviršek Hudnik, D. (2003) *Large Housing Estates in Slovenia. Overview of Developments and Problems in Ljubljana and Koper*. Utrecht: Faculty of Geosciences, Utrecht University.

Chignier-Riboulon, F., Commerçon, N., Trigueiro, M. and Zepf, M. (2003) *Large Housing Estates in France. Overview of Developments and Problems in Lyon*. Utrecht: Faculty of Geosciences, Utrecht University.

Coleman, A. (1985) *Utopia on Trial: Vision and Reality in Planned Housing*. London: Hillary Shipman.

Cox, K. (1983) Residential Mobility, Neighborhood Activism and Neighborhood Problems. *Political Geography Quarterly*, 2, pp. 99–117.

Crump, J. (2002) Deconcentration by Demolition: Public Housing, Poverty, and Urban Policy. *Environment and Planning D*, 20, pp. 581–96.

Dekker, K. (2006) *Governance as Glue: Urban Governance and Social Cohesion in Post-WWII Neighbourhoods in the Netherlands*. Utrecht: Koninklijk Nederlands Aardrijkskundig Genootschap.

Dekker, K. and Bolt, G. (2006) Social Cohesion in Post War Estates in the Netherlands: Differences between Social-Economic and Ethnic Groups. *Urban Studies*, 42, pp. 2447–70.

Dekker, K. and Van Kempen, R. (2005) Large Housing Estates in Europe: A Contemporary Overview. In: R. Van Kempen, K. Dekker, S. Hall and I. Tosics (Eds), *Restructuring Large Housing Estates in European* Cities, pp. 19–45. Bristol: The Policy Press.

Evans, K. (1998) Community Safety in High Crime Neighbourhoods: A View from the Street. In: A. Marlow and J. Pitts (Eds) *Planning Safer Communities*, pp. 181–8. Lyme Regis: Russell House Publishing.

Firey, W. (1947) *Land Use in Central Boston*. Cambridge (MA): Harvard University Press.

Forrest, R. and Kearns, A. (2001) Social Cohesion, Social Capital and the Neighbourhood. *Urban Studies*, 38 (12), pp. 2125–45.

Forrest, R. and Murie, A. (1983) Residualisation and Council Housing: Aspects of the Changing Social Relations of Housing Tenure. *Journal of Social Policy*, 12, pp. 453–68.

Forrest, R. and Murie, A. (1988) *Selling the Welfare State: The Privatisation of Public Housing*. London: Routledge.

Galster, G. C. (1999) The Evolving Challenges of Fair Housing since 1968: Open Housing, Integration, and the Reduction of Ghettoization. In: *Cityscape: A Journal of Policy Development and Research*, 4, pp. 123–38.

Galster, G. C. (2005) *Neighborhood Mix, Social Opportunities, and the Policy Challenges of an Increasingly Diverse Amsterdam*. Amsterdam: Amidst, University of Amsterdam.

Galster, G., Andersson, R., Musterd, S. and Kauppinen, T. (2008) Does Neighborhood Income Mix Affect Earnings of Adults? New Evidence from Sweden. *Journal of Urban Economics*, 63, pp. 858–70.

Galster, G. C., Quercia, R. G. and Cortes, A. (2000) Identifying Neighborhood Thresholds: An Empirical Exploration. *Housing Policy Debate*, 11, pp. 701–32.

Galster, G. and Godfrey, E. (2005) By Words and Deeds: Racial Steering by Real Estate Agents in the US in 2000. *Journal of the American Planning Association*, 71, pp. 251–68.

Goetze, R. (1979) *Understanding Neighborhood Change: The Role of Expectations in Urban Revitalizations*. Cambridge (MA): Ballinger.

Goodchild, B. and Cole, I. (2001) Social Balance and Mixed Neighbourhoods in Britain since 1979: A Review of Discourse and Practice in Social Housing. *Environment and Planning D*, 19, pp. 103–21.

Grigsby, W., Baratz, M., Galster, G. and Maclennan, D. (1987) The Dynamics of Neighbourhood Change and Decline. *Progress in Planning*, 28, pp. 1–76.

Hall, S., Murie, A. and Knorr-Siedow, T. (2005a) Large Housing Estates in their Historical Context. In: R. Van Kempen, K. Dekker, S. Hall and I. Tosics (Eds), *Restructuring Large Housing Estates in European Cities*, pp. 63–83. Bristol: The Policy Press.

Hall, S., Murie, A., Rowlands, R. and Sankey, S. (2005b) *Large Housing Estates in United Kingdom. Success and Fail Factors of Policies.* Utrecht: Faculty of Geosciences, Utrecht University.

Hamnett, C. (2003) Gentrification and the Middle-Class Remaking of Inner London. *Urban Studies,* 40, pp. 2401–26.

Harloe, M. (1995) *The People's Home? Social Rented Housing in Europe and America.* Oxford: Blackwell.

Hastings, A. and Dean, J. (2002) Challenging Images: Tackling Stigma through Estate Regeneration. *Policy and Politics,* 31, pp. 171–84.

Healey, P. (1997) *Collaborative Planning: Shaping Places in Fragmented Societies.* London: Macmillan.

Healey, P., Cameron, S., Davoudi, S., Graham, S. and Madanipour, A. (1995) *Managing Cities: The New Urban Context.* Chichester: John Wiley.

Heeger, H. (1993) *Aanpak Van Naoorlogse Probleemcomplexen* [Dealing with Post-War Housing Estates]. Delft: Delftse Universitaire Pers.

Henderson, J. and Karn, V. (1984) Race, Class and the Allocation of Public Housing in Britain. *Urban Studies,* 21, pp. 115–28.

Hoover, E. M. and Vernon, R. (1959) *Anatomy of a Metropolis.* Cambridge (MA): Harvard University Press.

Hoyt, H. (1939) *The Structure and Growth of Residential Neighbourhoods in American Cities.* Washington DC: Federal Housing Administration.

Jacquier, C. (2001) National and City Contexts, Urban Development Programmes and Neighbourhood Selection. The French Background Report. In: J. Vranken, P. De Decker and I. Van Nieuwenhuyze (Eds), *Urban Governance, Social Inclusion and Sustainability: National Context Reports,* pp. 1–94. Antwerp: Garant.

Jones, E. (1960) *A Social Geography of Belfast.* Oxford: Oxford University Press.

Judd, D. and Parkinson, M. (Eds) (1990) *Leadership and Urban Regeneration.* London: Sage.

Kearns, A. and Paddison, R. (2000) New Challenges for Urban Governance. *Urban Studies,* 37, pp. 845–50.

Kennett, P. and Forrest, R. (2003) From Planned Communities to Deregulated Spaces: Social and Tenurial Change in High Quality State Housing. *Housing Studies,* 18, pp. 47–63.

Knorr-Siedow, T. and Droste, C. (2003) *Large Housing Estates in Germany. Overview of Developments and Problems in Berlin.* Utrecht: Faculty of Geosciences, Utrecht University.

Kooiman, J. (Ed.) (1993) *Modern Governance.* London: Sage.

Lee, P. and Murie, A. (2002) The Poor City: National and Local Perspectives on Changes in Residential Patterns in the British City. In: P. Marcuse and R. Van Kempen (Eds) *Of States and Cities: The Partitioning of Urban Space,* pp. 59–87. Oxford: Oxford University Press.

Lipsky, M. (1980) *Street-Level Bureaucracy: Dilemmas of the Individual in Public Services.* New York: Russell Sage.

Lupton, R. (2004) *Poverty Street: The Dynamics of Neighbourhood Decline and Renewal.* Bristol: Policy Press.

Marcuse, P. and Van Kempen, R. (2000) *Globalizing Cities: A New Spatial Order?* Oxford: Blackwell.

Massey, D. S. and Denton, N. A. (1993) *American Apartheid: Segregation and the Making of the Underclass*. Cambridge: Harvard University Press.

Mcarthur, A. (2000) Rebuilding Sustainable Communities. Assessing Glasgow's Urban Village Experiment. *Town Planning Review*, 71, pp. 51–69.

Megbolugbe, I. F., Hoek-Smit, M. C. and Linnenman, P. D. (1996) Understanding Neighbourhood Dynamics: A Review of the Contributions of William G. Grigsby. *Urban Studies*, 33, pp. 1779–95.

Meusen, H. and Van Kempen, R. (1994) *Dutch Social Rented Housing: A British Experience?* Bristol: University of Bristol, School for Advanced Urban Studies.

Ministry Vrom (Ministry of Housing, Spatial Planning and the Environment) (2007) Cijfers Over Wonen 2006 [Figures about Housing 2006]. The Hague: Ministry Vrom.

Molotch, H. L. (1972) *Managed Integration: Dilemmas of Doing Good in the City*. Berkeley: University of California Press.

Molotch, H. (1976) The City as Growth Machine: Toward a Political Economy of Place. *American Journal of Sociology*, 82, pp. 309–30.

Murie, A. & Musterd, S. (2004) Social Exclusion & Opportunity Structures in European Cities and Neighbourhoods. *Urban Studies*, 41, pp. 1441–59.

Murie, A. (2005) Restructuring Large Housing Estates. Paper presented at the RESTATE Conference on 'Restructuring Large Housing Estates in Europe: Policies, Practices, & Perspectives', Ljubljana, Slovenia, 19–21 May 2005.

Murie, A., Knorr-Siedow, T. and Van Kempen, R. (2003) *Large Housing Estates in Europe: General Developments and Theoretical Backgrounds*. Utrecht: Faculty of Geosciences, Utrecht University.

Musterd, S. (2008) Residents Views on Social Mix: Social Mix, Social Networks and Stigmatisation in Post-War Housing Estates. *Urban Studies*, 45 (4), pp. 897–915.

Musterd, S., Andersson, R., Galster, G. and Kauppinen, T. (2008) Are Immigrants' Earnings Influenced by the Characteristics of their Neighbours? *Environment and Planning A*, 40, pp. 785–805.

Musterd, S., Ostendorf, W., Van Antwerpen, J. and Slot, J. (2003) *Measuring Neighbourhood Trajectories in Understanding Processes of Social Exclusion: Amsterdam, the Netherlands*. Amsterdam: University of Amsterdam/Municipality of Amsterdam.

Musterd, S. and Van Kempen, R. (2005) *Large-Scale Housing Estates in European Cities. Opinions of Residents on Recent Developments*. Utrecht: Faculty of Geosciences, Utrecht University.

Musterd, S. and Van Kempen, R. (2007) Trapped or on the Springboard? Housing Careers in Large Housing Estates in European Cities. *Journal of Urban Affairs*, 29 (3), pp. 311–29.

Musterd, S. and Ostendorf, W. (1998) *Urban Segregation and the Welfare State. Inequality and Exclusion in Western Cities*. London: Routledge.

Myers, D. (1990) Filtering in Time: Rethinking the Longitudinal Behavior of Neighborhood Housing Markets. In: D. Myers (Ed.), *Housing Demography: Linking Demographic Structure and Housing Markets*, pp. 274–96. Wisconsin: The University of Wisconsin Press.

Newman, O. (1972) *Defensible Space. Crime Prevention through Urban Design*. New York: Macmillan.

Onderzoeksinstituut Otb (1989) Exploitatieproblemen In De Naoorlogse Woningvoorraad: Diagnose En Therapie [Operational Management Problems in the Post-War Housing Stock: Diagnosis and Treatment]. The Hague: Ministerie Van Vrom.

Pahl, R. (1975) *Whose City?* Harmondsworth: Penguin.

Pahl, R. (1977) Managers, Technical Experts and the State. In: M. Harloe (Ed.), *Captive Cities*, pp. 49–60. London: Wiley.

Palm, R. (1985) Ethnic Segmentation of Real Estate Practice in the Urban Housing Market. *Annals of the Association of American Geographers*, 75, pp. 58–68.

Pareja Eastaway, M., Tapada Berteli, T., Van Boxmeer, B. and Garcia Ferrando, L. (2003) *Large Housing Estates in Spain. Overview of Developments and Problems in Madrid and Barcelona.* Utrecht: Faculty of Geosciences, Utrecht University.

Park, R. E. (1925) The City: Suggestions for the Investigation of Human Behavior in the Urban Environment. In: R. E. Park, E. W. Burgess and R. D. Mckenzie (Eds), *The City*, pp. 1–46. Chicago: The University of Chicago Press.

Phillips, D. and Karn, V. (1992) Race and Housing in a Property Owning Democracy. *New Community*, 18, pp. 355–69.

Popkin, S. J., Levy, D. K., Harris, L. E., Comey, J. and Cunningham, M. K. (2004), The Hope VI Program: What about the Residents? *Housing Policy Debate*, 15 (2), pp. 385–413.

Power, A. (1997) *Estates on the Edge. The Social Consequences of Mass Housing in Northern Europe.* London: Macmillan.

Prak, N. L. and Priemus, H. (1986) A Model for the Analysis of the Decline of Postwar Housing. *The International Journal of Urban and Regional Research*, 10, pp. 1–7.

Purdue, D. (2001) Neighbourhood Governance: Leadership, Trust and Social Capital. *Urban Studies*, 38 (12), pp. 2211–24.

Rex, J. and Moore, R. (1967) *Race, Community, and Conflict.* London: Oxford University Press.

Sampson, R. J. and Raudenbusch, S. W. (2004) Seeing Disorder: Neighborhood Stigma and the Social Construction of 'Broken Windows'. *Social Psychology Quarterly*, 67, pp. 319–42.

Sendi, R. (2006) Improving Public Spaces. In: R. Van Kempen, A. Murie, T. Knorr-Siedow and I. Tosics (Eds), *Regenerating Large Housing Estates: A Guide to Better Practice*, pp. 109–19. Utrecht: Faculty of Geosciences.

Skifter Andersen, H. (2003) *Urban Sores. On the Interaction between Segregation, Urban Decay and Deprived Neighbourhoods.* Aldershot: Ashgate.

Slob, A., Bolt, G., Van Kempen, R., Rus, A., and Vervloedt, H. (2005) Spatial Knock-On Effects in Urban Policies: 'Old' Theories and New Research. Paper presented at The ENHR-Conference in Reykjavik, Iceland, 29 June–3 July 2005.

Squires, G. and Velez, W. (1987) Neighbourhood Racial Composition and Mortgage Lending: City and Suburban Differences. *Journal of Urban Affairs*, 9, pp. 217–32.

Swyngedouw, E. (2000) Authoritarian Governance, Power, and the Politics of Rescaling. *Environment and Planning D*, 18, pp. 63–76.

Temkin, K. and Rohe, W. M. (1996) Neighbourhood Change and Urban Policy. *Journal of Planning Education and Research*, 15, pp. 159–70.

Temkin, K. and Rohe, W. M. (1998), Social Capital and Neighbourhood Stability: An Empirical Investigation. *Housing Policy Debate*, 9, pp. 61–88.

Turkington, R. W. (1997) Reclaiming Large Housing Estates: The British Experience. Paper presented at the Conference 'A Future for Large Housing Estates' Sofia, Bulgaria, 19–21 October 1997.

Turkington, R., Van Kempen, R. and Wassenberg, F. (Eds) (2004) *High-Rise Housing in Europe. Current Trends and Future Prospects*. Delft: Dup Science.

Van Beckhoven, E., Van Boxmeer, B. and Garcia Ferrando, L. (2005) Local Participation in Spain and the Netherlands. In: R. Van Kempen, S. Hall, I. Tosics and K. Dekker (Eds) *Restructuring Large Housing Estates in Europe*, pp. 231–55. Bristol: The Policy Press.

Van Beckhoven, E. and Van Boxmeer, B. (2006) Resident Participation. In: R. Van Kempen, A. Murie, T. Knorr-Siedow and I. Tosics (Eds), *Regenerating Large Housing Estates: A Guide to Better Practice*, pp. 61–70. Utrecht: Faculty of Geosciences.

Van Beckhoven, E. and Van Kempen, R. (2003) Social Effects of Urban Restructuring: A Case Study in Amsterdam and Utrecht, the Netherlands. *Housing Studies*, 18 (6), pp. 853–75.

Van Beckhoven E. and Van Kempen, R. (2006) Towards More Social Cohesion in Large Post-Second World War Housing Estates? A Case Study in Utrecht, the Netherlands. *Housing Studies*, 21, 4, pp. 477–500.

Van Der Meer, C. E. (1996) *Monitoring Van Buurten: Signalering En Analyse Van Probleemcumulatie* [Monitoring Neighbourhoods: Signalling and Analysing the Accumulation of Problems]. Amsterdam: Ame.

Van Kempen, R. (2000) Big Cities Policy in the Netherlands. *Tijdschrift Voor Economische En Sociale Geografie*, 91, pp. 197–203.

Van Kempen, R. (2002) The Academic Formulations: Explanations for the Partitioned City. In: P. Marcuse and R. Van Kempen (Eds), *Of States and Cities: The Partitioning of Urban Space*, pp. 35–56. Oxford: Oxford University Press.

Van Kempen, R. (2002) Towards Partitioned Cities in the Netherlands? Changing Patterns of Segregation in a Highly Developed Welfare State. In: P. Marcuse and R. Van Kempen (Eds), *Of States and Cities: The Partitioning of Urban Space*, pp. 59–87. Oxford: Oxford University Press.

Van Kempen, E. and Musterd, S. (1991) High Rise Housing: Some Research and Policy Implications. *Housing Studies*, 6, pp. 83–95.

Van Kempen, R., Murie, A., Knorr-Siedow, T. and Tosics, I. (2006) *Regenerating Large Housing Estates: A Guide to Better Practice*. Utrecht: Faculty of Geosciences.

Van Marissing, E., Bolt, G. and Van Kempen, R. (2006) Urban Governance and Social Cohesion: Effects of Urban Restructuring Policies in Two Dutch Cities. *Cities*, 23, 4, pp. 279–90.

Varady, D. P. (1970) *Ethnic Minorities in Urban Areas: A Case Study of Racially Changing Communities*. Boston: Martinus Nijhoff Publishing.

Varady, D. P. (1986) *Neighborhood Upgrading, A Realistic Assessment*. Albany: State University of New York Press.

Veldboer, L., Kleinhans, R. J. and Duyvendak, J. W. (2001) The Diversified Neighbourhood in Western Europe and the United States: How do Countries Deal with the Spatial Distribution of Economic and Cultural Differences? *Journal of International Migration and Integration*, 3, pp. 41–64.

Vranken, J., De Decker, J. and Van Nieuwenhuyze, I. (2002) *Social Inclusion, Urban Governance, and Sustainability. Towards a Conceptual Framework*. Antwerp: University of Antwerp.

Wassenberg, F. (1993) *Ideeën Voor Naoorlogse Wijken* [Ideas for Post-War Neighbourhoods]. Delft: Delft University Press.

Wassenberg, F., Van Meer, A. and Van Kempen, R. (2007) *Strategies for Upgrading the Physical Environment in Deprived Urban Areas: Examples of Good Practice in Europe*. Berlin: Federal Ministry of Transports, Building and Urban Affairs.

Wilson, J. Q. and Kelling, G. (1982) The Police and Neighbourhood Safety: Broken Windows. *The Atlantic Monthly*, 127, pp. 29–38.

Wirth, L. (1938) Urbanism as a Way of Life. *American Journal of Sociology*, 44, pp. 3–24.

Woolley, T. (1985) British Postwar Housing in Trouble 'Social or Technical?'. In: N. Prak and H. Priemus (Eds), *Post-War Public Housing in Trouble. Papers Presented at the Congress Post-War Public Housing in Trouble*. 4–5 October, 1984. Delft, the Netherlands: Delft University Press.

Wyly, E. K. (2002) Mortgaged Metropolis: Evolving Urban Geographies of Residential Lending. *Urban Geography*, 23, pp. 3–30.

Yinger, J. (1999) Sustaining the Fair Housing Act. *Cityscape: A Journal of Policy Development and Research*, 4, pp. 93–106.

Part I Different Perception

3
Resident Satisfaction in Post-WWII Housing Estates

Karien Dekker and Ronald van Kempen

Introduction

Large housing estates in Europe are seen by many people as unattractive places to live. From the outside they indeed might not seem nice areas with their high-rise blocks, the concrete, the seemingly lack of liveliness. Also when walking through large housing estates, it is probably not love at first sight between potential visitors and the estate. Often estates are characterised by groups of young people hanging around in streets and shopping centres, surrounded by unattractive green areas and, in some estates by demolition processes, which gives some large housing estates an abandoned look. Conflicts between neighbours and people in the neighbourhood may seriously affect the quality of life in the area. Graffiti, in car thefts and house burglaries, or problems associated with drugs may be a liability for many different types of inhabitants of large housing estates.

In the first two chapters of this book we have made it clear that large differentiations exist between post-WWII large housing estates. Also, when talking about resident satisfaction, large differences are expected to occur, not only between estates, but also between categories of people. In other words, large housing estates are not always, and not seen by every resident, as problematic places to live in. These areas definitely also have their assets, such as large green areas that can be used as playgrounds and for sports, neighbours that have known each other for many years, etc. Old people might like the short distances to shops; younger people might like the relatively low prices of the dwellings; ethnic minorities might value the relatively large numbers of people from the same ethnic group. In fact, we expect that a number of the estates' inhabitants may be satisfied with living in the estates.

In this chapter we will focus on satisfaction and dissatisfaction in large housing estates. We will indeed show that definitely not everybody is negative about living in large housing estates, that people do value certain aspects of the dwellings, as well as some physical and social aspects of the neighbourhoods. We will also indicate that the reasons for this positive evaluation are different and related to both individual characteristics, housing characteristics, as well as the local context. The following questions will be answered:

- How satisfied are the inhabitants of the large housing estates with their housing and their neighbourhood? Which aspects are evaluated positively, and which negatively?
- Which aspects determine satisfaction with the housing situation and the neighbourhood?
- Which differences can be noted in the North-Western, Southern and Central part of Europe?

The answers to these questions will give a picture of the function of the estates in their respective housing markets. On the basis of earlier research and the previous chapters, we expect that major differences with respect to these functions will exist between the three regions: North-Western Europe, Southern Europe and Central Europe. Data in this chapter was obtained through the RESTATE survey that was carried out in 29 estates in ten different countries.

Satisfaction and dissatisfaction: Some expectations

Satisfaction can be defined as a state in which the expectations of a person are met. Satisfaction with a home means for example that the dwelling is large enough or has enough amenities in the eyes of that person. Satisfaction with the estate can mean that the person likes the neighbours, the physical state of the area or its location with respect to the city centre. It is clear that an estate with people who are satisfied with their dwelling and their estate functions better than an estate with dissatisfied people.

Why are some people more satisfied with their dwelling and their estate than others? First of all, housing satisfaction and estate satisfaction are often considered differently and hence analysed separately. However, in the assessment of the neighbourhood, satisfaction with the home is also included. Consequently, below we will discuss the possible explanations for housing and estate satisfaction working together. The literature shows that there are several plausible explanations: individual and household characteristics, characteristics of the dwelling, and characteristics of the estate. Moreover, in the different regions of Europe different 'sets' of important variables can be discerned.

First of all, many explanations are based on the individual and household characteristics. These relationships find their roots in the expectations people have with respect to their estate and their dwelling at various life stages. First, household composition is an important variable (Adams and Gilder, 1976; Clark and Onaka, 1983). Single and two-person households are expected to be more positive about their dwelling and the estate than households with children. In most countries, living in large housing estates implies living in blocks of flats, quite often even high-rise flats. In general it can be expected that parents with children like living in a single-family house with a garden more than living somewhere above the ground. Already in 1952 Bauer claimed (for the USA) that families with children prefer to live on the ground level. Also in Denmark criticism was ventilated as early as the 1960s. For example, Morville (1969) found a negative correlation between the time young children play outside and height of their homes (quoted in Vestergaard, 2004). Brodsky et al. (1999) found that the presence of children had a negative effect on identification with the neighbourhood. Their research was carried out in several poor neighbourhoods that were not considered suitable environments for children. Others have found that children are an important intermediary in generating social interaction in a neighbourhood (see, e.g., Campbell and Lee, 1992; Guest and Wierzbicki, 1999), which in turn leads to stronger feelings of neighbourhood satisfaction (Dekker and Bolt, 2005).

The expectation that single and two-person households are more positive can probably also be associated with the fact that this category of residents is frequently characterised by a relatively short sojourn in the neighbourhood. Age is important here. In particular young singles and couples often have the idea that they will only stay temporarily in the present dwelling. More often than older people they see the present dwelling as a springboard for a further housing career (Musterd and Van Kempen, 2007). Because they do not feel very attached to the area, they also do not feel very negative; they just accept their current situation. (Campbell and Lee, 1992; Van Beckhoven and Van Kempen, 2003).

Household composition is thus usually associated with age. However, the explanatory value of age for neighbourhood satisfaction is difficult to assess, because different ways of reasoning are possible. One way of reasoning is that older people are more positive about the estate because they have generally lived there for a long time and are thus very much used to the area, the residents and the surroundings. An alternative reasoning is that these older people could be more negative because they have experienced all kinds of negative changes in the estate: the population might have changed and friends may have moved away or died; the dwellings and buildings may have started to show signs of deterioration; other kinds of areas may have become more attractive, causing uneasiness among those who are, for financial reasons, not able to move to one of those better places (see also Chapter 4).

The socio-economic background of a household can also play a role in explaining satisfaction. A low income can prevent a household from selecting its dwelling and its place to live (Deurloo et al., 1994; Clark and Dieleman, 1996). Being forced to stay in a place may lead to a negative attitude. But at the same time it might lead to a process of cognitive dissonance, resulting in a more positive attitude towards the present dwelling and neighbourhood. Having a higher income generally means that there are more possibilities of moving to a better dwelling and neighbourhood. Again, there are two sides to this (acceptance of the present situation or negative attitudes).

Lower-income groups also tend to have more friends, acquaintances and relatives in the neighbourhood than do higher-income groups (see e.g., Lee and Campbell, 1999; Dekker and Bolt, 2005). The expectations are that this results in more satisfaction with the neighbourhood for those with lower incomes.

The level of income is associated, among other things, with the labour market situation and an individual's educational level. Highly educated people usually have a wide network of activities and people, and their ties have a wider geographical range (Fischer, 1982). As a result, they often make little use of neighbourhood facilities: they are oriented towards the whole city or urban region for their activities and networks (Guest and Wierzbicki, 1999; Blokland, 2005). Professional status is associated with education. Categories like the unemployed and disabled people are restricted in their activity patterns and therefore stay closer to their area (Fischer, 1982; Guest and Wierzbicki, 1999). When more time is spent in the area, again more negative attitudes may develop.

Minority ethnic groups are often associated with low incomes. However, an important question is whether ethnicity has an independent influence on housing and neighbourhood satisfaction. We might expect that in situations where concentrations of people from the same ethnic group emerge, individuals belonging to that ethnic group might find support from people of the same group living in the same, or have more possibilities for contact (Flint and Rowlands, 2003), making life in the estate more agreeable. From the literature it becomes clear that especially recent immigrants who cannot speak the language of the guest country and immigrants with a low education level have the propensity to converge on neighbourhoods where many of their fellow-countrymen already live (Enchautegui, 1997, Fong and Gulia, 1999). Despite the advantages of living in areas with people of similar lineage, neither whites nor minority ethnic groups prefer a completely 'black' neighbourhood. As research in the US has shown, whites prefer a white neighbourhood whereas minority ethnic groups are happier in areas with a mixed population composition in terms of ethnicity (Charles, 2003).

The characteristics of a dwelling itself may be important for the evaluation of the housing situation. When the quality of a dwelling or a building is bad, it is logical that a negative opinion results. When a house is refurbished it might be expected that the inhabitant becomes more satisfied.

From the literature it also becomes clear that homeowners are generally more positive than tenants about their home. First, homeowners have in most cases deliberately chosen their present dwelling and neighbourhood. Second, owned properties might be of a higher quality than rented dwellings (Saunders, 1990; Boelhouwer, 1988). Finally, the simple fact that homeowners have put their own money into their homes may in general make them more positive than tenants. In short, there are enough reasons to expect that homeowners are more satisfied with their dwelling than tenants, also in large housing estates.

Satisfaction with the estate is often related to the characteristics of the estate. A changing population in the area may be assessed negatively; for example because the remaining inhabitants may have lost friends and neighbours, or because the new population categories are seen as a kind of economic or social threat. The influx of ethnic minorities is especially often seen by natives as a negative development. The same holds for an influx of people with a lower socio-economic status.

Although the physical appearance of the large housing estates all over Europe may be similar, they are perceived differently by their residents.

First, in countries such as Italy and Spain, living in high-rise housing seems to be quite normal among many different cross-sections of the population (Wassenberg et al., 2004). Residents in Southern Europe are therefore expected to have higher levels of satisfaction. It is also in the Southern European countries that a large share of the residents owns their home (for percentages of homeowners in the estates see Dekker and Van Kempen, 2005).

Second, as we stated above, homeowners are often more satisfied than tenants, which is another reason to expect higher levels of satisfaction in Southern Europe. The high levels of homeowners in Central Europe have a different expected outcome. In this part of Europe all residents became homeowners after the fall of communism, but if they are low-income households they have difficulties paying for the maintenance of their home. Therefore we expect that the high level of homeowners in Central Europe will not have a positive outcome on satisfaction.

And third, the high numbers of ethnic minorities on estates in Western Europe (see Dekker and Van Kempen, 2005 for percentages of ethnic minorities on the estates) will negatively influence the degree of satisfaction in this part of Europe. However, this may be different for immigrants in estates with a certain share of co-immigrants. For immigrants the estates with a moderate share of ethnic minorities may be desirable places to live.

The questionnaire and the survey

We used the results of a survey carried out in all 29 estates forming part of the RESTATE project. The same survey was used for all the estates, which makes it possible to compare them, the cities, and the countries. The survey was carried out between February and June 2004. In each case, a random sample was drawn, usually from the whole estate. For some estates, address lists were used as the basis for the sample; in other cases, the researchers first had to take a complete inventory of addresses themselves (for some deviations from this general method, see Musterd and Van Kempen, 2005).

In most cities, survey teams were hired to carry out the survey. Briefings were organised to instruct the survey teams. In some cases (as for example in Amsterdam and Utrecht) interviewers were recruited from specific ethnic groups in order to raise the response rate among, for example, the Turkish and Moroccan residents on the estates. In other cases, family members translated questions during a face-to-face interview. The questionnaire could be completed by the respondents themselves, but also by the interviewers in a face-to-face interview.[1]

Representativity

How representative is the survey? Are some population categories over- or under-represented? In general, older people and natives are over-represented, while younger people and non-natives are under-represented. For the young people, this discrepancy probably derives from the extent of their activities outside the home, making them more difficult to reach. The under-representation of the non-native population is presumably related to language and cultural differences. All the authors of the country reports assured us that, despite these over- and under-representations, the survey results are valuable for the analyses of their own individual situation.

Satisfaction with the home and the neighbourhood in European estates

Measuring satisfaction

To measure satisfaction, the respondents were asked to judge separately the satisfaction with their home and with their neighbourhood on a scale from 1–10. Non-responding residents were given the average score. For the descriptive statistics the ratio variables of satisfaction were recalculated into an ordinal variable: dissatisfied respondents (scores 1–4), neutral respondents (scores 5–6) and satisfied respondents (scores 7–10). For the explanatory statistics, the original scale of 1–10 on which satisfaction was measured allowed regression analysis. Satisfaction with the home and satisfaction with the neighbourhood were used as dependent variables in the regression models.

Independent variables

The independent variables in the models included a set of *social-demographic* variables containing two measures: household composition (with or without children, where 1 = without children), and a continuous variable for the respondent's age (in years). The log function of age in years was taken to avoid the possible impact of outliers. Three indicators of *socio-economic status* were also included: the first indicator was based on an evaluation of the respondents themselves, on how their income compares to the national average. This was divided into a dichotomous variable (medium low – low = 1, versus average – high). Second, a dichotomous variable for the respondents' level of education (0–12 years, and 13 years or more = 1) was used, and third, a dichotomous variable which represents the degree of social inclusion (those who have a paid job, versus those who do not have a paid job = 1) was included. The models also included *ethnicity* as a dichotomous variable (natives and non-natives, where 1 = non-native groups).

The *housing situation* was reflected in four dichotomous variables. First, the time lived in the house was represented in a dichotomous variable, differentiating recent in-movers (>= 2001 = 1) from more long-term residents (<2001). Second, the respondents were asked if their home has been refurbished (1 = yes). Then a differentiation was made between those that live on the ground floor (= 1) and those on higher floors. Finally, home-ownership was measured (homeowners and tenants, where tenants = 1). The ratio variable satisfaction with the home was included as an independent variable in the model that explains satisfaction with the neighbourhood.

The *neighbourhood characteristics* were represented in four variables that are based on the statistics provided by the authorities (see Dekker and Van Kempen, 2005; Musterd and Van Kempen, 2005): the proportion of unemployed in the neighbourhood, the proportion of ethnic minorities in the neighbourhood, the proportion of owner-occupied housing in the neighbourhood. Finally, the respondents were asked to indicate on a list which of a wide range of problems they experienced. The answers 'yes' were counted, after which the average count of the residents per neighbourhood was taken.

Analytical strategy

Bivariate analyses (chi square) were used to describe the differences in satisfaction between the three regions of Europe. Then, to test which variables determine these levels of satisfaction, six regression models were estimated: one for each European region analysing first satisfaction with the home and then satisfaction with the neighbourhood. The choice of the independent variables was based on the expectations that were formulated in the theoretical part of this chapter.

Aspects most and least liked

Already in the introduction to this chapter, we noticed that not all estates should automatically be regarded as bad places to live in. Also, for many inhabitants the estates will have at least some, and in some cases even many, advantages. How satisfied are the inhabitants of the large housing estates with their housing situation and their neighbourhood? Which aspects are evaluated positively, and which negatively?

The following (open) question provided some insight into which aspects are liked best by the respondents: 'Which aspect of the neighbourhood do you like most?'[2] In 12 of the 29 estates the availability of green spaces was seen as the most positive aspect of the estate, by more than 40 per cent of the respondents (Figure 3.1). The Italian estates Sant 'Ambrogio and Comasina can be found at the top here. In other

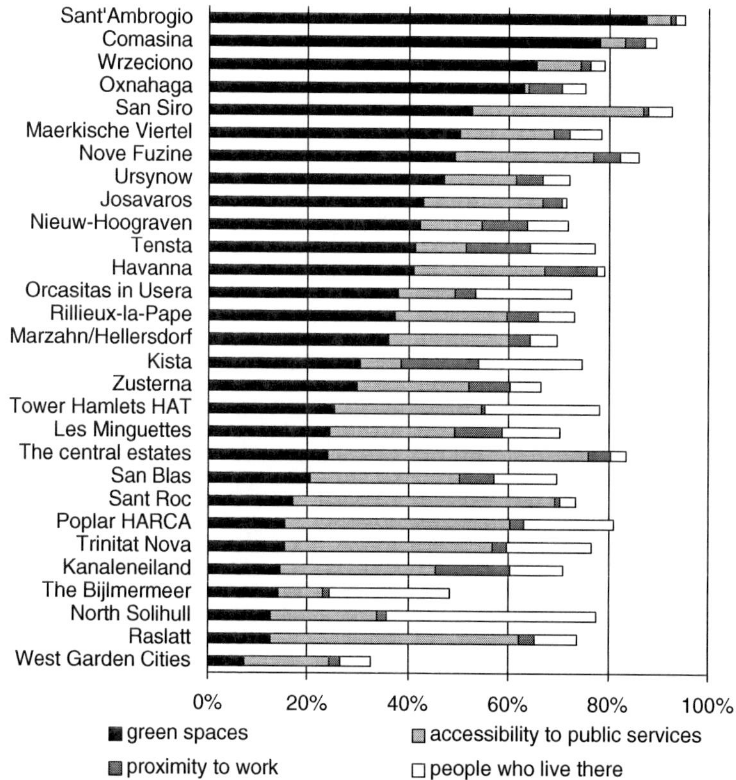

Figure 3.1 Neighbourhood aspects most liked in 29 post-WWII estates in European cities (sorted by percentage 'green spaces').

estates, like the Central Estates in the UK, Sant Roc in Spain and Raslatt in Sweden, accessibility to public services (such as shops, the library, medical services) was mentioned as an important positive aspect. In North Solihull and Tower Hamlets HAT in the UK and the Bijlmermeer in the Netherlands the people that live there are seen as the most positive factor of the estate.

The respondents were also asked which aspects of the neighbourhood they liked least (Figure 3.2). About 70 per cent stated they experienced problems mostly with social aspects related to the population (37 per cent) and the quality or quantity of the services (31 per cent). Especially in Sant Roc (Spain) and the Western Garden Cities (the Netherlands) aspects relating to the population were mentioned, such as the noise of other

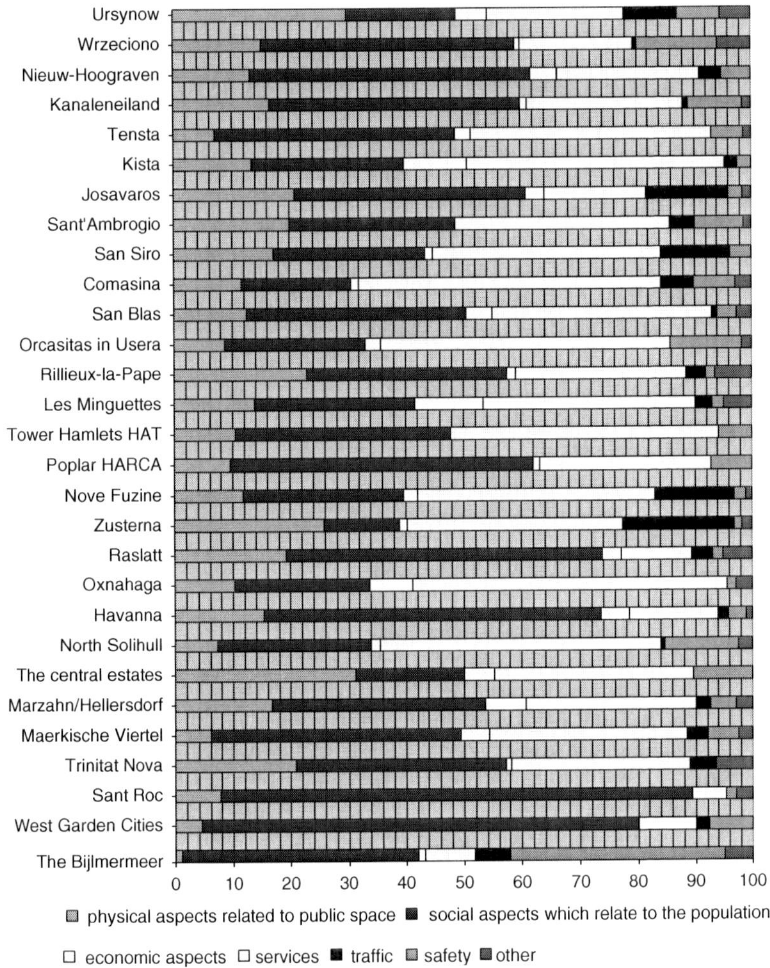

Figure 3.2 Neighbourhood aspects least liked in 29 post-WWII estates in European cities.

residents, and youngsters hanging out in the street. The lack of services, such as public transport or supermarkets, was mentioned most of all in Oxnehaga (Sweden) and Orcasitas in Usera (Spain).

As stated in the introduction, it is expected that the satisfaction with the home and with the neighbourhood would show major differences between the three regions of Europe. Therefore the estates were grouped according to region: North-West Europe (the UK, the Netherlands,

Sweden, and France), Central Europe (Germany, Hungary, Poland, and Slovenia) and Southern Europe (Italy and Spain).

The findings showed indeed that the satisfaction with the home and with the neighbourhood differs significantly per region of Europe. Generally speaking, inhabitants of the Southern European estates are the most satisfied residents, while North-Western Europeans are the least satisfied (Tables 3.1 and 3.2).

In Southern Europe 56 per cent is satisfied with the neighbourhood. Especially the public space and accessibility of public services are valued positively. More problematic is the availability of commercial services and public transport.

In Central Europe at least half of the population is satisfied with their neighbourhood, mentioning the public space, the accessibility of public services, as well as the proximity to school or work as the most positive points. The proportion of respondents that mentions traffic problems is higher in Central Europe compared to the other regions: often these respondents mention the lack of parking spaces leading to cars being parked all over the place.

In Western Europe the respondents are less satisfied with their neighbourhood than in the other regions of Europe (44 per cent is satisfied). Especially the green spaces are mentioned less frequently as a positive aspect, which may be related to the slightly higher number of people who state they feel unsafe.

All over Europe high proportions of respondents refer to social problems in the estate. The high density of people, combined with

Table 3.1 Satisfaction with the home for North-West, Central and Southern Europe, and all cases in Europe (column percentages)

	Western Europe	Central Europe	Southern Europe	All cases in Europe
Satisfaction with the home***				
Dissatisfied (1–4)	13.8	12.8	7.9	12.4
Neutral (5–6)	26.1	24.2	20.0	24.4
Satisfied (7–10)	60.1	63.0	72.1	63.2
Total	100.0	100.0	100.0	100.0
Development of satisfaction				
Lower	24.4	26.6	21.2	24.6
Same	59.9	56.2	54.0	57.4
Higher	15.7	17.2	24.8	18.0
Total	100.0	100.0	100.0	100.0

Source: RESTATE survey (2004). Statistically significant difference: *** = $p < 0.01$.

Table 3.2 Satisfaction with the neighbourhood for North-West, Central and Southern Europe, and all cases in Europe (column percentages)

	Western Europe	Central Europe	Southern Europe	All cases in Europe
Satisfaction with neighbourhood***				
Dissatisfied (1–4)	21.4	19.2	14.1	19.3
Neutral (5–6)	34.7	24.9	29.7	30.2
Satisfied (7–10)	43.9	55.9	56.2	50.4
Total (N = 4689)	100.0	100.0	100.0	100.0
Satisfied with…				
Green spaces	21.7	43.3	40.7	32.9
Accessibility to public services	21.3	20.3	25.3	21.6
Playgrounds for children	5.1	3.5	2.7	4.1
Proximity to work or school	9.7	12.0	5.5	9.8
People who live here	12.0	4.1	8.8	8.5
Other	30.3	16.8	17.0	23.0
Total	100.0	100.0	100.0	100.0
Dissatisfied with…				
Physical aspects	13.0	17.0	13.5	14.8
Social aspects	39.8	35.6	38.1	37.8
Economic aspects	3.7	3.9	1.8	3.4
Services	31.5	27.9	35.4	30.7
Traffic	1.9	7.6	3.3	4.5
Safety	8.2	5.2	5.3	6.4
Other	1.8	2.8	2.7	2.4
Total	100.0	100.0	100.0	100.0

Source: RESTATE survey (2004). Statistically significant difference: *** = $p < 0.01$.

differences in lifestyles, creates liveability problems in the eyes of the respondents. Many respondents refer to the 'influx of immigrants', 'youngsters hanging around', 'noisy neighbours', 'extreme right residents', or 'homeless people' as problematic issues in the neighbourhood. Partly these complaints have to do with the concentration of a large number of people in a small area with little private outer space. Partly, the complaints are also the result of a quickly changing population composition in the estates.

Aspects determining the satisfaction with the housing situation and the neighbourhood

Which aspects determine the satisfaction with the housing situation and the neighbourhood? As we indicated in the theoretical part of this chapter, it can be expected that the level of satisfaction and dissatisfaction is related to several factors: individual and household characteristics as well as housing characteristics are expected to be related to satisfaction with the home. With respect to satisfaction with the neighbourhood there will probably be an important explanatory role for neighbourhood characteristics as well. Not all housing characteristics are expected to relate to neighbourhood satisfaction.

Table 3.3 presents the variables that are used in the logistic regression analyses presented below. Many people residing in the North-Western European estates have characteristics that may be associated with low levels of satisfaction: more non-natives, more low-educated and more unemployed. These estates are also characterised by a high percentage of new residents, a high proportion of tenants and relatively few refurbished homes. A large group of residents is between 31 and 44 years old, an age group in which family life and making a career on the labour market is often considered important.

The Central European estates are inhabited by people who can be associated with higher satisfaction on the one hand: fewer unemployed and fewer non-natives when compared to the North-Western European estates. On the other hand, the level of education is rather high in these estates when compared to the other regions of Europe. Generally high levels of education are not associated with high levels of satisfaction. In addition, the housing characteristics can be associated with higher levels of satisfaction than in the North-Western estates: more refurbished homes, fewer new residents, and more homeowners. This may be related to the fact that many respondents in these estates are middle aged (24 per cent is between 45–54 years old). However, relatively few people live on the ground floor, which may lead to less satisfied residents with children because it is more difficult for the children to play outside if they do not live on the ground floor. Also the relatively long distance to the city centre may be a negative aspect of these estates.

The Southern European estates are characterised by a population that can generally be associated with high levels of satisfaction: many natives, many low educated, many unemployed people, and many elderly (33 per cent is 65 years old or more). Also the housing situation may be of positive influence: many people have lived here for a long time, about half of the homes have been refurbished and most people are homeowners rather than tenants

In order to evaluate the relative effect on housing satisfaction of these individual and household characteristics, the housing situation and the neighbourhood characteristics, a regression model is estimated (Table 3.4).

Table 3.3   Descriptive statistics for the variables used in the regression models, for North-West, Central and Southern Europe

		Model 1	Model 2	North-West Europe		Central Europe		Southern Europe	
Dependent variables				Mean	SD	Mean	SD	Mean	SD
Satisfaction with the home		X		6.69	2.10	6.92	2.24	7.55	2.24
Satisfaction with the neighbourhood		X		6.00	2.16	6.50	2.40	6.69	2.36
Independent variables									
Individual- and household characteristics				Mean	SD	Mean	SD	Mean	SD
Age				3.75	0.37	3.77	0.38	3.89	0.40
Household composition	With children	X	X	0.47		0.51		0.45	
	Without children	X	X	0.53		0.50		0.55	
Ethnicity	Natives	X	X	0.30[3]		0.90		0.89	
	Non-natives	X	X	0.70		0.10		0.11	
Income	High-average	X	X	0.55		0.57		0.53	
	Medium low-low	X	X	0.45		0.43		0.47	
Years of education	0–12 years	X	X	0.71		0.63		0.80	
	13 years or more	X	X	0.29		0.37		0.20	
Work	Paid work	X	X	0.45		0.51		0.36	
	No paid work	X	X	0.55		0.49		0.64	

Characteristics of the home				Mean		Mean		Mean	
Time lived in the house	< 2001	X	X	0.69		0.78		0.85	
	>= 2001	X	X	0.31		0.22		0.15	
Refurbished home	No	X		0.71		0.40		0.55	
	Yes	X		0.29		0.60		0.45	
Floor	> First floor	X		0.79		0.90		0.88	
	First floor	X		0.21		0.10		0.12	
Home-ownership	Homeowner	X	X	0.12		0.53		0.74	
	Tenant	X	X	0.88		0.47		0.26	
Neighbourhood characteristics				Mean	SD	Mean	SD	Mean	SD
% Unemployed		X		10.97	6.83	12.24	5.34	22.70	7.30
% Ethnic minorities		X		49.20	22.04	10.97	7.26	5.54	4.59
% Owner-occupied housing		X		20.21	14.15	69.68	29.43	62.72	22.34
Index experience of problems		X		0.26	0.23	0.32	0.20	0.31	0.21

Source: Survey, 2004.

Table 3.4   (Model 1): Regression-analyses 'satisfaction with the home' for North-West, Central and Southern Europe

	North-West Europe		Central Europe		Southern Europe	
	B	Sig.	B	Sig.	B	Sig.
(Constant)	6.652	.000***	6.440	.000***	6.875	.000***
Age	.022	.000***	.015	.000***	.014	.017**
Without children	.251	.024**	.205	.085*	−.065	.710
Non-natives	−.646	.000***	.660	.000***	−.230	.464
Medium-low income	−.503	.000***	−.446	.000***	.100	.592
>= 13 years of education	.124	.283	−.132	.297	−.635	.004***
No paid work	.052	.652	.035	.773	−.265	.217
Moved into this house >= 2001	.113	.340	.445	.002***	.325	.228
Lives in a refurbished home	.306	.006***	.085	.469	.602	.001***
Lives on ground floor	.242	.094*	−.222	.241	.148	.577
Social rent	−.737	.000***	−.618	.000***	−.210	.293
N	1405		1521		661	
Df	10		10		10	
Sign F	.000		.000		.000	
R square	.145		.050		.053	

* p > 0.10; ** p > 0.05; *** p > 0.01
Source: Survey, 2004.

Housing characteristics are of great importance to the *satisfaction with the home*. Foremost the ownership structure influences the satisfaction with the home. Tenants tend to be less satisfied with their home than homeowners in North-Western and Central Europe, but not in Southern Europe. This may be related to the relatively high proportion of homeowners in Southern European estates, which may reduce a possible negative effect of the presence of tenants in the opinion of the owners. Homeowners in North-Western and Central Europe tend to be more satisfied with their home than tenants, despite the generally low satisfaction with the estates in these regions of Europe.

Also the refurbishment of homes has a positive effect on satisfaction with the home: people living in refurbished homes are, not surprisingly, more satisfied than people not living in refurbished homes. This effect is stronger in Southern Europe, less strong in North-West Europe and not significant in Central Europe. The high proportion of refurbished homes in Southern Europe may be an important reason for the positive evaluation of the homes.

The effect of the other independent variables on satisfaction with the home is not so strong, or they have divergent directions. Non-natives, for example, were associated with lower levels of home satisfaction than natives in North-West Europe, while their co-immigrants in Central Europe are more satisfied than natives. A contextual effect plays a role here: while non-natives in North-Western European countries are in a situation in which many natives are able to move to better places, such as newer urban neighbourhoods and suburban homes, the non-natives in Central Europe generally do not enjoy such possibilities, because newer alternatives are less available.

A regression model for *satisfaction with the neighbourhood* has also been calculated which includes neighbourhood characteristics as independent variables, and leaving out two very specific home-related variables (refurbishment of the home and the floor on which the home is situated) (Table 3.5). Here we included satisfaction with the home as an explanatory variable, since other studies have shown that individuals are usually not satisfied with the neighbourhood if they are dissatisfied with their home (Musterd and Van Kempen, 2007).

The regression model shows the effect of individual, housing and neighbourhood characteristics on neighbourhood satisfaction. More important than any other variable is the impact of satisfaction with the home in explaining variations in satisfaction with the neighbourhood. As expected, satisfaction with the home raises satisfaction

Table 3.5   (Model 2): Regression-analyses 'satisfaction with the neighbourhood' for North-West, Central and Southern Europe

	North-West Europe		Central Europe		Southern Europe	
	B	Sig.	B	Sig.	B	Sig.
(Constant)	4.075	.000***	5.453	.000***	5.162	.000***
Age	−.001	.749	−.002	.554	−.003	.629
Without children	−.276	.005***	.072	.528	−.062	.723
Non-natives	.347	.001***	.366	.051*	.106	.739
Medium-low income	−.027	.792	−.067	.561	.251	.184
= 13 years of education	−.065	.533	−.197	.103	−.080	.720
No paid work	−.032	.756	−.028	.808	−.097	.657
Moved into this house = 2001	−.097	.362	−.432	.002***	−.217	.440
Social rented dwelling	−.181	.197	.167	.233	−.146	.510
Satisfaction with the home	.547	.000***	.380	.000***	.326	.000***
Share unemployed in the neighbourhood	−.022	.003***	−.040	.011**	−.040	.033**
Share ethnic minorities in the neighbourhood	−.009	.001***	−.004	.677	−.016	.452
Share owner-occupied housing incl. cooperatives	−.011	.009***	.002	.239	.014	.026**
Experienced number of problems	−.147	.000**	−.200	.000***	−.111	.000***
N	1309		1512		645	
Df	13		13		13	
Sign F	.000		.000		.000	
R square	.408		.265		.155	

* p < 0.10; ** p < 0.05; *** p < 0.01
Source: Survey, 2004.

with the neighbourhood. Clearly, the home and the neighbourhood are interrelated environments for residents.

Surprisingly, households with children in North-Western Europe are more satisfied with their neighbourhood than households without children. In the models without the control for housing satisfaction (not shown) families are less satisfied with their neighbourhood. It is likely that the houses are too small to house the families, or do not in other aspects live up to the desires of the families, but once this housing dissatisfaction is controlled for, these families are positive about the estates. The large green areas provide large spaces for children to play in, or for teenagers to meet. We controlled for the number of problems that are experienced, so the level of deprivation – which may cause dissatisfaction – is already taken into account. Having children does not really matter for the satisfaction in other parts of Europe.

We expected that the time lived in the neighbourhood positively influences the level of satisfaction with it. In the Central European estates this expectation was indeed confirmed, but in the other regions of Europe residents who moved in before 2001 are just as satisfied as residents who moved in more recently. We are not sure how to interpret this finding. Usually the time lived in a neighbourhood is related to age and home-ownership, both of which were already included in the model. Other possible explanations are the level of deprivation of the neighbourhood, but it is not likely that this has dramatically improved and can therefore counterbalance the negative impact of a short sojourn.

In line with our findings, age is a very important predictor of neighbourhood satisfaction (analyses not shown), but this is no longer the case when housing satisfaction is taken into account. Clearly, elderly care most about their own home and less about their neighbourhood.

There are more important differences between the regions of Europe in the aspects that influence neighbourhood satisfaction. In North-West Europe ethnic minorities tend to be less satisfied with their neighbourhood, especially in the Dutch and the Swedish cases. For example, in the Bijlmermeer (NL) ethnic minorities mention problems which relate to the population composition more often than natives. In the Swedish Oxnehaga, ethnic minorities are less positive about the physical environment than natives. Ethnicity has no impact in Southern Europe, and only a slight impact in Central Europe, but the number of ethnic minorities in Central Europe is very low.

Contrary to our expectations, tenure is not an important predictor of neighbourhood satisfaction. However, if the impact of satisfaction with the house is not included in the model (analyses not shown) tenure is important, especially in North-West Europe where the share of social rented dwellings is high. In Central Europe about half of the residents own their home (including condominiums) and the effect is slightly less strong. In Southern Europe, where most people own their homes, there is no effect of tenure. Clearly, the negative effects of renting the home mainly relates to satisfaction with the home, and not satisfaction with the neighbourhood.

The expectation that residents in deprived neighbourhoods are less satisfied with their neighbourhood holds true. Both the number of problems and unemployment are indicators of deprivation. When the number of problems rises, satisfaction declines in all regions of Europe. Slightly less strong, but also spread over all regions, is the negative relation between the proportion of unemployed people and satisfaction.

Conclusions

Residents of large housing estates evaluate the extent to which their dwelling and their neighbourhood live up to their expectations; if their expectations are met, they are satisfied with the situation. These subjective evaluations are important because dissatisfaction can be a reason to move elsewhere, whereas satisfaction can lead to a higher quality of life. Urban policies often aim at improving the quality of the neighbourhoods; an understanding of which aspects are liked and whom are satisfied can help to direct these policies. To add to our understanding of satisfaction with the neighbourhood and the dwelling, the following questions were answered in this chapter: How satisfied are the inhabitants of the large housing estates with their housing and their neighbourhood? Which aspects are evaluated positively, and which negatively? Which aspects determine the satisfaction with the housing situation and the neighbourhood? Which differences can be noted in the North-Western, Southern and Central part of Europe? The answers to these questions were presented using the 2004 RESTATE survey that was held in 29 estates in ten countries.

The chapter presents evidence that large housing estates in European cities are definitely not always and not by everyone seen as bad places to live in. Residents in Southern Europe are more satisfied than those in Central and North-WestNorth-Western Europe. On average two-thirds of the people are satisfied with their estate, especially the green spaces and the accessibility of public services are assets. Of course there are some problematic points too: the population is often mentioned as a negative point, and so is the lack of services.

Most aspects which determine the satisfaction with the housing situation and the neighbourhood are different for the three regions of Europe. The residents that are most likely to be satisfied with their dwelling in North-Western Europe are of elderly age, have no children, are of native origin, have a relatively high income and live in a refurbished owner-occupied home. In Central Europe people of elderly age, with no children, of non-native origin, high income, who have recently moved into a home they own are more satisfied. In Southern Europe people of elderly age, low educated, living in a refurbished home are more satisfied.

This study suggests that neighbourhood satisfaction is very much influenced by satisfaction with the dwelling; favourable feelings about the dwelling positively influence the assessment of the neighbourhood. But also individual and neighbourhood characteristics influence variations in neighbourhood satisfaction. As expected nobody likes to live in a deprived neighbourhood since, in all parts of Europe, neighbourhoods with many problems have less satisfied residents. However, the impact of compositional characteristics (share of ethnic minorities, share of unemployed, share of homeowners) is very small compared to the impact of satisfaction with the home on satisfaction with the neighbourhood.

It is not easy to present suggestions for policy improvements. Many policies in large housing estates in North-Western Europe focus on the demolition of social rented dwellings and thereby changing the composition of the population. Our findings show that tenants are less satisfied with their home and with their neighbourhood. This might lead to the conclusion that more owner-occupation in a large housing estate would be a good policy option. If satisfaction of the inhabitant were the only criterion, this would not be too bad a policy. However, transforming an estate with an overwhelming majority of rented dwellings into an owner-occupied area would have serious implications. Many of the original inhabitants would not be able to buy a home, for financial reasons. In general the large housing estates fulfil an important function on the urban housing markets: demolition and total reconstruction will destroy a very important housing area for low-income households.

From the introduction to this chapter it became clear that outsiders and people living in the estates might differ in the opinion about the estates. The external reputation of a large housing estate is in many cases not very positive. Unfortunately we do not have data on opinions of outsiders. For the future of the large housing estates, the opinion of the outsiders might be important because, if there is a general trend or negative idea, nobody might like to live in the estates in the future.

Vacancies will then probably not be filled, and large vacancy rates may in the end lead to all kinds of negative consequences for the neighbourhood, as Prak and Priemus (1985) have already showed.

Correlation between survey answers

While the starting point here is that the experience of the respondent with respect to policy action is expected to influence the scores on the indicators of social cohesion, it should be acknowledged that the converse is also possible. In fact it is likely that there is a continuous, dynamic interplay between the positive evaluation of policies, social networks, the tolerance of difference and neighbourhood attachment. The analyses should thus be interpreted with care. One might argue that a structural model in which satisfaction with policies, social networks, the tolerance of difference and neighbourhood attachment affect one another might be preferable to the one-way causal analysis presented in this article. We chose not to construct this type of model here for the following reason: it is the manner in which satisfaction with policies influences social networks, the tolerance of difference and neighbourhood attachment that is being studied. The aim is to analyse the extent to which policies that are noted by the residents add to their scores on the indicators of social cohesion. We do not aim to find out the extent to which policies and the indicators of social cohesion are interrelated.

By focusing on the mutual relationship between positive evaluations of policies, social networks, the tolerance of difference and neighbourhood attachment, we rule out the option of identifying which factors specifically influence the social cohesion of residents. The consequence of this choice is that, strictly speaking, the regression models cannot be regarded as causal models. They should be interpreted as what van Ham and Mulder (2005) call 'sophisticated descriptive statistics'. This is not necessarily a disadvantage of the analyses. The aim is to establish whether the social cohesion is associated with a positive evaluation of policy action, not whether a similar level of social cohesion would have been reached had exactly the same persons not had any positive experience of policy outcomes.

Notes

1. For an overview of response rates, see Musterd and van Kempen (2005).
2. This means that only aspects of the estate were mentioned here, not aspects of the dwelling.
3. Half of the respondents in the North-WestNorth-Western European countries did not answer this question compared to 9 per cent in Central Europe and 7 per cent in Eastern Europe. The figures as given here are, however, representative for the population when compared to the official statistics.

References

Adams, J. S. and Gilder, K. S. (1976) Household Location and Intra-Urban Migration. In: D. T. Herbert and R. J. Johnston (Eds) *Social Areas in Cities, Volume 1: Spatial Processes and Form*, pp. 159–92. London: Wiley.

Bauer, C. (1952) Clients for Housing: The Low-Income Tenant – Does He Want Supertenements? *Progressive Architecture*, 33 (5), pp. 61–4.

Boelhouwer, P. J. (1988) *De verkoop van woningwetwoningen: de overdracht van woningwetwoningen aan bewoners en de gevolgen voor de volkshuisvesting.* Utrecht: Universiteit Utrecht.

Blokland, T. (2005) *Goeie buren houden zich op d'r eigen: buurt, gemeenschap en sociale relaties in de stad.* Den Haag: Dr. Gradus Hendriks Stichting.

Brodsky, A. E., O'Campo, P. J. and Aronson, R. E. (1999) PSoc in Community Context: Multi-Level Correlates of a Measure of Psychological Sense of Community in Low-Income, Urban Neighbourhoods. *Journal of Community Psychology*, 27 (6), pp. 659–79.

Campbell, K. E. and Lee, B. A. (1992) Sources of Personal Neighbor Networks: Social Integration, Need, or Time? *Social Forces*, 70, pp. 1077–100.

Charles, C. A. (2003) Dynamics of Residential Segregation. *Annual Review of Sociology*, 29, pp. 167–207.

Clark, W. A. V. and Dieleman, F. M. (1996) *Households and Housing: Choice and Outcomes in the Housing Market.* New Brunswick: Center for Urban Policy Research.

Clark, W. A. V. and Onaka, J. L. (1983) Life Cycle and Housing Adjustment as Explanations of Residential Mobility. *Urban Studies*, 20, pp. 47–57.

Dekker, K. and Bolt, G. S. (2005) Social Cohesion in Post-War Estates in the Netherlands: Differences between Socioeconomic and Ethnic Groups. *Urban Studies*, 42 (13), pp. 2447–70.

Dekker, K. and Van Kempen, R. (2005) Large Housing Estates in Europe: A Contemporary Overview. In: R. Van Kempen, K. Dekker, S. Hall and I. Tosics (Eds), *Restructuring Large Housing Estates in European Cities*, pp. 19–45. Bristol: Policy Press.

Deurloo, M. C., Clark, W. A. V. and Dieleman, F. M. (1994) The Move to Housing Ownership in Temporal and Regional Contexts. *Environment and Planning A*, 26, pp. 1659–70.

Enchautegui, M. E. (1997) Latino Neighborhoods and Latino Neighborhood Poverty. *Journal of Urban Affairs*, 19 (4), pp. 445–67.

Fischer, C. S. (1982) *To Dwell among Friends, Personal Networks in Town and City, Chicago and London.* Chicago: The University of Chicago Press.

Flint, J. and Rowlands, R. (2003) Commodification, Normalisation and Intervention: Cultural, Social and Symbolic Capital in Housing Consumption and Governance. *Journal of Housing and the Built Environment*, 18, pp. 213–32.

Fong, E. and Gulia, M. (1999) Differences in Neighborhood Qualities among Racial and Ethnic Groups in Canada. *Sociological Inquiry*, 69 (4), pp. 575–98.

Guest, A. and Wierzbicki, S. (1999) Social Ties at the Neighborhood Level: Two Decades of GSS Evidence. *Urban Affairs Review*, 35, pp. 92–111.

Lee, B. A. and Campbell, K. E. (1999) Neighbor Networks of Black and White Americans. In: B. Wellman (Ed.), *Networks in the Global Village: Life in Contemporary Communities*, pp. 119–46. Boulder, CO: North-Westernview Press.

Morville, J. (1969), *Børns brug af friarealer* [Children's Play on Flatted Estates]. Copenhagen: Statens Byggeforskningsinstitut.

Musterd, S. and Van Kempen, R. (2005). *Large-Scale Housing Estates in European Cities: Opinions and Prospects of Inhabitants*. Utrecht: Faculty of Geosciences, Utrecht University.

Musterd, S. and Van Kempen, R. (2007) Trapped or on the Springboard? Housing Careers in Large Housing Estates in European Cities. *Journal of Urban Affairs*, 29 (3), pp. 311–29.

Prak, N. L. and Priemus, H. (1985) A Model for the Analysis of the Decline of Postwar Housing. *The International Journal of Urban and Regional Research*, 10, pp. 1–7.

Saunders, P. (1990) *A Nation of Home Owners*. London: Unwin Hyman.

Van Beckhoven, E. and Van Kempen, R. (2003) Social Effects of Urban Restructuring: A Case Study in Amsterdam and Utrecht, the Netherlands. *Housing Studies*, 18 (6), pp. 853–75.

van Ham, M. and Mulder, C. (2005). Geographical Access to Childcare and Mothers' Labour-force Participation. *Tijdschrift voor Economische en Sociale Geografie. Royal Dutch Geographical Society KNAG*, 96 (1), pp. 63–74, 02.

Vestergaard, H. (2004), Denmark: Limited Problems but Intensive Action. In: R. Turkington, R. Van Kempen and F. Wassenberg (Eds), *High-Rise Housing in Europe: Current Trends and Future Prospects*, pp. 49–60. Delft: DUP Science.

Wassenberg, F., Turkington, R. and Van Kempen, R. (2004), Prospects for High-Rise Housing Estates. In: R. Turkington, R. Van Kempen and F. Wassenberg (Eds), *High-Rise Housing in Europe: Current Trends and Future Prospects*, pp. 265–80. Delft: DUP Science.

4
Estates of Content: Regeneration and Neighbourhood Satisfaction

Wouter P. C. van Gent

Introduction

To tackle urban social problems, policy makers in several European countries are increasingly relying on so-called integrated, multi-sector, area-based initiatives (or policies) (Parkinson, 1998). Policies, such as the Dutch Big Cities Policies and the British New Deal for Communities, focus on tackling urban social problems at the neighbourhood level and strive to regenerate a selection of 'worst' neighbourhoods. Often the objectives of neighbourhood regeneration efforts are to tackle social economic deprivation as well as to improve 'liveability' in the targeted areas. Liveability is a subjective notion among residents that refers to place-based elements which are related to the daily living environment. These elements may include the quality of the housing stock, urban design, physical appearances, cleanliness, quality of public space, safety, and perhaps some degree of social interaction among neighbours. Likewise, a great deal of interventions are aimed at improving the liveability of the environment by improving and renovating public space and apartment blocks, by improving access to services, preventing the senses from drowning in odours, and by dealing with crime. The expectation is that regeneration will have a positive influence on the residents' perception of their neighbourhood. This is reflected in the importance of the perception, or satisfaction, of residents in regeneration policy evaluations (e.g. Leidelmeijer and Van Kamp, 2003; Neighbourhood Renewal Unit, 2005). Thus, residents' perceptions of the situation and direction of the neighbourhood is an important outcome of neighbourhood policies that aim to increase liveability.

In the previous chapter, resident satisfaction was the central item. In this chapter we will go one step further. Here we will make an explicit link with urban policy. Instinctively one may think that, in the end, neighbourhood regeneration will positively affect neighbourhood satisfaction. However, satisfaction as a key predictor of liveability, and as a measure to judge the success of neighbourhood regeneration efforts in the public and private sector, is not as straightforward as it may seem. Feelings of satisfaction are very much related to the type of neighbourhood that residents are living in and to residents' own expectations and socio-economic status (Pan Ké Shon, 2007). In other words, it depends on the context of the estate.

The aim of this chapter is to explore the relation between neighbourhood regeneration and perception among residents concerning the neighbourhood. More specifically, the aim is to illuminate the causal relation of neighbourhood regeneration together with other possible determinants on satisfaction with the neighbourhood. To account for the other determinants, the research strategy includes a causal analysis based on logic. This relatively novel type of analysis makes it possible to use both quantitative and qualitative case study data. Furthermore, it allows the assessment of the effects of neighbourhood regeneration on neighbourhood satisfaction while controlling for other possible determinants. The analyses were conducted on 29 European post-WWII housing estates that have been subject to some form of neighbourhood regeneration. The main questions to be addressed are: first, what factors affect neighbourhood satisfaction and dissatisfaction in large-scale post-war housing estates, and second, how do these factors relate to neighbourhood regeneration policies?

Studying satisfaction

There have been a number of studies into residents' perceptions and satisfaction in recent years (e.g. Kearns and Parkes, 2003; Pan Ké Shon, 2007; Parkes et al., 2002; Shields and Wooden, 2003; Sirgy and Cornwell, 2002; see also Chapter 4). But also in the past, many studies have sought which residential perceptions are associated with satisfaction and dissatisfaction (e.g. Baldassare, 1982; Cook, 1988; Davis and Fine-Davis, 1981; Fried, 1984; Herting and Guest, 1985; Michelson, 1977; Miller et al., 1980). Despite these studies, a solid theoretical explanation of the causality of satisfaction and discontent is often lacking (Priemus in Leidelmeijer and Van Kamp, 2003). Studies usually employ indicators that relate to a set of residential and neighbourhood characteristics, such as demographic composition, ethnicity, income and employment, social cohesion, access to facilities and services, safety and the (built) environment.

Apart from neighbourhood characteristics, satisfaction is also dependent on personal dispositions (see also Chapter 4). Demographic indicators reveal some regularity in feelings of satisfaction. Younger people are generally more dissatisfied with their neighbourhood than the elderly (Davis and Fine-Davis, 1981; Miller et al., 1980). Cook (1988) found a negative relationship between neighbourhood satisfaction and expected changes in standard of living, which might explain why certain young people are generally less satisfied, since they feel a large discrepancy between expectations and current situation (Davis and Fine-Davis, 1981; Parkes et al., 2002).

US evidence indicates that when residents in disadvantaged areas do not expect any change in their personal situation, they may reduce their aspirations and adapt their expectations of their living environment, which would limit dissatisfaction levels and may even produce a modicum of satisfaction (Galster, 1985). This phenomenon is referred to as cognitive dissonance reduction in social psychology. However, cognitive dissonance theory is only one of multiple theories in social psychology emphasising that people try to achieve consistency among conditions (see Schultz and Lepper, 1996). Consistency may also be achieved through free choice. So the amount of choice on the housing market affects the reliability of neighbourhood satisfaction.

Although the choice of type of dwelling and neighbourhood will always be constrained by income and personal wealth (the 'iron law' of the housing market, Priemus, 1978), it is unclear what degree of 'residential entrapment' will impinge upon resident perceptions and opinions. Kearns and Parkes (2003) found that residents in 'distressed' areas in the UK are neither more immune or accustomed to negative conditions, nor more sensitive to negative influences, than the general population. However, the type of neighbourhood does seem to matter for the overall satisfaction levels. A French study shows that perception of the neighbourhood is the result of the interplay between various factors (Pan Ké Shon, 2007). These factors include both personal inclinations as well as characteristics of the neighbourhood. The importance of these characteristics differs per type of neighbourhood. Working class and poor neighbourhoods appear to have a negative effect on the expectations and perceptions of individuals in all socio-occupational classes. In other words, there seems to be one or more conditions in these neighbourhoods that affect the perception of all residents. The study points to age structure, ethnic composition and its meaning in French society, and lack of access and segregation as possible explanations, and to the need for place-based policy interventions in poor and working class neighbourhoods to improve liveability and satisfaction.

Three mechanisms that affect neighbourhood satisfaction

Drawing on Buck (2001), who has distinguished several causal pathways of neighbourhood effects on adult residents, I propose that residents' perceptions can originate through social, physical, and institutional mechanisms. These mechanisms will provide us with the variables for analysis.

Physical mechanism: Quality and design

Some have argued a direct relation between design and criminal or antisocial behaviour, as poor design give opportunities for criminal behaviour and obstructed lines of sight forestall social control (e.g. Newman, 1972; see also Chapter 2). The assumption is that impersonal and dreary architecture as well as unsafe design negatively affect the residents and their perception. However, there does not appear to be a singular causal relation between the built environment and neighbourhood satisfaction. The social functioning of a neighbourhood seems to depend largely on the residents, and thus on social mechanisms, and not on design and management (Van Kempen and Musterd, 1991). Van Kempen (1994) argues that the relation between residential attitudes and design is complex and is also determined by the housing market, building type and especially location. Other authors draw a link between the neighbourhood's physique and its reputation, which affects identity and perception (Dickens, 1994). Another argument is that residents experience distress and possibly dissatisfaction, when they lack social and environmental control (control over place to dwell and over who they meet and live next to), which is often the case in more densely populated areas (Baldassare, 1982).

To be clear, extremities such as severe dilapidation of buildings, neglect of public spaces, and unsafety, do reflect on people's perception of their neighbourhood and their satisfaction with it. Herting and Guest (1985) found that static appearances matter more than more mobile variables such as noise, air pollution and traffic. Parkes et al. (2002) stated that satisfaction with housing and the general appearance of the area are most strongly related to neighbourhood satisfaction. Sirgy and Cornwell (2002) found that satisfaction with the neighbourhood's physical features such as upkeep of buildings and yards, landscapes, etc. are important for life satisfaction and thus affect decisions to move. Furthermore, housing satisfaction plays a determining role in the perception of the neighbourhood (Lu, 1999). Davis and Fine-Davis (1981) also found a relation between the prevailing conditions of property in the vicinity and neighbourhood satisfaction. Furthermore, the perception of the environment's safety has a lasting impact on a neighbourhood's reputation and on the mindset of residents (Cook, 1988; Davis and Fine-Davis, 1981).

Social mechanism: Social cohesion, and social mixing

There seems to be consensus that social relations and community life positively affect life satisfaction (e.g. Baldassare, 1982; Prezza and Constantini, 1998; Sirgy and Cornwell, 2002). This also seems to be true on a neighbourhood scale. Various studies have found that residents appreciate social contacts and good relations with their neighbours (Davis and Fine-Davis, 1981; Herting and Guest, 1985; Sirgy and Cornwell, 2002). Social contacts with friends and family also positively affect residents' perception of the neighbourhood (Drukker and Van Os, 2003; Pan Ké Shon, 2007). The assumption is that social behaviour prevents isolation and encourages the acquisition of social capital in the neighbourhood (see e.g. Forrest and Kearns, 2001). Furthermore, it was found that dissatisfaction over a lack of social cohesion could be a reason for moving (Van Beckhoven and Van Kempen, 2006). In addition to social contacts, social cohesion is also shaped by factors such as the degree to which residents feel involved in decision-making for the entire neighbourhood, membership of local associations, and attachment to the neighbourhood. The assumption is that these factors positively affect the residents' perception of the neighbourhood. However, the residents may not necessarily constitute a single group, but may be divided along social or ethnic lines (see Dekker and Rowlands, 2005).

In light of our interest in neighbourhood regeneration, the social mix of a neighbourhood has to be mentioned here as well. Social mixing policies refer to the practice of attracting more affluent households with the (implicit) goal of improving liveability, alongside other objectives, such as reducing poverty, increasing manageability and stimulating economic growth. The assumption then is that the presence of middle class residents positively affects the lower classes (Ostendorf et al., 2001). The effects of social mixing would play out through various social mechanisms, such as the role model function, socialisation and political leadership of the middle class, quality of housing, self-government of homeowners, increased area reputation, increased social interactions and social capital networks (Kleinhans, 2004; Marcuse, 1994). Although the empirical evidence supporting these assumptions is ambivalent (Galster, 2007), social mixing strategies have been widely employed in the regeneration of post-war housing estates, especially in Western European estates.

There has been little research into the effect of social mixing on neighbourhood satisfaction. Views on the effects of social mixing range from the possibility of social harmony to potential powder keg. Parkes et al. (2002) found a weak relationship between social renters' satisfaction and a low proportion of social rental dwellings in the neighbourhood. However, the precise causality is unclear. In the literature, social mix is generally related to socio-economic differences between residents. However, there may also be a cultural component to the concept. Especially in Western European policy, social mixing relates to 'desegregating' migrant communities. A German study found that an ethnic presence matters for life satisfaction. Immigrants living in ethnic neighbourhoods are less satisfied with their standard of living and with their neighbourhood than immigrants in non-ethnic neighbourhoods. On the other hand, immigrants in neighbourhoods were no more likely to feel isolated from goods and services, to be concerned with crime, or to be living in buildings that are to be renovated than immigrants in non-ethnic neighbourhoods (Drever, 2004).

Institutional mechanism: Access to services and amenities

The institutional model suggests that the availability of public services is important (Buck, 2001). A common institutional context may affect the perception of the neighbourhood either directly or indirectly. Good public service delivery benefits the status and reputation of the neighbourhood, public health and equal opportunities. Basic public services usually include sufficient schools, welfare and health care. The availability of facilities such as shops, entertainment, financial and postal services are important as well. Besides their convenience, their mere presence signifies a thriving area, while their absence could damage reputation much the same as vacancies. Access to services also relates to wider access to financial (employment), cognitive (knowledge and information), political (to defend formal rights and fight discrimination) and social (social networks, leisure) resources. Access to public transport may prevent residents from feeling trapped in the neighbourhood (Murie et al., 2003), which could create dissatisfaction.

Davis and Fine-Davis (1981) found that perception of public transport contributes to neighbourhood satisfaction, especially in low density areas. Along with safety, the availability of education is an important condition for neighbourhood satisfaction for single-parent women (Cook, 1988). Other studies found that access to services, work and amenities plays only a minor role in feelings of satisfaction (Herting and Guest, 1985). Parkes et al. (2002) argue that the importance of access to facilities and amenities to satisfaction plays indirectly, through opportunities for social interaction.

Comparing neighbourhoods

To gauge the effect of neighbourhood regeneration on neighbourhood satisfaction, a relatively new method of analysis was chosen. This method was used to compare case studies of post-war housing estates. These case studies came from the RESTATE (2005) project, which focused on the situation in 29 large-scale post-WWII housing estates, and on actions to counteract negative trends and problems in these housing estates. These estates were subjected to neighbourhood regeneration efforts at the time of research.

The aim of the analysis was to distil several key or decisive causal factors across the estates. The strategy and method irrevocably meant that much of the complexity, specificity and richness of the original case studies will be lost in favour of generalisation across Europe. The models should be seen as abstract-simple, allowing us to think about and reflect on regeneration.

While the selection of cases was quite diverse, there were some similarities. Most of the estates were built on the urban fringe with a similar layout: large multiple storey, multi-family dwellings with large green public spaces. The dwellings were usually relatively spacious and bright. Common negative points included (Musterd and Van Kempen, 2005):

- physical decay of dwellings
- lack of access to essential services
- architecture and urban design support anonymity
- high unemployment rates
- separation of functions leading to multiple problematic effects, such as unsafe spots, conflicts over maintenance of public spaces and little employment opportunities
- traffic and parking problems
- safety problems, vacancies, drug use, youngsters, and antisocial behaviour
- stigmatisation

These characteristics are not all true for all estates, especially for those in Central and Eastern Europe (see also Chapter 3). However, it is clear that the large-scale post-war estates belong to a specific 'population' of European neighbourhoods.

Neighbourhood regeneration efforts can influence the opinion of residents either directly or indirectly. Residents may not always be fully aware of the regeneration efforts, but their perception of the neighbourhood can still be influenced positively or negatively by the regeneration's effects. For instance, not all residents may be aware of youth programmes that aim to reduce antisocial behaviour, but a subsequent decrease in antisocial behaviour may positively influence the perception of the neighbourhood. This analysis incorporated qualitative data on neighbourhood regeneration in order to examine its direct effect on residents' perception of the neighbourhood.

In the analysis, neighbourhood satisfaction levels were aggregated to the neighbourhood level. This was slightly problematic since it meant that some of the richness of the individual data was lost. Furthermore, the composition of population in terms of demography and socio-occupational status was not equally distributed per case. Furthermore, to control for some compositional differences, the economic situation of the estate was included in the analysis. As noted above, residents' perceptions depend on the overall socio-economic status of a neighbourhood (Pan Ké Shon, 2007).

Qualitative comparative analysis: Explanation

This chapter employs the fuzzy-set qualitative comparative analysis (fs-QCA) method, developed by Charles Ragin (1987; 2000). The fs-QCA method has three major advantages. First, it is very suitable to handle small-N research designs (5–50 cases) and thus it allows the 29 estates to be compared. Second, the method is equipped to handle both quantitative and qualitative data. Third, it allows us to discern multiple causal combinations to reflect the diversity of the estates.

Unfortunately, the space available does not permit a full explanation of the method (see Ragin, 2003; Rihoux and Ragin, 2004; Shalev, 2006; Skaaning, 2005). It is important to know that the method is based on logic. Essential is that there are two types of causality in logic; *necessary causality* and *sufficient causality*.

Necessary causality can be explained by the following example: the ability to breathe is necessary for a human to survive. There can be no outcome without the cause, that is, there are no living humans that do not have the ability to breathe. In more technical terms: the necessity of breathing for surviving is colloquially equivalent to 'whenever breathing occurs or is true, so is surviving'. However, to survive humans may need other things as well.

Sufficient causality can be explained as follows: a knockout punch in a boxing match will automatically mean a win for the last man standing, regardless of any points scored in preceding rounds. So a knockout is sufficient for a win, but a boxing match can also be won by points. The cause will always produce the outcome, but the outcome may be produced by other causes as well. So all knockouts are wins but not all wins are knockouts.

To establish full causation, the requirements for both types have to be met. Only then can we assert that the outcome is true or present if and only if the causal conditions are true or present. The fs-QCA is a method for making inferences about both the necessary and sufficient conditions for a particular outcome to happen or a phenomenon to be present (Ragin, 2000). To give an example, to open a door, it is necessary that is unlocked, because, obviously, a locked door cannot be opened. However, unlocking alone is not sufficient to open it. It will either have to be opened manually or, in other cases, mechanically. These statements would lead to a necessary and sufficient model for opening a door with two causal combinations, or scenarios:

- Unlock *and* Manual
- Unlock *and* Mechanical

The analytical strategy of the method requires two steps to be taken; first, the analysis of *necessity* and second, the analysis of *sufficiency*. To determine *necessity* of a single condition means establishing whether all instances of the outcome share an antecedent condition (e.g. doors were unlocked). Instances of the relevant outcome without the suspected cause undermine necessity (e.g. any instances of locked doors that were opened). The second step is establishing the *sufficiency* of the cause. The question here is whether the suspected cause is by *itself* capable of producing the outcome? The cause should always produce the outcome in question. Evidence of instances where the cause is present but not followed by the outcome, undermines sufficiency (e.g. instances where a door was unlocked and it was operated either manually or mechanically, but did not open). The result of these two steps is a model with one or more combinations of causal variables which predict the outcome (neighbourhood satisfaction). For the reader's convenience these causal combinations are termed scenarios below.

Data and variables

The two steps above were carried out by simple arithmetic operations on a data-set. However, the fs-QCA method acknowledges the ambiguities and diversity of social reality and hence the two tests to establish causality are probabilistic. The use of probabilistic criteria, such as significance, allows the tests to be more flexible in case of small abnormalities in the data that are the result of the messiness of social processes.

To further allow for this messiness, fuzzy-set logic is used instead of Boolean logic which handles concepts as either true or false, 1 or 0. Fuzzy-set logic allows for a degree of truth through membership scores between 0 and 1. To be clear, fuzzy-set logic is not any less precise than any other form of logic: it is an organised and mathematical method of handling inherently imprecise concepts, such as social cohesion and environmental quality.

Thus, the data-set features membership scores for all variables. Membership scores express the presence or absence of a variable. Different degrees of property are expressed in scores between 0 and 1, whereby the maximum membership score of 1 implies that a case is 'fully in' a category, while 0 means 'fully out'. The score 0.5 indicates a qualitative breakpoint and means 'neither in nor out'. The membership scores can be based on either qualitative or quantitative data.

The qualitative data consisted of the assessments of the RESTATE researchers made in a series of standardised research reports written by researchers. These reports were mainly used to compose the membership scores for the 'appropriate neighbourhood regeneration' variable.[1] The scores for this variable were assigned based on assessments made by the RESTATE researchers on physical restructuring and various socio-economic interventions. However, because restructuring is often more costly, the physical dimension was weighted equally to the combined socio-economic interventions.

The quantitative data came from a survey, which was conducted in all the estates in the first half of 2004. The questionnaire focused on aspects of liveability, which resulted in questions on various forms of satisfaction, social contacts, attachment, reputation and participation. Questions were also asked about the development and policies in the estate. The membership scores for the remaining variables were based on this survey, including neighbourhood satisfaction.

In most cases the variables were composed of multiple survey questions and/or qualitative data from the research reports. Thirty-eight arithmetic and logical operations were done to construct a data-set with membership scores between 0 and 1 per variable for each estate (data-set not shown). For instance, the outcome variable, neighbourhood satisfaction, is composed by using two survey questions. The first asked for a more general feeling of neighbourhood satisfaction, while the second question inquired whether the respondent felt positive or negative about the future of the neighbourhood. Data from these two questions were converted to membership scores between 0 and 1 and subsequently averaged to create one variable where full membership would mean completely satisfied with the neighbourhood and optimistic about future developments. A low membership score, on the other hand, meant completely dissatisfied and pessimistic. The combination of these two questions signifies that the meaning of neighbourhood satisfaction relates to the perception of the neighbourhood and its direction.

Table 4.1 lists all the variables used and their empirical source. The causal variables used in the analyses were 'appropriate neighbourhood regeneration', which was based on the research reports, and seven other causal variables based on the literature above. The physical mechanism included dwelling satisfaction and a variable which expressed environmental quality. The social mechanism included one social cohesion variable and two variables on social mix. The institutional dimension was operationalised as access to services and public transport. Finally, the data-set included a 'prosperity' variable to compensate for any differences in overall socio-economic status of the estates.

Results

Below are presented the two best models to explain neighbourhood satisfaction and dissatisfaction. The models were calculated with the fs-QCA 1.1 software (Ragin et al., 2003). The models are the result of the tests of necessity and sufficiency and consist of multiple scenarios that explain neighbourhood satisfaction.

Causes for neighbourhood satisfaction

The best model to explain neighbourhood satisfaction tested six conditions: perceived social mix, environmental quality, social cohesion, appropriate neighbourhood regeneration, dwelling satisfaction, and neighbourhood

Table 4.1   Variables used

Causal Category	Fs-QCA variable	Empirical data
Physical	dwelling satisfaction	Survey question
	environmental quality	Written assessments by researchers on dilapidation, pollution or traffic problems and two survey questions on reasons to move and how future could look brighter
Social	social cohesion	Four survey questions: attachment to the neighbourhood, amount of social contacts within neighbourhood, quality of social contacts, participation in associations to improve neighbourhood
	perceived social mix	Survey question: degree of social mix in neighbourhood
	ethnic mix	Census data on demographic composition
Institutional	access	Nine survey questions on access to health care, public, schools, employment, parks, transport and shops
Other	neighbourhood prosperity	Survey data on employment and income
	'appropriate' neighbourhood regeneration	The assessments in reports on 'appropriateness' of physical (housing, public space and infrastructure) and social economic regeneration (economic development, health, safety, education, social initiatives)
Outcome	neighbourhood satisfaction	Two survey questions: rating of neighbourhood satisfaction and feelings on future development

prosperity. The two probabilistic tests of necessity and sufficiency[2] resulted in three possible 'scenarios' of neighbourhood satisfaction:[3]

1. dwelling satisfaction *and* social cohesion
2. dwelling satisfaction *and* environmental quality
3. dwelling satisfaction *and* appropriate neighbourhood regeneration[4]

Dwelling satisfaction is mentioned in all three scenarios because it is the only variable that was found to be 'almost always' necessary for neighbourhood satisfaction.[5] In other words, without a degree of dwelling satisfaction there can be no neighbourhood satisfaction. However, to achieve neighbourhood satisfaction other variables come into play. It was found that three other factors together with dwelling satisfaction explained the degree of satisfaction: neighbourhood regeneration, environmental quality, and social cohesion. In some estates, the combination of social cohesion and dwelling satisfaction explained and caused neighbourhood satisfaction, while in other estates it was appropriate neighbourhood regeneration or environmental quality combined with dwelling satisfaction.

Table 4.2 displays the results of the fs-QCA for each estate as membership scores for the three scenarios. The most relevant scenario for each estate was determined by the highest membership scores (bold in the table). However, when the difference between the highest scenario score and satisfaction was too high, the model was not able to explain the degree of satisfaction in that estate. Thus, neighbourhood satisfaction in four estates remains unexplained (scores in brackets).

It is interesting to see that neighbourhood regeneration, in combination with dwelling satisfaction, explains the degree of satisfaction in about half of the estates and causes high neighbourhood satisfaction in six cases. It may very well be that in the third scenario, estates where satisfaction is low, more or better-targeted investments will increase satisfaction and liveability. Of course, these investments would eventually also lead to better environmental quality and better housing. However, considering that regeneration was attempted in all cases, it should not be forgotten that in other estates good environmental quality or social cohesion proved to be more decisive. Furthermore, the table shows that some cases also have high membership scores for other scenarios. Märkische Viertel in Berlin, for instance, belongs to scenario 3 but its membership score for scenario 2 is almost as high. This means that environmental quality along with dwelling satisfaction and the effectiveness of regeneration seems to play a role in that estate.

Satisfaction with dwelling has already been identified in previous studies as an important indicator or predictor for neighbourhood satisfaction. However, the fuzzy-set analysis of necessity indicates that satisfaction with dwelling is not a mere indicator but a necessary condition for satisfaction in the housing estates. This finding underlines the importance for individuals of private living space over neighbourhood characteristics. In other words, good housing seems to be a *sine qua non*

Table 4.2   Membership scores per scenario and neighbourhood satisfaction

Estate	Scenario 1	Scenario 2	Scenario 3	Satisfaction	Difference
The Bijlmermeer	0.21	0.43	**0.69**	0.80	0.11
West Garden Cities	0.17	0.12	**0.58**	0.61	0.04
Sant Roc	**(0.81)**	0.22	0.26	0.34	−0.47*
Trinitat Nova	**0.73**	0.37	0.42	0.87	0.14
Märkische Viertel	0.04	0.49	**0.50**	0.41	−0.09
Marzahn/Hellersdorf	0.16	0.47	**0.50**	0.44	−0.06
The central estates	0.07	0.12	**0.47**	0.59	0.12
Hodge Hill	0.12	**0.21**	0.09	0.13	−0.08
Havanna	0.13	0.09	**0.38**	0.51	0.13
Oxnahaga	0.37	0.48	**0.72**	0.58	−0.14
Raslatt	0.21	0.36	**0.72**	0.76	0.04
Zusterna	0.17	**(0.29)**	0.19	0.50	0.21*
Nove Fuzine	0.20	**0.63**	0.19	0.63	0.00
Poplar HARCA	0.16	0.40	**(0.63)**	0.34	−0.29*
Tower Hamlets HAT	0.24	0.47	**0.60**	0.53	−0.07
Les Minguettes	0.27	0.13	**0.35**	0.40	0.06
Rillieux-l-Pape	**0.46**	0.40	0.35	0.46	0.00
Orcasitas in Usera	**0.91**	0.74	0.37	0.78	−0.13
San Blas	0.37	**0.47**	0.34	0.65	0.18
Comasina	0.13	**0.87**	0.38	0.67	−0.20
San Siro	0.30	0.28	**0.44**	0.54	0.11
Sant'Ambrogio	0.19	**0.57**	0.42	0.51	−0.06
Josavaros	0.00	**(0.30)**	0.16	0.60	0.29*
Kista	0.23	**0.53**	0.47	0.33	−0.20
Tensta	0.35	0.32	**0.51**	0.36	−0.14
Kanaleneiland	0.13	0.02	**0.35**	0.44	0.09
Nieuw-Hoograven	0.15	0.16	**0.66**	0.56	−0.10
Wrzeciono	0.28	0.26	**0.36**	0.52	0.17
Ursynow	0.29	**0.74**	0.50	0.71	−0.03

* Difference too great for model to explain the outcome.

for neighbourhood satisfaction. Efforts to increase liveability in a neighbourhood should pay attention to this.

The effect of social cohesion on satisfaction in a neighbourhood has been theorised and assumed before (Sirgy and Cornwell, 2002). However, social cohesion (in combination with dwelling satisfaction) is not the sole determinant of satisfaction. The scenario mainly explains neighbourhood satisfaction in estates in Southern Europe, where it seems that neighbours appreciate the social environment even when environmental quality is low and neighbourhood regeneration insufficient. Especially the Spanish estates stand out. This may be explained by the prevalent social ownership tenure structure. Because assets in social ownership housing are not released until after a certain period, families were bound to the estates for longer periods and had more opportunities for social contacts and more stakes in collective civic action (see Pareja Eastaway et al., 2004).

The second scenario indicates the importance of the physical environment in combination with dwelling satisfaction. These findings also correspond with previous findings, which point to the quality of the physical environment as a condition for satisfaction. This scenario includes cases that have not (yet) experienced the 'appropriate' regeneration, but still have a good environmental quality, keeping residents satisfied about their estate. It is noteworthy that the 'satisfied' estates are all in Southern and Eastern Europe.

The third scenario may include cases that also experience a high degree of social cohesion and environmental quality (see Table 4.2). However, appropriate neighbourhood regeneration, in combination with dwelling satisfaction, was found to be the common denominator. The 'satisfied' estates are Swedish, British and Dutch. As mentioned above, this scenario explains satisfaction in half of the cases, which means appropriate neighbourhood regeneration together with dwelling satisfaction, is a convincing cause of neighbourhood satisfaction. In other words, success in addressing the issues at hand and making sure that individual housing is of good quality seem to go a long way in making people overall satisfied about their neighbourhood and its liveability.

In summary, we have seen that dwelling satisfaction is relevant in all cases and other variables in some situations. The different scenarios reflect the diversity of estates from different parts of Europe. However, the differences are also visible between estates within the same national or metropolitan context. The English estates are a clear example of this. Furthermore, it is striking that social mix and neighbourhood prosperity are not conditions for neighbourhood satisfaction. Social mix, in particular, is a policy and development strategy which is being pursued to increase the liveability and social economic conditions in several estates. However, the perceived social mix does not seem to affect neighbourhood satisfaction. Social mix will be discussed further below. Finally, the importance of dwelling satisfaction and neighbourhood regeneration suggests that satisfaction about the neighbourhood can be achieved with the 'appropriate' interventions. This implies that policy makers, who are successful in addressing the relevant issues and problems, will be successful in creating liveable neighbourhoods.

Causes for neighbourhood dissatisfaction

Despite being related, 'neighbourhood dissatisfaction' is considered a different phenomenon from 'neighbourhood satisfaction'. Hence, it was found that the best model for dissatisfaction had a different set of variables: social cohesion, access, environmental quality, dwelling satisfaction, neighbourhood prosperity, appropriate neighbourhood regeneration and ethnic mix. Ethnic mix was included to substitute perceived social mix, because it improved the model's coverage.

It is already noteworthy that the 'appropriate neighbourhood regeneration' variable is absent in the found dissatisfaction model. So, while regeneration plays an important role in neighbourhood satisfaction, it does not for dissatisfaction. Nevertheless, the results below do have consequences for it. Besides the regeneration variables, the environmental quality variable is missing as well.

The two probabilistic tests of necessity and sufficiency[6] resulted in three possible 'scenarios' of neighbourhood dissatisfaction:

1. *no* social cohesion *and no* dwelling satisfaction
2. *no* social cohesion *and* ethnic mix
3. *no* social cohesion *and no* access *and* neighbourhood prosperity[7]

All three scenarios share a necessary cause. The absence of social cohesion seems to 'almost always' be necessary for neighbourhood dissatisfaction.[8] In other words, a high degree of social cohesion will 'almost never' be found in 'dissatisfied neighbourhoods'. From the literature, this result seems logical, although we should be cautious since the fuzzy-set featured only a few estates with high social cohesion membership scores.

In addition to an absence of social cohesion, neighbourhood dissatisfaction is caused by a lack of dwelling satisfaction, or an ethnically mixed population, or prosperity in combination with a lack of access to services and amenities. Table 4.3 displays the results of the fs-QCA for each estate as membership scores for the three scenarios. Again, the most relevant scenario for each estate is determined by the highest membership scores (highlighted in the table). The difference between the highest scenario score and dissatisfaction was found to be too high for nine estates, which means that dissatisfaction in these estates remains unexplained (scores in brackets).

It appears that most of the 'dissatisfied estates' belong to the second scenario. Most of the cases with low dissatisfaction, that is cases with relatively high satisfaction, belong to the third scenario. The model seems to have been successful in covering most of the high dissatisfaction estates, which are all located in Western European countries. In our data-set, dissatisfaction in Central European estates is low to moderate.

Thus, the analysis indicated three different scenarios where, in combination with lack of social cohesion, variables create dissatisfaction. The first is a low degree of satisfaction with the dwelling, which is in line with the satisfaction analysis and findings in other studies. Only one 'dissatisfied' estate fits this scenario. Apparently, the residents regard the quality of housing in the other 'dissatisfied' Western European estates as acceptable, or other issues take precedence.

The second scenario includes the presence of non-native residents (non-native to the host country). This result is very interesting, but we should be careful in asserting that the behaviour of ethnic groups in those estates is the source of dissatisfaction. This explanation would be too narrow and negligent of wider social processes. It is important to remember that the absence of social cohesion is the co-determinant in this scenario. Low social cohesion implies a lack of social contact, which can make a common understanding between groups difficult and may result in distrust. In addition to distrust between residents, there may be a second explanation for this model. The large-scale presence of non-native residents may translate into a negative neighbourhood reputation among outsiders, which in turn may breed dissatisfaction about the neighbourhood among residents who feel isolated, excluded or stigmatised. Unfortunately, it is beyond the scope of this analysis to test whether this is the case.

I will, however, give one example: the Bijlmermeer in Amsterdam has a large ethnic mix and low social cohesion, yet still has a high level of neighbourhood satisfaction. This may be because the (long-term) dominance of ethnic groups and low amount of native residents

Table 4.3   Membership scores per scenario and neighbourhood dissatisfaction

Estate	Scenario 1	Scenario 2	Scenario 3	Dissatisfaction	Difference
The Bijlmermeer	0.12	(0.79)	0.45	0.20	−0.60*
West Garden Cities	0.43	(0.64)	0.41	0.39	−0.25*
Sant Roc	(0.18)	0.06	(0.18)	0.66	0.48*
Trinitat Nova	0.15	0.07	0.27	0.13	−0.14
Maerkische Viertel	0.20	0.08	(0.24)	0.59	0.35*
Marzahn/Hellersdorf	0.31	0.04	0.73	0.56	−0.17
The central estates	0.32	0.39	0.43	0.41	−0.03
Hodge Hill	0.73	0.13	0.00	0.87	0.14
Havanna	0.37	0.01	0.48	0.49	0.01
Oxnahaga	0.00	0.27	0.30	0.42	0.12
Raslatt	0.12	(0.46)	0.10	0.24	−0.22*
Zusterna	0.17	0.18	0.40	0.50	0.10
Nove Fuzine	0.01	0.24	0.26	0.37	0.11
Poplar HARCA	0.37	0.59	0.40	0.66	0.07
Tower Hamlets HAT	0.20	0.32	0.46	0.47	0.01
Les Minguettes	0.48	0.63	0.34	0.60	−0.03
Rillieux-la-Pape	0.16	(0.32)	0.25	0.54	0.22*
Orcasitas in Usera	0.00	0.04	0.09	0.22	0.13
San Blas	0.26	0.14	0.00	0.35	0.09
Comasina	0.07	(0.10)	0.08	0.33	0.23*
San Siro	0.17	0.09	(0.24)	0.46	0.22*
Sant'Ambrogio	0.13	0.13	0.43	0.49	0.06
Josavaros	0.22	0.00	0.22	0.40	0.18
Kista	0.47	0.77	0.01	0.67	−0.10
Tensta	0.36	0.65	0.16	0.64	−0.02
Kanaleneiland	0.35	0.53	0.51	0.56	0.03
Nieuw-Hoograven	0.25	0.25	0.41	0.44	0.03
Wrzeciono	0.64	0.01	0.42	0.48	−0.17
Ursynow	0.24	0.01	0.23	0.29	0.05

* Difference too great for model to explain the outcome.

result in less misunderstanding within the area between native and non-native residents, between newcomers and long-term residents. In other words, there are no conflicts about who 'belongs' in the neighbourhood. In addition, the neighbourhood regeneration efforts may have improved the neighbourhood's reputation (see Aalbers et al., 2004).

As mentioned, the third scenario, which emphasises the lack of access in combination with prosperity, mostly accounts for 'satisfied' estates (see Table 4.3). However, one 'dissatisfied' estate, Marzahn/Hellersdorf in East Berlin, fits the expression. The high dissatisfaction score of this estate is mostly determined by a pessimistic view of the future. The important issues are lack of environmental quality, regional unemployment and the vastness of the urban design which impedes quick access to facilities and amenities (Knorr-Siedow and Droste, 2005). This last point is arguably the most relevant determinant for the Marzahn/Hellersdorf case. As previous studies have shown, lack of access to amenities, transport and services is in some cases a determinant of dissatisfaction. A low degree of access to services and public transport may deprive the neighbourhood of vital and necessary amenities and may induce feelings of isolation and exclusion in the area. As the lack of access in Marzahn/Hellersdorf is linked to the urban design, it is no surprise that residents link the lack of access to their perception of the neighbourhood.

In summary, while the dissatisfaction model was less powerful than the satisfaction model in terms of coverage, there were some very interesting findings. The necessity of low social cohesion for dissatisfaction underlines the importance of a degree of local social interaction, participation and attachment. In most cases, a high degree of social cohesion prevents neighbourhood dissatisfaction, unless there are problems with the housing units, a degree of ethnic mix, or a lack of access. Although neighbourhood regeneration is absent in the model, the results show that neighbourhood regeneration may be relevant as the answer to some of the causes of dissatisfaction. While social cohesion may be hard to stimulate and foster top-down, quality of housing and problems with access can be improved with regeneration interventions. When the causal relation between the presence of ethnic groups and dissatisfaction points to problems with cultural integration and distrust between immigrants and natives, neighbourhood regeneration may be able to contribute to the solution. However, an area-based focus will ultimately fall short when the issues are societal. When the negative reputation is the issue, neighbourhood regeneration can help to improve the face and image of the neighbourhood.

Conclusion

This chapter focused on the causation of neighbourhood satisfaction in general; and in the role of neighbourhood regeneration in particular. It appears that social, institutional and physical mechanisms all appear to matter in various combinations. More importantly, it was found that the degree of neighbourhood regeneration positively affects the overall perceptions about the quality and direction of the neighbourhood in half of the cases. In the other half, other factors such as social cohesion proved to be decisive.

In addition, we saw that neighbourhood regeneration can play an important part in relation to some of the causes of neighbourhood dissatisfaction. Social, economic and physical regeneration interventions can address place-based issues such as lack of access to amenities, housing quality and, to some degree, a lack of social cohesion. Some causes, however, seem to be connected to wider social processes such as cultural integration, stigmatisation, and perhaps social economic deprivation, which would be harder to tackle with neighbourhood regeneration interventions alone, as their territorial focus tends to be limited.

Another important finding was the great amount of diversity among our 'population' of estates. The diversity between the estates becomes immediately apparent in the different constellations of membership scores for each scenario. While some estates have high membership scores for only one scenario, others display high scores for other scenarios as well, indicating the presence of other social processes. Consequently, this means that any neighbourhood regeneration effort would have to pay attention to this diversity. In other words, a feeling for the diversity of estates, irrespective of whether this is in an international, national, or regional context, will help to make neighbourhood regeneration interventions more 'appropriate' and will ultimately yield better results in creating a liveable environments.

The right neighbourhood regeneration policies, however, will only positively influence neighbourhood satisfaction when residents are also satisfied with their dwellings. The analyses showed that to achieve neighbourhood satisfaction, dwelling satisfaction is 'almost always' necessary. Furthermore, we already know that households tend to prioritise internal conditions (homes) over external conditions (those in the neighbourhood) for improvement regardless of satisfaction rates with these features (Galster, 1985). This should be taken into account when using dissatisfaction as an indicator for policy. The quality of individual housing units is crucial for any regeneration to have a positive effect on the perceptions of the residents.

In relation to neighbourhood regeneration, the analyses reveal some interesting points that are relevant to the debate about social mixing. It appears that the perceived social mix is irrelevant for the causality of satisfaction. However, ethnic presence, a social-mix indicator, in combination with a low degree of social cohesion seems to be a condition for dissatisfaction in some Western European estates. In these estates the presence of ethnic groups seems to have a negative rather than a positive influence on the residents' perceptions. However, the Bijlmermeer case shows that it is unclear where the balance lies and whether there is perhaps some sort of tipping point when an ethnic presence is of no consequence to satisfaction. The findings are interesting since social mixing policies which strive for, among other things, liveability, are often part of the regeneration interventions, at least in Western Europe. The negative relation between social mixing and satisfaction helps to nuance the arguments surrounding the assumed positive effect of living in socially and ethnically diverse areas on people. However, it is clear that the effect of social mixing on neighbourhood satisfaction deserves more attention.

Notes

1. The term 'appropriate' is used here instead of 'successful' because the RESTATE project was not set up to perform strict *ex post* evaluations. However, its set-up did examine developments and problems in the estates and the way policies and practices connected with them. Thus, the term 'appropriate' is, in this case, more suitable.
2. Benchmark proportion is 'almost always' (minimum 75 per cent of cases display causal relation) and .05 significance level for all tests.
3. Containment rules, or minimisation, allow the elimination of expressions which are logically redundant. Because I strive for a degree of generalisation, containment was done by means of a Quine-McCluskey algorithm.
4. The coverage, that is, the percentage of the outcome explained by the causal condition (Ragin, 2003), of this model is .73. The coverage measure is comparable to the level of explained variances, such as R^2 in statistics (Skaaning, 2005).
5. Observed proportion of cases where cause $\geq$ outcome is 0.9. Significance is .046.
6. Benchmark proportion is 'almost always' (minimum 75 per cent of cases display causal relation) and .05 significance level for all tests.
7. The model's coverage measure is .69.
8. Observed proportion of cases where cause $\geq$ outcome is 0.93. Significance is .013.

References

Aalbers, M., Van Beckhoven, E., Van Kempen, R., Musterd, S. and Ostendorf, W. (2004) *Large Housing Estates in the Netherlands: Policies and Practices*. Utrecht: Faculty of Geosciences, Utrecht University.

Baldassare, M. (1982) The Effects of Neighborhood Density and Social Control on Residential Satisfaction. *The Sociological Quarterly*, 23 (Winter), pp. 95–105.

Buck, N. (2001) Identifying Neighbourhood Effects on Social Exclusion. *Urban Studies*, 38 (12), pp. 2251–75.

Cook, C. C. (1988) Components of Neighbourhood Satisfaction, Responses from Urban and Suburban Single-Parent Women. *Environment and Behavior*, 20 (2), pp. 115–49.

Davis, E. E. and Fine-Davis, M. (1981) Predictors of Satisfaction with Housing and Neighbourhood: A Nationwide Study in the Republic of Ireland. *Social Indicators Research*, 9, pp. 477–94.

Dekker, K. and Rowlands, R. (2005) Tackling Social Cohesion in Ethnically Diverse Estates. In: R. Van Kempen, K. Dekker, S. Hall and I. Tosics (Eds) *Restructuring Large Housing Estates in Europe*, pp. 105–26. Bristol: Policy Press.

Dickens, P. (1994) Modernity, Alienation and Environment: Some Aspects of Housing Tenure, Design, and Social Identity. In: B. Danermark and I. Elander (Eds) *Social Rented Housing in Europe: Policy, Tenure and Design*, pp. 123–38. Delft: Delft University Press.

Drever, A. I. (2004) Separate Spaces, Separate Outcomes? Neighbourhood Impacts on Minorities in Germany. *Urban Studies*, 41 (8), pp. 1423–39.

Drukker, M. and Van Os, J. (2003) Mediators of Neighbourhood Socioeconomic Deprivation and Quality of Life. *Social Psychiatry and Psychiatric Epidemiology*, 38, pp. 698–706.

Forrest, R. and Kearns, A. (2001) Social Cohesion, Social Capital and the Neighbourhood. *Urban Studies*, 38 (12), pp. 2125–43.

Fried, M. (1984) The Structure and Significance of Community Satisfaction. *Population and Environment*, 13 (6), pp. 61–86.

Galster, G. (2007) Should Policy Makers Strive for Neighborhood Social Mix? An Analysis of the Western European Evidence Base. *Housing Studies*, 22 (4), pp. 523–45.

Galster, G. C. (1985) Evaluating Indicators for Housing Policy: Residential Satisfaction vs Marginal Improvement Priorities. *Social Indicators Research*, 16, pp. 415–48.

Herting, J. R. and Guest, A. M. (1985) Components of Satisfaction with Local Areas in the Metropolis. *The Sociological Quarterly*, 26 (1), pp. 99–115.

Kearns, A. and Parkes, A. (2003) Living in and Leaving Poor Neighbourhood Conditions in England. *Housing Studies*, 18 (6), pp. 827–51.

Kleinhans, R. (2004) Social Implications of Housing Diversification in Urban Renewal: A Review of Recent Literature. *Journal of Housing and the Built Environment*, 19, pp. 367–90.

Knorr-Siedow, T. and Droste, C. (2005) *Large Housing Estates in Berlin, Germany, Opinions of Residents on Recent Developments, Report 4b*. Utrecht: Faculty of Geosciences, Utrecht University.

Leidelmeijer, K. and Van Kamp, I. (2003) Kwaliteit Van De Leefomgeving En Leefbaarheid, Naar Een Begrippenkader En Conceptuele Inkadering (Quality of the Living Environment and Livability). Amsterdam/ Bilthoven: RIGO/ RIVM.

Lu, M. (1999) Determinants of Residential Satisfaction: Ordered Logit vs Regression Models. *Growth and Change*, 30 (2), pp. 264–87.

Marcuse, P. (1994) Privatization, Tenure and Property Rights: Towards Clarity in Concepts. In: B. Danermark and I. Elander (Eds) *Social Rented Housing in Europe – Policy, Tenure and Design*, pp. 21–36. The Netherlands: Delft University Press.

Michelson, W. (1977) *Environmental Choice, Human Behavior, and Residential Satisfaction*. New York: Oxford University Press.

Miller, F. D., Tsemberis, S., Malia, G. P. and Grega, D. (1980) Neighborhood Satisfaction among Urban Dwellers. *Journal of Social Issues*, 36 (3), pp. 101–17.

Murie, A., Knorr-Siedow, T. and Van Kempen, R. (2003) *General Developments and Theoretical Backgrounds, Report 1*. Utrecht: Faculty of Geosciences, Utrecht University.

Musterd, S. and Van Kempen, R. (2005) *Opinions of Residents on Recent Developments, Report 4k*. Utrecht: Faculty of Geosciences, Utrecht University.

Neighbourhood Renewal Unit (2005) *New Deal for Communities 2001–2005: An Interim Evaluation*. Sheffield: CRESR, Sheffield Hallam University.

Newman, O. (1972) *Defensible Space: Crime Prevention through Urban Design*. New York: Collier.

Ostendorf, W., Musterd, S. and De Vos, S. (2001) Social Mix and the Neighbourhood Effect. Policy Ambitions and Empirical Evidence. *Housing Studies*, 16 (3), pp. 371–80.

Pan Ké Shon, J.-L. (2007) Residents' Perceptions of Their Neighbourhood: Disentangling Dissatisfaction, a French Survey. *Urban Studies*, 44 (11), pp. 2231–68.

Pareja Eastaway, M., Tapada Berteli, T., Van Boxmeer, B. and Garcia Ferro, L. (2004) *Large Housing Estates in Madrid and Barcelona, Spain; Policies and Practices, Report 3h*. Utrecht: Faculty of Geosciences, Utrecht University.

Parkes, A., Kearns, A. and Atkinson, R. (2002) *The Determinants of Neighbourhood Dissatisfaction*. Glasgow: ESRC Centre for Neighbourhood Research.

Parkinson, M. (1998) *Combating Social Exclusion. Lessons from Area-Based Programmes in Europe*. Bristol: Policy Press.

Prezza, M. and Constantini, S. (1998) Sense of Community and Life Satisfaction: Investigation in Three Different Territorial Contexts. *Journal of Community and Applied Social Psychology*, 8, pp. 181–94.

Priemus, H. (1978) *Volkshuisvesting; Begrippen, Problemen, Beleid* (Housing; Concepts, Problems, Policy). Alphen aan den Rijn: 1978.

Ragin, C. C. (1987) *The Comparative Method, Moving Beyond Qualitative and Quantitative Strategies*. Berkeley: University of California Press.

Ragin, C. C. (2000) *Fuzzy-Set Social Science*. Chicago: The University of Chicago Press.

Ragin, C. (2003) *Recent Advanced in Fuzzy-Set Methods and Their Application to Policy Questions*. Compasss Working Paper WP2003–9. www.compasss.org/wp.htm.

Ragin, C. C., Drass, K. A. and Davey, S. (2003) *Fuzzy-Set/ Qualitative Comparitative Analysis 1.1*. Tucson, Arizona: Department of Sociology, University of Arizona.

RESTATE (2005) *Restructuring Large-Scale Housing Estates in European Cities: Good Practices and New Visions for Sustainable Neighbourhood and Cities*. Utrecht: Faculty of Geosciences, Utrecht University.

Rihoux, B. and Ragin, C. C. (2004) *Qualitative Comparitative Analysis (Qca): State of the Art and Prospects*. Chicago: Annual Meeting of the American Political Science Association.

Shalev, M. (2006) Limits and Alternatives to Multiple Regression in Comparative Research. *Comparative Social Research*, 24, pp. 261–308.

Shields, M. and Wooden, M. (2003) *Investigating the Role of Neighbourhood Characteristics in Determining Life Satisfaction*. Melbourne: The University of Melbourne.

Shultz, T. R. and Lepper, M. R. (1996) Cognitive Dissonance Reduction as Constraint Satisfaction. *Psychological Review*, 103 (2), pp. 219–40.

Sirgy, M. J. and Cornwell, T. (2002) How Neighborhood Features Affect Quality of Life. *Social Indicators Research*, 59, pp. 79–114.

Skaaning, S.-E. (2005) Respect for Civil Liberties in Post-Communist Countries: A Multi-Methodoligical Test of Structural Explanations. Paper prepared for the XIV NOPSA Conference, Reykjavik, Iceland.

Van Beckhoven, E. and Van Kempen, R. (2006) Towards More Social Cohesion in Large Post-Second World War Housing Estates? A Case Study in Utrecht, the Netherlands. *Housing Studies*, 21 (4), pp. 477–500.

Van Kempen, E. T. (1994) High-Rise Living: The Social Limits to Design. In: B. Danermark and I. Elander (Eds) *Social Rented Housing in Europe: Policy, Tenure and Design*, pp. 159–80. Delft: Delft University Press.

Van Kempen, E. T. and Musterd, S. (1991) High-Rise Housing Reconsidered: Some Research and Policy Implications. *Housing Studies*, 6 (2), pp. 83–95.

5
A Resident's View on Social Mix

Sako Musterd

Introduction

Many players in the urban and housing policy arenas believe that social mix in urban areas does enhance the opportunities in life. It can be a key factor in bringing back socially cohesive urban neighbourhoods and this in turn has various positive spin-offs. Social mix therefore has become one of the supposedly promising and explicit targets in today's urban policies in countries including the Netherlands, Sweden, United Kingdom, France, Belgium, Denmark and others (Musterd et al., 2003, Kleinhans, 2004). More mixed communities would provide good role models next to weaker ones, and interaction between individuals would potentially create positive socialisation processes. Many scholars argue that mixed environments would enhance the quality of – albeit weak – social relations between people because successful people will mix with less successful people and the former is assumed to provide help, in one way or another, to improve the life chances of the latter (Wilson, 1987, Jargowsky, 1997). More mixed neighbourhoods would also imply a reduction in negative reputation that might be connected to rather homogeneous settings in which weak social positions prevail (see Friedrichs, 1998, Leventhal and Brooks-Gunn, 2000, Sampson et al., 2002).

However, there are also other opinions about the impact of social mix (for reviews of different and critical views see e.g. Jencks and Mayer, 1990, Ellen and Turner, 1997, Atkinson and Kintrea 2001). Several scholars argue that neighbourhood social mix will just create local societies in which different people do not interact with each other, let alone help each other in improving their life chances (Blokland, 2003). Social networks may even be weaker in socially mixed environments, and positive socialisation processes may simply not occur because people have too little in common to reach a sufficiently high level of interaction, which is required to get to positive socialisation (Murie and Musterd, 2004). The reputation of the area may indeed benefit from higher levels of mix; however, if that reputation or related stigmatisation is less connected with social dimensions and more with other dimensions, such as the physical characteristics of the estates, then social mix might not even reduce an existing negative reputation.

This chapter seeks to contribute to the knowledge of the association between the level of social mix in people's direct living environment and the strength of social networks, as well as the relationship with the reputation of the environment, by focusing on the level of social mix as it is perceived or constructed by the residents themselves. As will be shown, these perceptions are not strongly related to actual levels of social mix; the perceptions residents have of social mix may be independently related to the strength of social networks and to neighbourhood reputation. The following questions are addressed:

- What kinds of differences exist in terms of the perception of the level of social mix, the strength of social networks and the reputation of the area in different neighbourhood contexts?
- What is the relationship between the perception of the level of social mix and the strength of social networks?
- What is the relationship between the perception of the level of social mix and the reputation of the neighbourhood?

The empirical analysis focuses on post-war housing estates in European cities and the questions and answers therefore are also restricted to these estates. Many of the estates receive special policy attention in their own contexts. In France, Germany, the Netherlands, United Kingdom and Sweden, current urban restructuring processes are to a large extent targeted at these post-war housing estates and, since the current social policy focus is on social mix, many local and national governments are making efforts to create social mix in these post-war housing estates. The estates in Eastern and Southern European cities appear to be positioned differently in the wider housing markets in their contexts and the social mix discourses, as well as social mix policies, are so far limited, yet their housing markets are changing rapidly and so do the discourses and policies (see e.g. Sykora, 1999; Malheiros, 2002). Therefore, it makes sense to investigate the ideas presented in the estates across Europe. To some extent the post-war housing estates are similar – they were built in approximately the same historical period with common influences of design, engineering and views of what made successful communities. Nevertheless it is to be expected that there will be differences between these estates and the responses adopted towards estates in different settings. Richer countries have more means to finance rigorous restructuring programmes than poorer countries and, as said, there will also be differences between estates as regards the position they have in their respective housing markets; in addition attitudes towards specific social compositions of the population and also housing cultures will differ between countries.

Apart from focusing on differences in terms of perceptions of social mix, social networks and reputation, and apart from testing the most persistent assumptions about the relationship between perceived social mix, social networks and reputation, it is also highly relevant to consider the opinions of those who are living in estates characterised by different perceptions of levels of social mix. It is not important just to consider the resident's view on whether they see themselves as living in a socially mixed environment or not, but also whether they like that or not. It is striking that the residents themselves are hardly heard in this debate. In the second part of this chapter I will particularly investigate the resident's opinions with regard to social mix. These analyses take into account the respondents' individual characteristics, their household situation and their housing situation. Again three questions guide this section:

- What kinds of differences exist among the residents' opinions of social mix?
- To what extent are these different opinions related to the perception of their own social mix situation?
- How are different opinions with regard to social mix related to individual characteristics and to household and housing situations?

The aim of the chapter is to create results that help to confront the social mix strategies that are being developed by many policy makers with the actual relations with social networks and reputation and with the opinions and attitudes of the inhabitants themselves.

In the following sections, I first look at a selection of the literature covering the central concepts and relationships; this is done in two parts, following the structure set out earlier. The first part covers the relationship between social mix, social networks and reputation; the second section deals with the residents' opinions on social mix. These sections are followed by a short introduction to the data used. Subsequently, the empirical results are presented, separately for each of the two parts. The chapter ends with some conclusions and discussion.

Research on social mix, social networks and stigmatisation

The issue of social mix and its potential impact on social opportunities for individuals has received a lot of attention, first in the North American literature (see e.g. Wilson, 1987, Galster and Killen, 1995, and reviews in Briggs, 1997, Ellen and Turner, 1997, Leventhal and Brooks-Gunn, 2000, Galster, 2002) and increasingly also in the European literature, where this issue received ample attention from the late 1990s onwards (Friedrichs, 1998, Andersson, 2001, Atkinson and Kintrea, 2001, Ostendorf et al., 2001, Musterd et al., 2003, Friedrichs et al., 2005, Kearns and Parkes, 2003, Musterd and Andersson, 2005).

Part of the research literature is about socialisation processes through role models and the social links between the inhabitants of a neighbourhood. The most powerful examples that have had a great impact on the social mix debate come from Wilson's work on the negative socialisation processes in urban neighbourhoods where large and homogeneous (that is, not mixed) concentrations of unemployed, low-skilled, partly criminal, young black people were living (Wilson, 1987). The over-representation of negative role models would reduce the opportunities of others because group pressure results in a reduction in individuals' efforts to improve their skills that subsequently reduce their labour-market opportunities.

Although this research does not provide the opportunity to carry out a proper analysis of the impact of different socialisation processes we are – to some extent – able to investigate the social interactions between people in the neighbourhood context. This brings us to the insights of Granovetter's work on the role of (weak) social networks in shaping opportunities for getting a job (Granovetter, 1978). Weak connections between people without and people with the essential resources to establish the link with the labour market, are regarded to be of crucial importance. Although his focus is not on local networks, mixed environments might also create the proper conditions for the creation of weak, but real, social ties. People who are part of these weak social networks are assumed to help each other to improve their lives. However, when the internal social network ties are very strong, there may be a risk of losing contact with the wider society. Then, alienation from the rest of society will reduce opportunities to go forward in life.

According to some research, mixed environments also help to avoid negative stigmatisation of the area. Such stigmas may develop – and become highly persistent – if relatively large concentrations of deprived people are living together in a delineated space. However, it is unclear to what extent these areas are actually regarded as mixed or homogeneous, and how the perception of levels of mix relates to negative stigmatisation. In any case, once neighbourhoods get the reputation of being 'problem accumulation areas', they exert negative influence on the opportunities of individuals who are living there. Wacquant (1993) referred to this as 'territorial' stigmatisation; he discussed the case of *grands ensembles* in Paris. Even though a wide variety of inhabitants, with good or bad opportunities on the basis of individual skills, may live there, such reputations can remain for a very long time. Dean and Hastings (2000) reached similar conclusions in their study on stigmatisation in three housing estates in the UK. They argued, on the basis of empirical research, that: 'despite substantive change on the three estates, a poor local image persists. An estate's reputation does not automatically improve as the estate improves'. White (1998) argued that actually the fact that specific policies are being developed aimed at these 'problem areas' *may* have contributed to their negative image because these policies underlined their weak position. He referred to the fact that (in 1998) around 50 districts in the Paris agglomeration were designated as such, almost all of them in social housing estates. Other examples can be found elsewhere too.

In contrast to ideas dominated by the promotion of social mix because positive effects are expected to relate to that, there are also many authors who stress that it is far from evident that social mix is the most appropriate strategy to follow. This scepticism regards several aspects of the social mix and opportunities literature. Some of the critiques address the weak support for social mix policies in general terms; Cole and Goodschild (2000, p. 351), for example, argued that 'policy intervention is overtly premised on the assumption that more mixed communities will promote more positive social interaction for residents, despite the lack of evidence for this claim.' Others are more specific and point to difficulties with regard to proper measurement of effects, because various unmeasured variables and self-selection mechanisms may play a role (Tienda, 1991, Briggs, 1998); again others point to the possible positive effects on socially weaker households, but negative effects on stronger households; some refer to this in a more generalised way, by questioning what shape the relationship between the social composition of the environment and social outcomes has and for whom; knowledge of that shape – linearity, or various forms of non-linearity – is important for policy makers if they aim for positive sum outcomes as a result of their interventions; linear relations will result in a zero sum outcome; non-linear relations may result in positive sum or negative sum outcomes (Galster and Zobel, 1998, Galster, 2003, Musterd et al., 2003). Research has also shown that efforts aimed at mixing neighbourhoods can also cause serious displacement effects. If socially weaker households are among those who have to leave their house, because the housing stock becomes more differentiated through demolition, for example, at least some of them will not be able to return to their old neighbourhood, because the newly built housing simply is too expensive. This will result in a negative displacement effect, similar to that found in the gentrification literature (Atkinson, 2003). Van Beckhoven and Van Kempen (2002) have shown that a move to another neighbourhood results in a decrease of social relations and activities within the destination neighbourhood. In addition, mix also increases the social distance between – different – inhabitants and therefore may put up barriers to interaction between inhabitants. This may therefore also result in the development of non-communicating worlds apart in small territories. Atkinson and Kintrea (2001) speak about the unwillingness to make contact between different social groups. In turn, this may have negative impacts on the level of social cohesion in the neighbourhood. This may be welcome if cohesion is too strong and actually prohibiting interaction with the wider world, but may not be welcome if the cohesion is just at a level on which people are interacting smoothly with each other.

In short, the literature shows various views, attitudes and research findings with regard to the association between social mix (perceptions), social networks and stigmatisation. These views are far from clear and sometimes they are even contradictory. On top of that, not much is known about the perceptions of residents themselves. Therefore, the indistinct relation between the level of social mix as perceived by the residents and the strength of social networks, as well as the unclear relation between the perception of the level of social mix and the reputation of the neighbourhood, call for a further investigation of these relations

Research on resident's opinions on social spatial mix

Specific literature on assessing the residents' views on social mix strategies is scarce, yet some interesting studies can be referred to. Overall, they reveal that social mix strategies are not automatically regarded as positive from the perspective of residents. Kearns and Parkes noticed that: 'There is not a majority in the UK in favour of mixing communities by income, class or housing tenure, with owner occupiers being particularly opposed and people in rented housing areas more in favour' (2003: 847); On the basis of research in two Dutch cities, Van Beckhoven and Van Kempen add to the scepticism by stating that social interaction between old and new residents in restructured neighbourhoods points at weakening social structures. They argue, 'people like to live together with those who are "like them" and if this is not the case, the interest in each other is not very easily generated, let alone sustained' (2003: 871). This may also feed the mechanism that results in rather homogeneous neighbourhoods once residents are able to exert some choice in their housing selection. Blokland (2003) came to similar conclusions about the lack of interaction between people with very different social characteristics. The larger the social distance, the more moderate the contact is.

Thus in this section a first hypothesis to test is that perceived social mix is negatively related to social interaction; it is expected that this is also expressed by more negative attitudes towards social mix. However, at the same time, residents do not easily dissociate from their own (relative) decisions and thus are also likely to express some positive views about their own situation, irrespective of the situation they are in. This will be especially true for those who have recently moved to a new address or for those who have no opportunity to move away. This triggers the hypothesis that residents in these situations are (or have to be) more positive about their own social environment than the remaining households, irrespective of the perceived level of social mix.

A second hypothesis regards the impact of household type and housing situation. From Louis Wirth (1938) onwards, it is well known that more urban environments are housing smaller households. These households' first interests are not directed at their own direct environment; most of them are instead oriented towards urban facilities and many urbanites are highly outdoor-oriented. Most of them do not have children. As a consequence, it does not make much difference to them whether their direct housing environment is homogeneous or mixed in social terms. In contrast, less urban environments, with lower densities and fewer facilities, which also tend to be more peripherally located, will house more family households, often with children. For them, space in and around the dwellings is important, but also parents will pay more attention to the social composition of their environment. They seem to search for environments in which their children can play with 'similar' children. Although this is probably an over-generalisation, it seems worthwhile to test the hypothesis that middle- or upper-class households with children will express a more negative attitude towards socially mixed environments than other households.

The last hypothesis refers to the housing tenure situation. Following Kearns and Parkes (2003), I hypothesise that residents who are owner-occupiers try to create socially homogeneous environments, because mixed environments are regarded as likely to reduce the value of their housing assets. This hypothesis is related to the former hypothesis, since the owner-occupiers are often middle- or upper-class households, who also aim to build socially homogeneous environments. This could be reached through homogeneous tenure structures.

Data and methods

The tests of the hypotheses are carried out on the basis of interview results from the RESTATE project. These interviews were gathered in 29 post-war housing estates in 16 cities across Europe. The estates were selected on the basis of a number of criteria. They had to be a group of dwellings and buildings that was recognised as distinct and discrete geographical areas, planned by the state or with state support, comprising at least 2,000 units, and had to be built in the second half of the twentieth century. Mainly through face-to-face interviews, information was gathered using a similar questionnaire for each estate in which respondents were randomly selected. The core of the questionnaire focused on the residential situation and the resident's opinions. Data were collected in 2004. The overall response was 4756, and the minimum number of responses per estate was 100. The response rate varied per estate and averaged 47 per cent, ranging from 25 per cent in Bijlmermeer, Amsterdam and La Ville Nouvelle, Lyon to approximately 70 per cent in Tensta and Husby (both Stockholm), Öxnehaga and Råslätt (both Jönköping); non-responses included categories such as 'not at home', no time to cooperate, and not willing to answer questions. In general, older people were somewhat over-represented and young, black and minority ethnic people were somewhat under-represented. For the young this is probably connected to the fact that they have more outdoor activities compared to the elderly, and therefore they are more difficult to reach; the under-representation of non-natives obviously has to do with language and partly also with cultural differences. All researchers who were part of the international team reported that despite these response issues, the results of the survey are valuable for the analyses of their estate. These judgments were also based on the additional information available for each case through qualitative in-depth interviews with local stakeholders and on information available in the policy reports studied. A more elaborated report on the response/non-response per estate and data validity can be found in Musterd and Van Kempen (2005). In this paper some differences between estates are shown, yet the focus is on understanding the different opinions of individuals in the estates. Due to differences in terms of high-rise social housing's position in different state and local contexts, and due to cultural differences between countries and cities with regard to that type of housing situations, we expect different resident's opinions on social mix as well. The analyses are built on the assumption that the combined random samples broadly represent the residents in large-scale, post-war housing estates across Europe. The cohort of estates that was selected does not represent the whole range of neighbourhoods that exist in a city, but it represents a relatively similar cohort of housing that receives a lot of attention in current housing debates, or is about to receive that attention. The focus on such a 'narrow' cohort implies that several other sources of variation are not present. This allows us to say more about the type of housing we selected.

Social mix, social networks and stigmatisation; empirical evidence

The level of social mix in the estates was measured by how it was perceived by the respondents. The question was asked whether the estate was socially mixed, moderately mixed or socially homogeneous. The strength of the local social network was measured using three indicators: contacts with other residents; presence of friends and relatives living in the neighbourhood; and whether or not the residents give mutual help. We also constructed an index applying these three indicators. A value of 1 is added to the index if there are good contacts, friends and/or relatives in the neighbourhood, and if residents help each other (maximum 3). The index has been made relative.[1] A higher score implies a stronger local social network. The third dimension, stigmatisation, was measured by a question asking about the reputation of the estate. Although reputation can also be measured from 'outside' (external reputation) by asking key stakeholders about reputation, in this chapter I focused on the resident's perception of reputation: internal reputation.

A description of the three dimensions is required to answer the first question, focusing on the differences between estates in terms of the perceived level of social mix, the strength of social networks and the reputation of the area. Table 5.1 shows some general data with regard to the three central variables. Table 5.2 shows the scores for the variables that were used to construct the local social network index.

Table 5.1   Social mix, social networks and reputation

		Frequency	Per cent
Social Mix	socially mixed	1933	45.3
	moderately mixed	1229	28.8
	socially homogeneous	1108	25.9
	Total	4270	100.0
Local social network score	0 – weakest	990	20.8
	0.33 – weak	1486	31.3
	0.50 – moderate	175	3.7
	0.67 – strong	1390	29.3
	1 – strongest	709	14.9
	Total	4750	100.0
Estate reputation in the rest of the city	good	807	18.7
	moderate	1599	37.1
	bad	1905	44.2
	Total	4311	100.0

Source: RESTATE survey 2004.

Table 5.2   Variables used in the construction of the local social network index score

		Frequency	Per cent
Rate of contacts with other residents	good	2381	51.5
	moderate	1842	39.8
	bad	402	8.7
	Total	4625	100.0
Friends or relatives in the neighbourhood?	yes, both relatives and friends	1280	27.1
	yes, but only friends	1250	26.4
	yes, but only relatives	318	6.7
	no	1880	39.8
	Total	4728	100.0
Residents help each other?	help each other	1244	28.2
	go their own way	1767	40.1
	mixture	1396	31.7
	Total	4407	100.0

Source: RESTATE survey 2004.

The largest group of respondents (45 per cent) consider that they live in a socially mixed environment; less than a third say that they live in a moderately mixed neighbourhood, and a quarter say they live in a socially homogeneous neighbourhood. As was already argued in the introduction of this chapter, these perceptions do not necessarily reflect the actual social compositions of the estates. This becomes clear if the entropy values for five income classes are calculated per estate. The entropy is a measure for the variation of nominal variables;[2] a value of 0 represents total homogeneity (all incomes in one class); a value of 1 stands for complete heterogeneity. The calculated values run from levels in the 0.60s (estates in Birmingham, Warsaw, Utrecht and Amsterdam) to values above 0.90 (in Barcelona and Madrid). In fact, all values point to fairly heterogeneous estates, with only relative differences between the levels. Table 5.3 summarises the weak yet significant positive relationship between the perceived level of social mix and the actual level of social mix in the estates included in the research.

With regard to the local social network index, we can distinguish those with the weakest social network (21 per cent); those with a weak network (31 per cent); and those with a strong (29 per cent) or very strong (15 per cent) local social network. Finally, the reputation of the estates is more often bad than good.

In order to get a picture of the differences between the estates as regards the perceived level of social mix, strength of social networks and type of reputation, three K-means cluster analyses were run. The methodology applied will be illustrated for the classification of estates based on the perceived level of social mix. First, for each estate the proportion of respondents who said the estate was socially homogeneous, moderately mixed or socially mixed, was calculated. Subsequently a cluster analysis was run on two variables: the percentage scoring socially homogeneous and the percentage scoring socially mixed.[3] A three-cluster solution appeared to result in fairly homogeneous groups of estates. Figure 5.1 shows the cluster-averages of the percentages of respondents per estate who view their estate as socially homogeneous, moderately mixed or socially mixed. In the first cluster, with ten estates, the dominant respondent view is that these estates are socially mixed. The second cluster, with only three estates, is characterised by social homogeneity. The third cluster (16 estates) can be regarded as the 'middle'; these estates are characterised by a wide variety of opinions regarding the level of social mix.

In order to classify the estates also in a balanced way with regard to the strength of local social networks, and their reputation, similar types of cluster analyses were carried out for these two dimensions as well. In both

Table 5.3   Level of perceived social mix by levels of actual social mix (income entropy), percentages

Perceived social mix	Entropy				Total
	Homogeneous	Relatively homogeneous	Relatively heterogeneous	Heterogeneous	
Socially mixed	15.2	29.7	30.8	24.2	100
Moderately mixed	33.4	20.3	22.4	23.9	100
Socially homogeneous	30.0	22.7	19.7	27.6	100
Total	25.0	25.0	25.0	25.0	100

Cramer's V 0.15, p < 0.01
Source: RESTATE survey 2004.

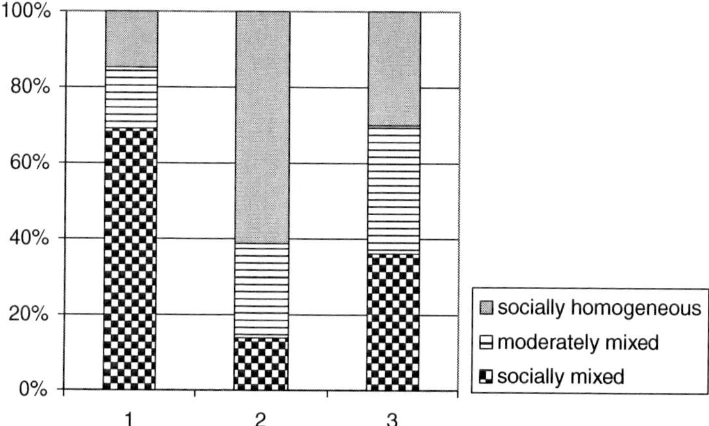

Figure 5.1   Profiles of clusters of estates according to the perceived level of social mix.

cases again, three clusters appeared to provide interpretable categories. For the analysis on the basis of the strength of local social networks, a cluster resulted that bundled 16 estates with residents with a relatively strong local social network; another cluster of seven estates was characterised by residents with relatively weak local social networks; and finally there was a cluster of six estates with a very high proportion of residents reporting strong(est) local social networks (Figure 5.2). Figure 5.3 shows the profiles of the three clusters that were constructed on the basis of the estates' reputation. Cluster 1 (ten estates) is characterised by a wide variety of opinions on the reputation of the estates, but also with a high portion scoring 'relatively bad'; the second cluster (ten estates) is characterised by a moderate or good reputation; the third cluster (nine estates) clearly is worst off, with a high average portion of residents who report a bad reputation.

It is interesting to see whether, at the level of estates, there is an association between the clusters based on the three dimensions we dealt with. In Table 5.4 the estates are presented with their cluster membership in each of the three classifications. The estates are sorted by cluster, based on the level of social mix. As shown, there is a tremendous variation in the levels of social mix in the post-war housing estates we considered. The highest scores in the highly mixed category were experienced in La Ville Nouvelle (Lyon), Märkische Viertel (Berlin) and Nove Fuzine (Ljubljana); in these estates at least 75 per cent of the residents perceived their estate to be socially mixed. The lowest levels of social mix (i.e. social homogeneity) were registered in Hodge Hill (Birmingham),

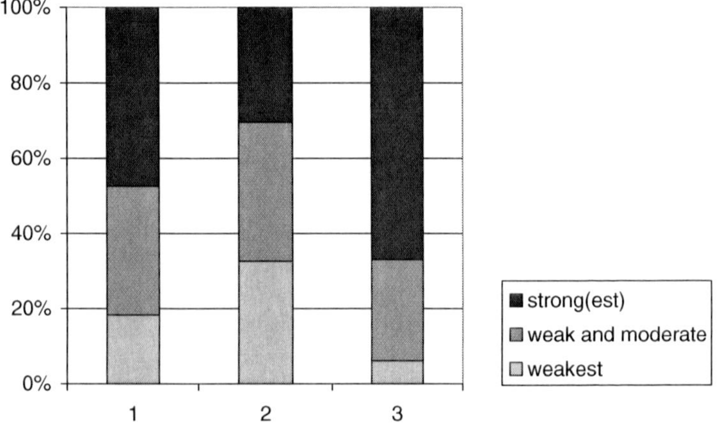

Figure 5.2   Profiles of clusters of estates according to strength of social networks.

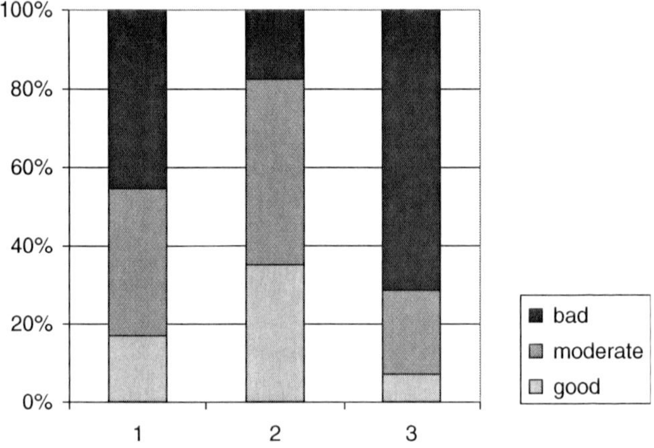

Figure 5.3   Profiles of clusters of estates according to reputation.

Kolenkit (Amsterdam) and Kanaleneiland (Utrecht); in these estates less than 20 per cent of the residents thought their estate was socially mixed. It can be seen that the estates that are regarded as socially mixed and those which are moderately mixed may or may not be estates in which residents report strong social networks; In each of these two mix types approximately 60 per cent of the estates is characterised by moderately strong social networks; there does not seem to be a significant relationship between the perceived level of social mix and the strength of social

Table 5.4   Estate classification based on three clustering processes

Estate	City	Estate socially mixed	Local social networks	Reputation
La Ville Nouvelle	Lyon	highly mixed	Strongest	relatively good
Wrzeciono	Warsaw	highly mixed	Strongest	relatively bad
Öxnehaga	Jönköping	highly mixed	moderately strong	relatively good
Sant'Ambrogio	Milan	highly mixed	moderately strong	relatively good
Bijlmer-East	Amsterdam	highly mixed	moderately strong	relatively bad
Märkisches Viertel	Berlin	highly mixed	moderately strong	relatively bad
Zusterna-Semedela	Koper	highly mixed	moderately strong	relatively bad
Råslätt	Jönköping	highly mixed	moderately strong	very bad
Marzahn/Hellersdorf	Berlin	highly mixed	relatively weak	relatively bad
Nove Fuzine	Ljubljana	highly mixed	relatively weak	very bad
Hodge Hill	Birmingham	relatively homogeneous	relatively weak	relatively bad
Kolenkit	Amsterdam	relatively homogeneous	relatively weak	very bad
Kanaleneiland	Utrecht	relatively homogeneous	relatively weak	very bad
Trinitat Nova	Barcelona	moderately mixed	Strongest	relatively bad
Simancas	Madrid	moderately mixed	Strongest	relatively bad
Sant Roc	Barcelona	moderately mixed	Strongest	very bad
Orcasitas	Madrid	moderately mixed	Strongest	very bad
Poplar HARCA	London	moderately mixed	moderately strong	relatively good
Bow HAT	London	moderately mixed	moderately strong	relatively good
Comasina	Milan	moderately mixed	moderately strong	relatively good
San Siro	Milan	moderately mixed	moderately strong	relatively good
Jósaváros	Nyíregyháza	moderately mixed	moderately strong	relatively good
Ursynów	Warsaw	moderately mixed	moderately strong	relatively good
Tensta	Stockholm	moderately mixed	moderately strong	relatively bad
Havanna	Budapest	moderately mixed	moderately strong	very bad
Les Minguettes	Lyon	moderately mixed	moderately strong	very bad
Husby	Stockholm	moderately mixed	moderately strong	very bad
Central Estates	Birmingham	moderately mixed	relatively weak	relatively good
Nieuw-Hoograven	Utrecht	moderately mixed	relatively weak	relatively bad

Source: RESTATE survey 2004.

networks. So, this finding does not support the hypothesis that the perception of social mix relates negatively to the strength of social networks in the estates. Reputation also does not seem to relate strongly to the level of social mix. Estates with relatively good, relatively bad and very bad reputations can be found both in highly mixed and in moderately mixed situations. It seems that the estates that are perceived to be socially relatively homogeneous (Hodge Hill, Kolenkit and Kanaleneiland) are worst off. They are all characterised by their relatively weak local social networks and all have a bad reputation. However, the conclusion should not be drawn too quickly that social mix would solve the problems in such estates. When we refer to all of the estates in the research that are characterised by a high level of social mix, 70 per cent are characterised by a bad reputation. The moderately mixed estates more often have a relatively good reputation (44 per cent). There is no clear European geography as regards the estates according to the perceived level of social mix, the strength of social networks and the reputation.

As said, our main focus in this contribution is on the individual level. Therefore, the analyses of the associations between perceived level of social mix, strength of local social network and reputation are also carried out directly, at the individual level, without taking the estate's position into account. In Table 5.5 the association between the perceived level of social mix and the strength of the social network is shown (Question 2). Again, these results do not support the hypothesis that the perception of social mix relates negatively with the strength of social networks. In contrast, there even appears to be a significant, albeit weak, reverse association. Residents who say they are living in socially mixed situations tend to report stronger social networks more often than residents who say they are living in a socially homogeneous neighbourhood. However, the differences are small; yet if social distances increase through a higher perceived level of social mix, this does not seem to be associated with

Table 5.5   Level of social mix by strength of local social network

	Weakest	Moderate	Strong and Strongest		n
Socially mixed	18%	33%	48%	100%	1933
Moderately mixed	20%	37%	43%	100%	1229
Socially homogeneous	24%	35%	42%	100%	1107
Total	20%	35%	45%	100%	4269

Cramer's V 0.05, p < 0.01
Source: RESTATE survey 2004.

Table 5.6   Level of social mix by reputation of the estate

	good	moderate	bad		n
Socially mixed	19%	36%	45%	100%	1782
Moderately mixed	19%	43%	38%	100%	1128
Socially homogeneous	17%	32%	52%	100%	1024
Total	18%	37%	45%	100%	3934

Cramer's V 0.07, p < 0.01
Source: RESTATE survey 2004.

weaker social networks. This is also the conclusion if we look, more specifically, at the rate of contacts with other residents in the neighbourhood. The proportion of people who report good contacts is significantly higher in neighbourhoods that are seen as socially mixed (58 per cent) than in neighbourhood that are regarded socially homogeneous (48 per cent). Table 5.6 shows some support for the second hypothesis, which is that social mix will be better for the reputation of the neighbourhood (Question 3). The portion of respondents that reports bad reputation is lower in situations that are perceived as socially mixed than in homogeneous contexts. However, again the difference is moderate.

Residents' opinions on social spatial mix; empirical evidence

The respondents in our research project do not uniformly value a high level of social mix as a positive thing (Questions 4–6). We asked the residents whether a high level of social mix is good or bad for interaction between residents. Of all the residents, 35 per cent thought that it was good for interaction, 45 per cent had a neutral opinion, while 20 per cent thought it was a bad idea. Interestingly, there appears to be a geographic differentiation in the pattern of answers. Estates in the northern and western parts of Europe (France, UK, Sweden, the Netherlands) show clearly higher scores on the answer 'a high level of mix is good', compared to southern and eastern parts of Europe (Figure 5.4).

If we again go to the individual level and combine the opinions on whether social mix is seen as good or bad with the perceived residential situation of the respondents themselves, it can be shown (Table 5.7) that, among those who say they are living in socially mixed estates, there is a relatively high percentage that says that a high level of social mix is a good thing, but also a relatively high percentage says that a high level of social mix is a bad thing for interaction between residents. According

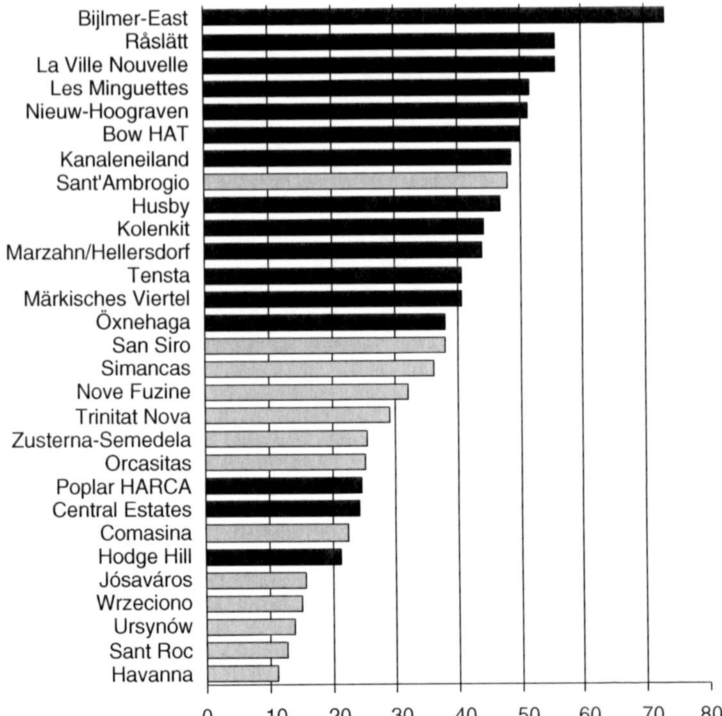

Figure 5.4 Percentage of residents per estate who regard a high level of social mix to be good for interaction between the residents. Black bars: northern and western parts of Europe; Grey bars: southern and eastern parts of Europe.

Table 5.7 Opinion about a high level of social mix by perceived level of social mix

	high level of social mix is good or bad for interaction between residents				
	good	neutral	bad		N
socially mixed	37%	40%	23%	100%	1789
moderately mixed	33%	53%	14%	100%	1146
socially homogeneous	33%	47%	19%	100%	959
Total	35%	45%	20%	100%	3894

Cramer's V 0.09, p < 0.01
Source: RESTATE survey 2004.

to the literature referred to in this chapter, this pattern may also be explained by other variables, such as individual demographic, cultural, and socio-economic characteristics of the respondent, household type, tenure type, duration of stay and the strength of local social networks. In order to get some understanding of these impacts, a logistic regression analysis was carried out in which the odds of expressing that a high level of social mix is good was regressed against a series of these variables (Table 5.8). There appeared to be remarkably little effect of gender, demographic situation (age and age of youngest child) and family type (with or without children). Also duration of stay in the dwelling did not matter. With regard to the socio-economic position we found that the middle incomes were showing the highest percentages of 'good' scores on the question about whether a high level of social mix is good or bad. The hypothesis that middle-class and upper-class household would be more negative with regard to higher levels of social mix could thus not generally be supported. We did find significant impact of ethnicity, the strength of the social network, and tenure. Regarding ethnicity we could distinguish between ethnic majorities and Mediterranean[4] households. Clearly the probability that a higher percentage of 'good' answers would be given is much higher for Mediterranean than for ethnic majorities. In fact, in our survey 47 per cent of the former category says that a high level of social mix is good, whereas only 27 per cent of ethnic majorities give that answer.

It is also interesting to see that those with a strong social network more often favour highly mixed estates compared to those with a weaker social network. However, when this relation is inspected in somewhat greater detail, the association disappears for those who are living in a socially homogeneous environment (Figure 5.5). An interpretation may be that in mixed or moderately mixed situations those who have strong social networks are indeed aware of the social mix of their environment and regard this to be a good thing *because* they associate this with a strong social network. Those with weaker social networks clearly have other opinions about the social mix (less frequently positive); they may even blame the social mix for their weak social networks. In socially homogeneous circumstances those with stronger social networks are obviously not so sure if they want more mix; there we find higher portions of those who have a weaker social network in favour of more mix. For them this may be regarded as a way out of their current situation.

Apart from ethnicity and strength of social networks, housing tenure type also appears to be related to the proportion of people who think

Table 5.8 Logistic regression of those who say that a high level of social mix is good with individual, household and dwelling characteristics as independent variables; odds ratios

	Exp(B)
Constant	0.878
Age (ref 65+)	
18–30	0.988
31–44	0.988
45–54	0.963
55–64	0.999
Local social network (ref strong and strongest)	
weakest	0.694
moderate	0.598**
Ethnicity (ref other)	
Majorities	0.492**
Mediterranean	1.388
Income (ref medium low)	
high	1.194
average	1.410*
Perceived level of social mix (ref socially homogeneous)	
socially mixed	1.017
moderately mixed	0.787
Duration of stay (ref 2001–4)	
before 1995	0.921
1996–2000	1.135
Tenure (ref owner occupier)	
social rent	1.410*
Private rent	1.899**
Family type (ref other)	
with children	0.705
Age youngest child (ref > 15 years)	
< 16 years	1.031
Gender (ref female)	
Male	1.214

Nagelkerke R = 0.12, *p < 0.05; **p < 0.01
Source: RESTATE survey (2004).

a high level of social mix is good for interaction. Clearly most owner-occupiers disagree, while those who are living in the private or social rented sector more often agree, with that. In support of the hypothesis that was formulated on the basis of work done by Kearns and Parkes,

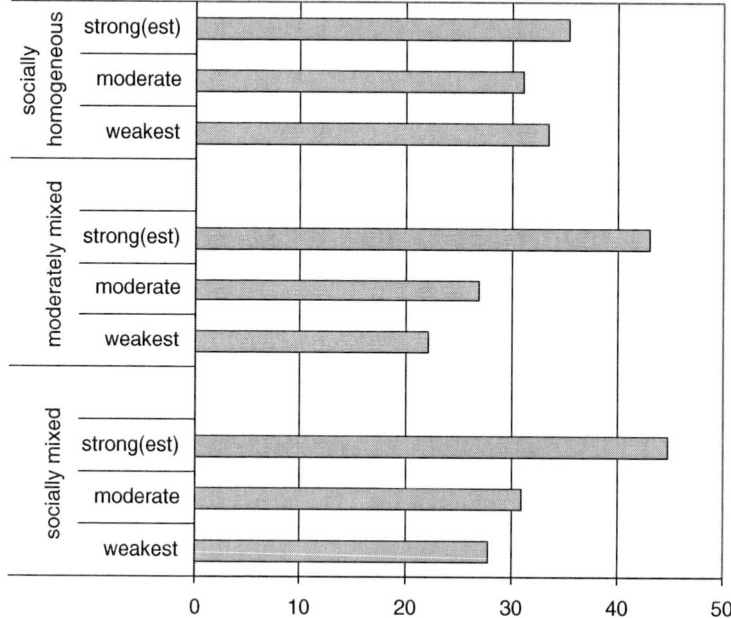

Figure 5.5 Percentage of respondents who say a high level of social mix is good for interaction between residents, by strength of the social network by level of social mix in the estate.

(2003), it can be shown (Figure 5.6) that owner-occupiers more often are of the opinion that a high level of social mix is bad for interaction between residents, and that social renters and private renters less frequently express that opinion. Further analyses revealed that the proportion having that opinion is higher when residents are living in socially mixed situations themselves, but that this is only true for social rent and owner-occupiers and not for private rent. Perhaps residents of privately rented accommodation are less sensitive to the environment they are living in, because they are more likely to live there only for a short period.

Finally, one other impact must be mentioned. The judgement of residents about people in the estate in general appeared to be an important effect. Residents were asked to report what aspect of the estate they liked least. The most frequently reported answer was: people in the estate. More than a quarter of all households had that opinion. Based on that answer, a new variable was created distinguishing between residents who had that opinion and others. This new variable turned out to relate significantly to a negative judgement about high levels of social mix.

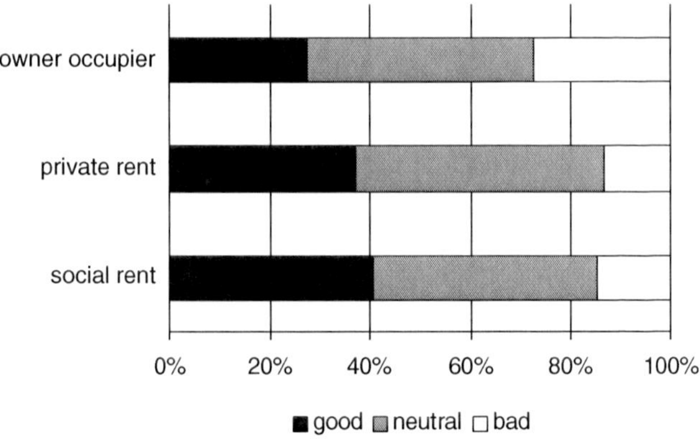

Figure 5.6 Judgement about the question whether a high level of social mix is good or bad for interaction between residents, per tenure category.

Almost 30 per cent of those who said that the aspect of the estate they liked least was people in the estate, felt that a high level of social mix was a bad thing for the interaction between residents; as opposed to only 20 per cent of those who did not report people in the estate as the least liked aspect. Further analyses of this relation in combination with the level of social mix they say they find themselves in, revealed an interesting statistical interaction effect. Residents who reported that people in the estate were the least liked aspect of the estate, and who regarded themselves living in a clearly socially mixed situation, were very negative about high levels of social mix: 38.5 per cent of them thought that was bad for interaction between residents. Those who were similarly negative about people in their estate, yet were living in a socially homogeneous situation, were much less frequently negative: 23 per cent. For those who did not mention the people in the estate as the least liked aspect of their estate, there did not seem to be a significant difference. Of those who lived in a socially mixed situation, 23 per cent reported that a high level of social mix was bad for interaction between residents, while 20 per cent of those who lived in a socially homogeneous situation held this view.

Conclusions and discussion

Even within post-war housing estates, which are just a section of the total housing stock, there appear to be widely differing social mix situations and also very different strengths of social networks. From the analysis aimed at answering the first three questions on the relationships between the level of social mix and the strength of social networks and reputation of the estate, an interesting finding could be derived, which is that increasing social distances through more social mix is not necessarily associated with weaker local social networks. The proportion of people who report good contacts with residents in their environment is statistically more significant and higher, although not much, in neighbourhoods that are regarded as socially mixed than in neighbourhoods that are seen as socially homogeneous. This was an unexpected finding because the literature tells us that social interaction is easiest in homogeneous environments. A second finding, which was more expected, was that social mix did show some relation with the reputation of the neighbourhood; the reputation benefits from mix, as was expected on the basis of existing literature. However, again differences are small and these findings should not automatically be interpreted as support for social mix policies, as became clear from the analyses in the second part of the chapter.

Questions 4–6 of the chapter, regarding opinions on creating a high level of social mix (especially with regard to what this would mean for the interaction with other residents) under various circumstances (individual, dwelling, level of social mix, strength of social networks, opinion on neighbours), revealed that respondents from estates in the northern and western parts of Europe show higher scores on the answer 'a high level of mix is good for interaction', compared with southern and eastern parts of Europe. These individual opinions did not relate to demographic dimensions (gender, age, age youngest child, household type) but did associate with socio-economic dimensions, ethnicity, and strength of social network. Middle-income households unexpectedly turned out to be less negative towards high levels of social mix compared to other income categories. Mediterranean respondents were much more in favour of social mix than majorities; owner-occupiers were most often negative about social mix. Those who had strong social networks were, again somewhat surprisingly, more in favour of social mix if they perceived themselves to live in fairly mixed situations, but not if they said they lived in socially homogeneous environments. In other words: those with strong social networks living in mixed environments seem to prefer mixed environments; those with strong social networks living in homogeneous environments are likely to prefer socially homogeneous environments. Thus, the framework people find themselves in seems to be important for their opinion on social mix. This is an important nuance of the literature we referred to before. In addition, however, how people judged the residents in their own post-war housing estates also turned out to be important. If people had negative opinions about the residents in their estate, they also reported more negative views of social mix. These reports were most frequently negative if they lived in a mixed situation themselves. This was even more the case if the respondents were owner-occupiers.

If the – surprising – results from the first empirical part of the paper are combined with those of the second part, it may be suggested that the causality between social mix and strength of social networks runs from the strength of social networks to the opinions on social mix, instead of the other way around. If that were true, those with strong social networks would, in general, be more positive about their own situation and this also applies when it is a socially mixed situation; they would also be positive about their own situation when it is homogeneous; However, since there are more contexts perceived as socially mixed than as homogeneous, the general picture of the association will be that strong social networks are associated with social mix. When we investigate the individual contexts in a more detailed way (as in the analyses of opinions in the second empirical part), it is revealed that the local social and housing contexts in the European estates we studied, as well as attitudes towards neighbours in these estates have major impacts on opinions about the value of social mix.

Although these findings may all have implications for housing mix policies, the associations with tenure may perhaps offer the most concrete link to current housing policies. We are living in an era that is characterised by an increasingly important role for private initiatives, private capital, private urban development and private housing. In that context owner-occupier housing is a logical choice for both suppliers and those who find themselves on the demand side. With regard to social mix initiatives, this has serious implications since we were able to support existing literature that claims that owner-occupiers in particular see social mix as something negative. This will also impact on the use of social mix as a tool to reduce negative stigma. In general it has wide implications for the dominant philosophies in current urban restructuring policies.

Notes

This chapter was previously published as Musterd, S. (2008) Residents Views on Social Mix: Social Mix, Social Networks and Stigmatisation in Post-war Housing Estates. *Urban Studies*, Volume 45, No. 4, pp. 897–915.

1. If the index is based on three valid scores, the denominator is 3; if only two valid scores can be measured, the denominator is 2. The relative score runs from 0–1.

2. In formal terms: $H(X) = -\Sigma p_i \ln p_i$, where p_i is the probability of an observation belonging to category I of X and $p_i \ln p_i = 0$ for $p_i = 0$. $H'(X) = H(X) / \ln I$ is the standardised value, where I is the maximum number of categories that is theoretically possible (here five income categories).
3. The middle category was left out to avoid redundancy of information, since the three together add up to 100 per cent.
4. This is the largest minority category in the research project and includes Moroccans, Algerians, Tunisians and Turkish migrants.

References

Andersson, R. (2001) Spaces of Socialization and Social Network Competition: A Study of Neighbourhood Effects in Stockholm, Sweden. In: H. T. Andersen and R. van Kempen (Eds), *Governing European Cities: Social Fragmentation and Urban Governance*, pp. 149–88. Ashgate: Aldershot.

Atkinson, R. and Kintrea, K. (2001) Disentangling Area Effects: Evidence from Deprived and Non-Deprived Neighbourhoods. *Urban Studies*, 38 (12), pp. 2277–98.

Atkinson, R. (2003) Special Issue: Gentrification in a New Century: Misunderstood Saviour or Vengeful Wrecker? What Really is the Problem with Gentrification? *Urban Studies*, 40 (12), pp. 2343–50.

Beckhoven, E. van and Van Kempen, R. (2002) Het belang van de buurt. De invloed van herstructurering op activiteiten van blijvers en nieuwkomers in een Amsterdamse en Utrechtse buurt. DGW/NETHUR partnership 20. Utrecht: NETHUR.

Beckhoven, E. and Van Kempen, R. (2003) The Social Effects of Urban Restructuring: A Case Study in Amsterdam and Utrecht. *Housing Studies*, 18 (6), pp. 853–74.

Blokland, T. (2003) *Urban Bonds*. Cambridge: Polity Press.

Briggs, X. De Souza (1997) Moving up Versus Moving Out: Researching and Interpreting Neighborhood Effects in Housing Mobility Programs. *Housing Policy Debate*, 8, 195–234.

Briggs, X. De Souza (1998) Brown Kids in White Suburbs. Housing Mobility and the Many Faces of Social Capital. *Housing Policy Debate*, 9, pp. 177–221.

Cole, I. and Goodschild, B. (2000) Social Mix and the 'Balanced Community' in British Housing Policy – a Tale of Two Epochs. *GeoJournal*, 51 (4), pp. 351–60.

Dean, J. and Hastings, A. (2000). *Challenging Images: Housing Estates, Stigma and Regeneration*. Bristol: Policy Press.

Ellen, I. and Turner, M. (1997) Does Neighborhood Matter? Assessing Recent Evidence. *Housing Policy Debate*, 8, pp. 833–66.

Friedrichs, J. (1998) Do Poor Neighborhoods Make their Residents Poorer? Context Effects of Poverty Neighborhoods on their Residents. In: H. Andress (Ed.), *Empirical Poverty Research in a Comparative Perspective*, pp. 77–99. Aldershot: Ashgate.

Friedrichs, J., Galster, G. and Musterd, S. (2005) Neighborhood Effects on Social Opportunities: The European and American Research and Policy Context. In: J. Friedrichs, G. Galster and S. Musterd (Eds) *Life in Poverty*

Neighbourhoods: European and American Perspectives, pp. 1–10. London and New York: Routledge.

Galster, G. (2002) An Economic Efficiency Analysis of Deconcentrating Poverty Populations. *Journal of Housing Economics*, 11, pp. 303–29.

Galster, G. (2003) Investigating Behavioral Impacts of Poor Neighborhoods: Towards New Data and Analytic Strategies. *Housing Studies* 18 (3), pp. 893–914.

Galster, G. C. and Killen, S. P. (1995) The Geography of Metropolitan Opportunity: A Reconnaissance and Conceptual Framework. *Housing Policy Debate*, 6 (1), pp. 7–43.

Galster, G. and Zobel, A. (1998) Will Dispersed Housing Programmes Reduce Social Problems in the US? *Housing Studies*, 13 (5), pp. 605–22.

Granovetter, M. (1978) Threshold Models of Collective Behavior. *American Journal of Sociology*, 83, pp. 1420–43.

Jargowsky, P. (1997) *Poverty and Place*. New York: Russell Sage Foundation.

Jencks, C. and Mayer, S. (1990) The Social Consequences of Growing Up in a Poor Neighborhood. In: L. Lynn and M. McGeary (Eds), *Inner-City Poverty in the United States*, pp. 111–86. Washington DC: National Academy Press.

Kearns, A. and Parkes, A. (2003) Living in and Leaving Poor Neighbourhood Conditions in England. *Housing Studies*, 18 (6), pp. 827–51.

Kleinhans, R. (2004) Social Implications of Housing Diversification in Urban Renewal: A Review of Recent Literature. *Journal of Housing and the Built Environment*, 19 (4), pp. 367–90.

Leventhal, T. and Brooks-Gunn, J. (2000) The Neighborhoods they Live In. *Psychological Bulletin*, 126 (2), pp. 309–37.

Malheiros, J. (2002) Ethni-Cities: Residential Patterns in the Northern European and Mediterranean Metropolises – Implications for Policy Design. *International Journal of Population Geography*, 8 (2), pp. 107–34.

Murie, A. and Musterd, S. (2004) Social Exclusion and Opportunity Structures in European Cities and Neighborhoods. *Urban Studies*, 41 (8), pp. 1441–59.

Musterd, S., Ostendorf, W. and Vos, S. de (2003) Environmental Effects and Social Mobility. *Housing Studies*, 18 (6), pp. 877–92.

Musterd, S. and Van Kempen, R. (2005) *Large-Scale Housing Estates in European Cities: Opinions of Residents on Recent Developments, RESTATE Report 4k*. Utrecht: Faculty of Geosciences, Utrecht University.

Musterd, S. and Andersson, R. (2005) Housing Mix, Social Mix and Social Opportunities. *Urban Affairs Review*, 40 (6), pp. 761–90.

Ostendorf, W., Musterd, S. and Vos, S. de (2001) Social Mix and the Neighbourhood-Effect: Policy-Ambition and Empirical Support. *Housing Studies*, 16 (3), pp. 371–80.

Sampson, R., Morenoff, J. and Gannon-Rowley, T. (2002) Assessing 'Neighborhood Effects': Social Processes and New Directions in Research. *Annual Review of Sociology*, 28, pp. 443–78.

Sykora, L. (1999) Processes of Socio-Spatial Differentiation in Post-Communist Prague. *Housing Studies*, 14 (5), pp. 679–701.

Tienda, M. (1991) Poor People and Poor Places: Deciphering Neighborhood Effects on Poverty Outcomes. In: J. Haber (Ed.), *Macro–Micro Linkages in Sociology*, pp. 244–62. Newbury Park: Sage.

Wacquant, L. J. D. (1993) Urban Outcasts: Stigma and Division in the Black American Ghetto and the French Urban Periphery. *International Journal of Urban and Regional Research*, 17, pp. 366–83.

White, P. (1998) Ideologies, Social Exclusion and Spatial Segregation in Paris. In: S. Musterd and W. Ostendorf (Eds) *Urban Segregation and the Welfare State: Inequality and Exclusion in Western Cities*, pp. 148–67. London: Routledge.

Wilson, W. J. (1987) *The Truly Disadvantaged*. Chicago (IL): University of Chicago Press.

Wirth, L. (1938) Urbanism as a Way of Life. *American Journal of Sociology*, 44, pp. 1–24.

Part II Difference in Place

6
Public Space in Large Housing Estates

Richard Sendi, Manuel B. Aalbers and Marcele Trigueiro

Introduction

In recent years, much concern about the quality of life of the residents of large, post-war housing estates in Europe has focused on the various socio-economic aspects of the resident populations and the way these aspects impact on their living conditions. Social aspects of the debate have been dominated by issues concerning social mix and the behaviour of housing estate residents, while issues concerning social interaction and social cohesion have received much less attention. We adopt a different approach and use the example of public space to address the issue of social interaction in large, post-war housing estates. We identify the major characteristics of public space within these residential areas, adopt the notion of 'social space', and use empirical examples to explain the importance of proper public space design, management, and maintenance; the meaning of social space to the residents; and its importance in fostering social interaction and social cohesion.

Social scientists have often admitted to the difficulty of defining clearly and adequately the notion of 'public space'. Burgers (2000) points out two main reasons for this. Firstly, public space, and most of the events that take place there, cannot be classified under one specific institutional category. Secondly, there is the problem of describing behaviour in public space, which makes the very concept of public space hard to specify. Along similar lines, Atkinson (2003) argues that the idea of a single public itself is difficult to sustain since there are many publics whose legitimacy may be defined as much by the context of the place as by the social character of the individuals. If public space is defined as 'space to which normally people have unrestricted access and right of way', Atkinson continues, it is difficult to make the argument that any space has ever held such a status. For the purpose of our discussion, we shall nonetheless adopt the definition that describes public space as 'open, publicly accessible spaces where people go for group or individual activities' (Carr et al., 1992, p. 50). Irrespective of the different publics, be it with regard to socio-economic class, age, ethnic background, tradition, or behaviour, public space exposes different urban residents to one another and connotes the social-cultural values shared by the inhabitants of a residential environment.

While most of the literature on public space focuses on the centres of cities, this discussion focuses on public space in large-scale, post-war residential neighbourhoods. This is space which resulted from the very rigorous Modernistic urban planning approaches whose principles denied any relationship with land that was mainly devoted to green areas. We build upon and extend the distinction made by Madanipour (2004) who contrasts 'marginal public spaces', which are usually located in neighbourhoods where disadvantaged populations live, with the central or major public spaces of the city that have citywide significance (city squares, boulevards, parks, and the like). Marginal public spaces, he argues, rarely enjoy any of this significance: 'They are not on the list of priorities of local authorities to deal with, whether in terms of political legitimacy, economic competitiveness, and social cohesion of the city or its image and marketability' (Madanipour, 2004, p. 269). In addition to this definition of marginality, public spaces in large housing estates may also be considered marginal due to their nature. Such is the unplanned 'open space' often referred to as 'space left over after planning' (sloap). Drawing on the findings of a Europe-wide research project, Madanipour describes a rather grim situation regarding the use of public space in large housing estates. He refers to the vulnerability of residents due to social, political, cultural, economic, age, gender, and ethnic differences. He points to their entrapment 'within a limited space, bearing enormous pressures from within and without, and with limited capacity to connect to the outside world' (Madanipour, 2004, p. 271). The ensuing situation, he continues, leads to cracks that are visible in public spaces in the form of neglect and decline as well as tensions along the lines of social fragmentation and stratification. 'As there is competition for the limited resources available, public spaces become battlegrounds. While some tend to dominate the public spaces, others are intimidated, leading to a lack of safety and withdrawal from public areas and from engagement with others' (Madanipour, 2004, p. 271).

The discussion in this chapter focuses on public space in post-WWII large housing estates in Europe. The data presented here was gathered through a survey that was conducted in all the 29 estates described in Chapter 3. As has been stated in the introductory chapter, the popularity of large-scale housing estates as residential areas started to decline in western European countries in the 1970s while, on the other hand, they continued to be constructed in large quantities in Eastern European countries until the early 1990s. And while geo-political factors set Europe apart from other continents, the same factors also shape the divide between Eastern and Western Europe. In some cases, this seems to be the dominant divide in our ten case countries (e.g. ownership of public space) while, in some cases, the divide may not always be as dominant as may be expected. Issues of safety in public space for example transcend the common East–West divide and may be more important in one eastern country (Poland) than in another (Slovenia) and more important in one western country (UK) than in another (Sweden). At times, the differences between estates in one country may appear larger than the differences between estates in different countries. Therefore, we have not prioritised a geo-political analysis or explanation over other analyses and explanations. Such analyses have been undertaken elsewhere (Allen and Cars, 2001; Andersen and Leather, 1999; Burrows and Rhodes, 1999; Coleman, 1985; Cooper and Hawtin, 1997; Diacon, 1991; Emms, 1990; Murie et al., 2003; Pearl, 1997; Power, 1997; Turkington et al., 2004, Turner et al., 1992; Van Kempen et al., 2005).

We draw a alternative scenario that may be considered a European one, full of differences between estates, but also with some commonalities. Our aim is not to explain these differences but to highlight the common patterns and solutions in public space use, design and redesign. We do this cautiously, avoiding swift unwarranted generalisations. Our interest is less of a theoretical and more of a practical nature. We do not aspire to theorise the current state of public space, but hope that our analysis of public space in European large housing estates provides a fresh perspective on issues concerning the design and use of public space and how these impact on the residents' social interaction and social cohesion. Emphasis is put on the identification of the most important aspects of public space design that we believe to be vital and helpful in the implementation of programmes and activities intended to promote social interaction in large housing estates. It is arguied that appropriate public space design and use may significantly contribute to improvements in the quality of life of the millions of Europeans living in these estates.

We start with a description of the different attributes of public space with the aim of defining clearly the specific categories of public space that exist in large housing estates. We adopt the notion of 'social space' (De Chiara et al., 1995) to discuss what is perhaps the single most important function of public space in large housing estates. We then look at the different attitudes and approaches to the use of public space with respect to the demographic and ethnic characteristics of housing estate inhabitants. This is followed by a discussion on the key aspects of public space including management, maintenance, and renewal, resident participation, and safety. In conclusion, certain actions and measures are suggested that need to be taken in order to create more attractive environments within these residential neighbourhoods.

The plurality of public space

There is no single public space in large housing estates, not just because different estates have different public spaces but also because there are significant differences within each individual housing estate. These differences may be due to the design or nature of a particular public space, its intended use, and the conduct of the users. One of the key features of public space is that is it highly contingent on the actual site. Even a more abstracted notion of public space or a generalised ideal type of public space in large housing estates has to face this intrinsic plurality. The plurality of public space can be defined in purely functional terms. For example, a parking lot and a playground are both public spaces, but they differ in design, location, and use. Public spaces are normally intended for different functions and, therefore, for different users. But even two similarly designed playgrounds within a particular housing estate may not be equal with respect to use and perception. Public space may be overused, underused, misused, or simply not used. Furthermore, unintended users may also use these spaces, which may lead to conflict. The story of public space in large housing estates is therefore like the red thread of this book, that is, a story of differentiation.

In this discussion, we depart from the general premise that describes public space in large housing estates as those areas that play a variety of roles through their various uses and which, due to their design aspects, may impact on the image of the estate. These areas provide an intermediary link between the dwelling and the outer world. In fact, they represent places of casual interaction between residents. As common facilities intended to provide practical advantages and a place for residents to become acquainted, they are normally planned to create a sense of community for their users. Social contact may occur in entrance courts, community buildings, community spaces, playgrounds, and other places within the estate. Other such spaces may include benches and canopy trees for shade and other social activity. These areas provide residents with a place to relax and converse with neighbours. In this way, public space can be seen as a 'social space'. Very essential parts of social space are the outdoor facilities clustered about the neighbourhood centre and the various playing courts and open green spaces located within the residential area (usually referred to as 'neighbourhood space'). Our discussion focuses mainly on this external, freely accessible space that provides the opportunity for unlimited outdoor social contact. Indoor, semi-public space (entrances, staircases, elevators, common rooms, etc) that allows only limited access is referred to only in passing.

The main emphasis in the development of outdoor social space should be to provide adequate lawn areas and other open spaces that offer a setting for a variety of activities for all residents irrespective of age or other criteria. Such space must be designed to enable 'sociality' and to promote the quality of urbanity. Sociality, according to Haider and Kaplan (2004), refers to the degree to which the open space encourages social contact or interaction among people. Sociality is also related to accessibility or the physical, visual, and symbolic ease of experiencing and negotiating an environment, which can motivate interaction through the exploratory use of an open space. Sociality or the social potential of a public space also refers to the emergence of new (and desirable) social practices in public space. Why and how people feel connected to and take pride in their immediate environment greatly contributes to the satisfaction and feeling of belonging of the inhabitants of a housing estate. The design and organisation of social space in a residential environment has a great impact on the image that the neighbourhood projects to both its residents and those outside it. If not properly planned, managed, and maintained, social spaces may be a cause of various negative features (physical and social) within a residential neighbourhood. On the other hand, well-planned, well-organised, and well-maintained social spaces play a vital role in the development of a good residential environment and may contribute greatly to the creation of a sense of neighbourhood or community cohesiveness among the residents (De Chiara et al., 1995).

In the development of outdoor facilities that constitute an essential part of social space in residential neighbourhoods, public space design prescribes the necessity of paying particular attention to the specific requirements and interests of the different users, in particular with respect to the various age groups (Bengston, 2004; Elsley, 2004; Schwab and Standler, 2004). It is vital that these facilities are planned and arranged in a manner that keeps user conflict to a minimum. Public space that engages all residents, both adults and children, while providing a degree of autonomy to the different user groups is generally more desirable than settings that force interaction among the various categories of users. The final objective should be to create an environment that enables public space to function effectively as a social space for all the inhabitants of a residential neighbourhood.

According to Pipard (1995), who conducted a study of La Darnaise, one of the districts of the post-war housing estate Les Minguettes in Lyon, this estate provides a good example of the variety of forms of social contact that may take place within social spaces. The rhythm of the estate is determined by the school rhythm and by the rhythm of the workers. Indeed, its inhabitants are present in external areas, and in particular in public spaces, more intensely after school hours. People gather in groups generally constituted of persons of the same age, sex, and cultural origin. The population of foreign origin, in particular people originating from North Africa, were found to represent the socio-cultural group that uses the social space most frequently. Furthermore, social spaces display a cultural phenomenon of appropriation whereby some groups may be identified as potential users of certain spaces. It is generally possible to establish a connection between some groups and the spaces that they frequently use. The women and children frequently gather in gardens and playgrounds and in the Minguettes Park. The men meet on the benches, lawns, and pavements in front of the shopping centre. Young people meet on the benches, on the pavement around the table tennis area, and in building entrances, while the teenagers collect at the school exit and in the gardens and on the lawns of Minguettes Park (Commerçon et al., 2003). Such a setting appears to function well.

Lawson (2001) argues that such appropriation of space derives from the need for specific social groups to belong to and identify places as either exclusively theirs or at least associated with them. This argument is based on the belief that every social group that has any degree of cohesion also has social norms. According to Lawson, 'Social norms are extremely powerful in that they give security to people in the group, allowing them to behave in a regulated way without fear of their behaviour being thought to be inappropriate by their neighbours, colleagues and friends' (Lawson, 2001, p. 23). It is therefore argued that social norms form some of the most fundamental components of the language of space.

The case study of the La Ville Nouvelle estate provides further proof of the importance of the appropriate design and organisation of public space. The absence of public spaces for socialising and community activity had previously resulted in some groups of young people misbehaving and engaging in unruly activities that caused feelings of insecurity among the inhabitants. Realising the problem, several projects were undertaken that created 44 different public gardens and parks. Planned mainly for young children, some of these spaces are also equipped to meet the needs of teenagers. The subsequent reduction in urban delinquency that has been observed could be attributed to the re-qualification of urban spaces (Commerçon et al., 2003).

In some of the estates, however, very little or no consideration at all has been given to the provision of appropriate outdoor facilities. The example of the two Polish case study estates is indicative of the possible negative consequences of such failures. The absence of meeting places for different groups of inhabitants, a lack of recreation areas for families and young people, and a lack of places for youngsters and older people to spend their free time peacefully and safely, have led to serious inter-generational conflicts in both estates. Asked whether the management company had plans to create any places for meeting in the estate such as benches and playgrounds, a representative of one of the housing cooperatives in Ursynów responded,

> 'Benches become clusters of noisy youths and drinkers. Our inhabitants are getting older and less tolerant. They do not want the benches in front of their windows. They cannot stand the noise. Presently, because of the protests against youths, we are pulling down the sport baskets. Soon we will have to build facilities for the elderly and fence them off. These two age groups cannot tolerate each other. We respond to the needs of the older generation because they are the majority. This is democracy'
>
> (Węcławowicz et al., 2005, p. 48).

Responding to the needs of a particular user group while ignoring the rest (and wrongly justifying such actions as 'democracy') is obviously not going to lead to improved intergenerational relationships. On the contrary, it may result in greater tension. In addition to the requirement to satisfy intergenerational needs, socio-cultural considerations also constitute a very important aspect of accessibility to and the use of public space in large housing estates. According to one of the basic principles of public space design, access to social space must be guaranteed for all regardless of age, colour, race, creed, or economic status (Butler, 1968).

Many European large housing estates' populations are made up of lower-income households, often, especially in Northern and Western Europe, of various cultural and ethnic backgrounds. The problems associated with low income and the different cultural and ethnic characteristics often lead to conflicts that may also be manifested in the treatment and use of social space. Madanipour (2004) identifies several causes of social-space related tensions. Some are due to different patterns of use where some households are accustomed to conducting various activities in the social space and others are not. There are also those who hang around longer in social spaces such as the unemployed, the homeless, drug abusers and street drinkers, and teenagers and migrants who may have no other place for socialising (Sendi et al., 2004).

Research findings provide evidence to suggest that tensions over public space tend to follow ethnic lines in many housing estates in Northern and Western Europe. In the Marzahn estate in Berlin, for example, the different age groups of the Russian immigrant community occupy social space and greenery, often at distinct meeting places. Conflicting 'behaviours' (language, the manner of speaking, body language), norms, and values related to their 'pre-modern' structures and being different to the 'free' West German lifestyles were cited as frequent causes of misunderstandings (Knorr-Siedow and Droste, 2003).

Marzahn is not the only estate that has been affected by contrasting values and norms that have often resulted in more serious forms of ethnically based social tensions. In the Bijlmer estate in Amsterdam, for example, drug dealing, drug abuse, fear and high crime rates, vandalism, garbage disposal and littering in public spaces, and youth delinquency are strongly associated with the various fringe groups of refugees, migrants, illegal foreigners, and others who found refuge in the district in the mid 1980s. It is argued that Bijlmer's anonymity and badly organised public and semi-public spaces also provided convenient places for illegal immigrants to loiter and hide (Aalbers et al., 2003).

It is important to recognise that natives and immigrants tend to use social space in different ways. As described above in the case of Les Minguettes, some ethnic and immigrant groups use public space much more intensively than natives. Not only do they spend more time outside, some of them also gather in larger groups. In San Roc (Barcelona), Roma use public spaces relatively more than non-Roma groups since in general they live with large households in small dwellings. It has been observed that their activities on the street and in public spaces often cause problems and lead to conflicts with other residents (Pareja Eastaway et al., 2003).

Besides the conflicts generated by ethnic and cultural differences, tensions are also caused by emotional links. Madanipour (2004) describes these occurrences in cases where the old residents consider newcomers as intruders invading their 'acquired' territory. Such, for example, are the tensions that have arisen due to the gentrification processes described later on in the case of the Wrzeciono estate (Warsaw). Similar tensions have been observed in the Comasina estate in Milan: 'Nowadays, public spaces are becoming new arenas of conflict between new and old residents in the estates in Milan; the same public space is interpreted in different ways by different groups (native and immigrants, young and old generations, men and women)' (Zajczyk et al., 2005, p. 40).

Attributes of public space in large housing estates

Social space design in the majority of the large, post-war housing estates was based primarily on Le Corbusier's CIAM (Congrès Internationaux d'Architecture Moderne) planning principles. Essentially, residential areas would be planned as neighbourhoods full of light, fresh air, and plenty of open space in between the blocks of buildings. There would be hardly any industry or offices in the area, but plenty of houses and greenery. Indeed, these areas were – and often still are – characterised by the separation of uses (see also Chapter 1).

Open and green space

The building of large housing estates often coincided with post-war reconstruction, as well as with the establishment of the welfare state in Western European countries and to a lesser extent in Central and Eastern European countries. Although many original housing construction plans turned out to be too expensive and parts of them were cut for budgetary reasons (often resulting in higher residential densities), the provision of large amounts of green space remained a key feature of these developments. As such, most of these areas are today still considered very green in comparison with other parts of the city, as was confirmed by several examples in the resident survey undertaken in the various case study estates across Europe. In the majority of the estates studied, the abundance of open public green space within these neighbourhoods was described as their most attractive feature. The Bow estate of Tower Hamlets in London is described as 'an oasis of open space in an otherwise under-provided borough' (Hall et al., 2003, p. 39) and Marzahn in Berlin as 'living in a landscape' (Knorr-Siedow and Droste, 2003, p. 99). In the Jósaváros estate in Nyíregyháza (Hungary), green space accounts for about 56 per cent of the total area of the estate, a proportion that 'demonstrates the fact that the estate was originally well designed and built' (Erdösi et al., 2003, p. 63). Cerisier in the Les Minguettes estate in Lyon is still essentially constituted by a green area and a very large public space, even though the current urban renewal project will definitely change this characteristic (Trigueiro, 2006). In one part of the Bijlmer estates in Amsterdam, 72 per cent of the residents mentioned the high proportion of green space as the most attractive factor in their housing environment (Wassenberg, 2002). Likewise, the residents of the Wrzeciono estate in Warsaw described the green areas as the element that positively 'distinguishes their estate from the rest of the city and for many of them this is a main feature of their estate, which makes it attractive to live in' (Węcławowicz et al., 2005, p. 43).

In addition to the green areas available within the boundaries of large housing estates, many of them enjoy the advantage of being located next to large expanses of natural vegetation and other attractive natural features. In the case of the Fužine estate in Ljubljana, the Ljubljanica River that borders the estate's southern and western edges 'creates great spatial ambiance and offers a quality landscape and many opportunities for recreation and spare time activities' (Ploštajner et al., 2004, p. 27). In the case of the Ursynow estate in Warsaw, the natural environment in the area is described as exceptional: 'The built-up area is surrounded by a green belt. There is no industrial pollution. The whole belt of housing estates is in close proximity to the green areas of forest, meadows, and fields' (Węcławowicz et al., 2003, p. 43).

In some estates, on the other hand, residents are not satisfied with the green and other public spaces available. Respondents in the Žusterna-Semedela estate in Koper (Slovenia) cited green spaces and children's playgrounds as the most disliked aspect of their residential environment. This has much to do with bad design as well as with improper maintenance. Some estates do not have much green space at all. The Märkische Viertel estate in Berlin, for example, is described as 'blocks on a concrete parking lot' (Knorr-Siedow and Droste, 2003, p. 99). In the Havanna estate in Budapest, the monotonous, prefabricated panel construction is described as 'high-rise apartment blocks with an artificial layout of greenery' (Erdősi et al., 2003, p. 78). There is a high density of large buildings, often with hundreds of dwellings in each.

It is therefore important to realise that the presence of open and green areas does not alone guarantee a good quality environment. Green areas that are inappropriately managed or poorly maintained may become a safety problem. In the Wrzeciono estate in Warsaw, for example, the residents consider the surrounding park and the neglected and vandalised recreational facilities and playgrounds as dangerous (Węcławowicz et al., 2005). It may also be argued that the abundance of open space itself could be problematic as it makes it harder to maintain a high-quality public space. Good design and the appropriate management and maintenance of public space play a very importance role in this regard.

Design matters

As we have argued above, public space should be designed in a way that allows it to function as social space. The important question is how do we achieve this? The literature presents two conflicting schools of thought on this subject. These are described here as the 'strict zoning approach' and the 'liberal approach'. While many architects and urbanists, including defensible space protagonists such as Newman (1973) and Coleman (1985), tend to overestimate the importance of design for a well-functioning neighbourhood or city (the strict zoning approach, which has also been described elsewhere in the literature as *physical determinism* or *spatial fetishism*), other authors, such as Jacobs (1961) and Lawson (2001) (the liberal approach) draw attention to the various misconceptions behind such designs and the unintended limitations they impose on the potential users.

Alice Coleman's analysis of the situation of high-rise housing in England is premised on Newman's earlier work that established a strong relationship between housing-estate design and criminality and anti-social behaviour in American cities. Both of them argue that crime levels in housing estates can be considerably reduced through good neighbourhood design that increases the feeling of safety. According to Newman, good design may be measured, for example, by the quality of lobby visibility from the main entrance door. Good design may also be achieved through apartment layouts that facilitate the surveillance of outside areas from the inside. 'Surveillance from within' as he calls this design approach, requires locating kitchen windows in each apartment so that they face the building entries, which enables adults to keep a watch on their children at play outside. The aim is to provide people with a feeling of territoriality and, therefore, make residents feel safer. Defensible space strategies have been widely applied in housing estates and often focus on reducing feelings of insecurity through re-designing public and especially semi-public spaces such as elevators, staircases, hallways and porches. But while these strategies may often *reduce feelings* of insecurity, critics have suggested they do little to improve actual insecurity because most problems of insecurity are not physical, but social in nature (Aalbers et al., 2005; Laé, 1991; Van Kempen, 1994).

Jacobs (1961), on the other hand, argues strongly against planning practices that seek to isolate residential areas from the surrounding city fabric. She stresses the importance of casual sidewalk contacts between residents that are not dictated by strict zoning rules. On the subject of children's play areas, for example, she observes that

> 'Garden City planners, with their hatred of the street, thought the solution to keeping children off the streets and under wholesome surveillance was to build interior enclaves for them in the centres of super-blocks. Today, many large renewal areas are being planned on the principle of enclosed park enclaves within blocks. The trouble with this scheme, as can be seen in such already existing examples, is that no child of enterprise or spirit will willingly stay in such a boring place after he reaches the age of six. Most want out earlier. These sheltered, "togetherness" worlds are suitable, and in real life are used, for about three or four years of a small child's life, in many ways the easiest four years to manage. Nor do the adult residents of these places even want older children to play in their sheltered courts'

(Jacobs, 1961, p. 80).

Lawson (2001) presents a similar line of thinking, arguing that layouts that create 'safe' areas of grassy spaces overlooked by the living room windows of all the surrounding houses and marked by signs reading 'children's play area' are based on the assumption that children will behave logically. He admits that children of course behave logically, but stresses that it is the logic of the child not the logic of the designer that prevails here. Lawson also talks of the 'tyranny of functionalist space' which he describes as being rooted in the functionalism of the modern movement. He points out that the idea that functions must be located in space and have space that is somehow precisely adjusted to their needs prevails among professional public space designers rather than in the minds and actions of ordinary people.

The problem with these two approaches to housing-estate design is that both of them present strong arguments which appear, at the same time, to be in direct conflict with one another. There is no doubt that public spaces in large housing estates need to be properly designed in order for them to play their various roles in fostering resident interaction and social cohesion. As such, the criticism levelled at the defensible space protagonists does not mean that physical solutions are by definition entirely redundant. As our examples highlighted, inappropriate neighbourhood layout may lead to an undesirable spatial organisation that is unpleasant and unattractive to its residents and, as such, does not encourage social interaction. Despite the abundance of green space in the neighbourhood, the Jósaváros estate in Nyíregyháza was found to have several design deficiencies:

'On Ungvár Avenue, the main boulevard, there are many 'transit gates' for pedestrians walking under or beside the buildings. Garbage accumulates around these gates and the paths become smelly and unpleasant. Ósző˝lő˝ Street, on the western border of the estate, is too narrow; cars parked there hinder traffic all day long'

(Erdösi et al., 2003, p. 73).

On the other hand, however, the liberalists are trying to make us aware that human beings do not always have to accept, or behave in accordance with, what professional spatial designers consider to be appropriate for them. Design deficiencies were, for example, described in the Armstrong area of the Les Minguettes estate in Lyon. The green areas in this neighbourhood appear to have been designed to follow a functional hierarchy, with lawns and trees more or less surrounding the buildings. However, this functionalist rigour failed to achieve the legibility of these public spaces (Trigueiro, 2006). 'Legibility', according to Lynch (1960), refers to the ease with which the constituent elements or parts of a residential environment can be recognised as a consistent pattern. He describes a legible environment as well formed, distinct, remarkable, engaging the senses, and inviting participation. In Armstrong, on the contrary, great confusion can be perceived due to unreadable urban forms and the lack of reference marks. There are no architectural elements that create a hierarchy of spaces. The public spaces of Armstrong are uninviting and are currently unused by the residents. This example shows that the functionalist design principles that were applied in the area failed to achieve the desired objectives.

Notwithstanding the implicit misconceptions of strict zoning approaches, it must be realised that the liberalist approach carries some weight only insofar as it makes us aware that people will not interact with others simply because spatial designers want them to. We need to recognise that children play where they enjoy playing, for example the game of hide and seek behind cars in the parking area. Similarly, adults sit where they want to sit and not necessarily where designers put seats. This means that spatial designers need to take into account specific circumstances and try as much as possible to reconcile them with the natural needs of the potential users. Beyond that, the liberalist approach tends to be over simplistic. Children, especially young children, need to be protected and looked after. One cannot just let small children play on the streets unsupervised. Lawson does, nonetheless, give some useful hints on public space design.

'The trick of designing, then, seems to be a more intelligent and mature view of time, change and human behaviour in space. The designer needs to know above all else when to make a move in space that frames or invites behaviour, and when to leave the space more ambiguous. This is extremely hard to get right, and perhaps we can never expect fully to do so. There is probably no substitute for experience and observation in teaching us how this all works'

(Lawson, 2001, p. 225).

Management, maintenance and improvement

Just as buildings require appropriate management and maintenance, so do public spaces. The life or lifelessness of public spaces depends very much on their quality and whether they welcome potential users to walk, stay, sit, or otherwise enjoy them (Gehl, 2004). The desired pleasant environment can be guaranteed only through the proper management and maintenance of public space or through the introduction of changes and improvements where deficiencies exist. Public space management and maintenance systems vary from country to country, primarily according to ownership structure and the legal and institutional framework. In this area, many large housing estates in Central and Eastern Europe experience comparatively greater problems than in most other European countries. Part of the problem throughout Europe is that maintenance costs for (semi-) public spaces in some estates are higher as a result of a physical environment with many semi-public spaces and a high proportion of green open space. The costs are further increased by the residents' low levels of attachment to these places and the consequent low levels of resident responsibility for these places. As a result, littering, graffiti, and vandalism further contribute to high maintenance costs (Aalbers et al., 2003).

In Central and Eastern European (CEE) countries, management and maintenance problems are closely related to the as yet unresolved ownership rights pertaining to the land within housing estates. The privatisation of the majority of the former public housing stock in most CEE countries in the early 1990s resulted in sitting tenants becoming owners of their previous rental dwellings. In the majority of cases, however, the land on which the buildings stand still remains in the ownership of some third party (municipality, company, individual landlord, etc.). In addition to housing privatisation, the restitution of property nationalised after the war to its rightful owners (this process also started in the early 1990s) enabled certain individuals to regain ownership of the land on which some of the estates were constructed.

These and many other changes that took place in relation to large housing estates, after the introduction of a market economy system in East European countries in the early 1990s, have been discussed in detail by various authors (Clapham et al., 1996; Dimitrovska Andrews and Sendi, 2001; Lowe and Tsenkova, 2003; Mandic, 1994; Priemus and Mandic, 2000; Schwedler, 1996; Sendi, 1995; Struyk, 1996; Tanninen et al., 1994; Turner et al, 1992, Van Kempen et al., 2005). In some cases, these developments have resulted in very ambiguous situations that allow the various actors involved to avoid undertaking necessary tasks under the pretext of not knowing exactly who is responsible for what. Under these circumstances, the condition of public space in some of the housing estates was found to be appalling. In the Havanna estate in Budapest, neglect of the public spaces, especially the playgrounds and basketball courts, was specified as the most negative aspect of the estate (Erdösi et al., 2003). In the Jósaváros estate in Nyíregyháza, it was found that the pavements had not been mended for many years and had become uneven and cracked with large potholes full of water appearing after rain. The street lighting was not working in some public places, and street furniture such as benches was often broken or missing. In the two Slovenian case study housing estates, Fužine and Žusterna-Semedela, the residents blame the local government (the official land-owner) for the inadequate up-keep and maintenance of public spaces while the local government expects the residents, in their capacity as homeowners, to assume greater responsibility in this regard.

There have been significant changes in the attitudes and approaches to public space management and maintenance in northern, western, and southern European countries. Although unresolved ownership issues are usually not a problem, these countries also have their share of problems related to a lack of responsibility. In many estates, more than one actor (local government, housing associations/companies, special service agencies) is involved in managing the environment. Furthermore, in many countries residents are becoming increasingly less responsible for the public space within their estate. The example of the Kanaleneiland estate in Utrecht provides an interesting illustration of the changing attitudes towards public space management and maintenance. The estate was previously known as the 'Island of Roses', where the residents together with the local government and housing associations felt responsible and participated in the up-keep of their environment. However, nowadays the feelings of responsibility have disappeared, several playgrounds have been closed, and the environment suffers from pollution and vandalism (Aalbers et al., 2003). This type of denial of responsibility is common in other estates as well. Concern for and the maintenance of public spaces also seem to be problematic in the two Spanish case study housing estates. Some parts of the Simancas estate in Madrid experience problems concerning the responsibility for keeping up the public spaces within the estate. According to the local government, public spaces that are used only by the inhabitants of the surrounding blocks are the responsibility of the inhabitants. The inhabitants, on the other hand, argue that the squares are public and therefore a government responsibility. In the San Roc estate in Barcelona, inhabitants are also dissatisfied with the maintenance of public spaces, which were found to be in very poor condition. This situation is not only the result of the self-exclusion of the local government but also a result of management problems caused by a lack of co-ordination between the local government and the Autonomous Community board that exists within the neighbourhood (Pareja Eastaway et al., 2003).

However, in both Eastern and Western Europe, there has been considerable improvement in the management and maintenance of public space in some estates in recent years. In the Havanna estate in Budapest, the Urban Management Company, which manages the public spaces, undertook an extensive regeneration programme that has resulted in significant improvements in the condition of public spaces (Erdösi et al., 2003). Playgrounds have been renovated in accordance with EU standards (with the help of EU funding), trees have been planted, and pavements refurbished. In the case of the Bijlmer estate in Amsterdam, those involved in the renewal programme discovered that the management of public space was the weakest link in the renewal operation. This led to the creation of 'management groups' whose task is to keep public spaces liveable before, during, and after restructuring interventions. The new approach consists of extra intensive management during the (physical) renewal period and efficient management when the renewal is completed. The keywords are 'do more', 'organise better', and 'involve residents more' (Aalbers et al., 2004). This has resulted in better public space maintenance practices.

In Italy, on the other hand, it has been found that while owner-occupiers are willing to invest in the improvement of both private and public space in order to improve the standard of the estate, tenants are frustrated by the lack of interest shown by the housing management companies on which they must rely for improvements. The Comasina estate in Milan shows a strong sense of social cohesion especially with regard to the several initiatives of self-organised homeowner groups for maintaining and managing the properties recently bought. There is a growing number of activities promoted by these groups, which include cleaning and redecorating common areas in their blocks and even maintaining the green areas of the estate (Zajczyk et al., 2005).

In the case of Central and Eastern Europe, the privatisation and restitution of property (including land on which some of the large housing estates are located) has particularly had an influence on public space development and improvement activity. Apart from the problems relating to the management and maintenance discussed above, it has been observed that public space is also experiencing growing pressure from potential investors who are constantly looking for any 'spare' space that may be exploited for new construction. The Wrzeciono estate in Warsaw offers an example of such developments. Following the collapse of most of the heavy industry that resulted in job losses for many people in Poland, the maintenance of the buildings in the estate started to fall behind. Under the circumstances of a general crisis and lack of money, the state management companies and the housing associations started to sell off the 'spare' land within the estate. New upper market housing was constructed and new residents, more prosperous than the original residents of the estate, moved into the new buildings. Most of these new residential buildings are separated from the rest of the estate by high walls, heralding the appearance of gated communities inside large housing estates. These developments have had several consequences, mostly negative. Firstly, they have encroached upon and substantially reduced the original size of the green areas that the residents specified in the survey as the main feature that makes their estate attractive to live in. Secondly, the gentrification that has occurred in the housing estate has created large contrasts between old buildings and new ones, resulting in many conflicts between the former and new residents, especially regarding the appropriation of space by the gated communities (Węcławowicz et al., 2003). This may be an example of the situation described earlier (Madanipour, 2004) in which the scarce public spaces become a battleground in the competition between different users. Thirdly, the new developments have created architectural barriers that cause many problems for internal transport and communication, make access to some places difficult, hinder fire brigade access, and make the daily life of the handicapped and the elderly difficult (Węcławowicz et al., 2003, p. 65).

Another important aspect of public space management, maintenance, and improvement is the active involvement of the residents. Although resident participation is often considered a high priority, it is seldom actually implemented in practice. A lack of interest on the part of local authorities and social housing companies/associations is only part of the explanation. In Western Europe, and probably even more so in Eastern Europe, a lack of interest on the part of the local residents takes a considerable share of the blame. Most residents focus attention on their homes or private space and are indifferent to or ignore problems outside. Their attitude could be expressed as 'the boundary of my property is the boundary of my participation'. The involvement of residents with anything outside their apartments is generally very limited. Many residents explain their unwillingness to participate in outside activities as fearing involvement in various problematic situations outside their homes. Others feel that their participation (especially in decision-making processes) would not make any difference in any case. In Poland, people 'generally do not trust officials, they are not engaged in general social matters. Only 7–10 per cent of householders take part in meetings.' (Węcławowicz et al., 2004, p. 26). The situation is similar in Slovenia where citizens 'do not believe that participation is meaningful and that their actions can in any way influence the final decisions that lead to implementation' (Černič Mali et al., 2005, p. 11). Regrettably, this attitude of residents is often proven justified by the actions of decision-makers. In Cerisier in the Les Minguettes estate in Lyon, a renewal project that included the construction of 90 new dwellings on a current green area was approved in spite of the furious protests against its implementation staged by the residents (Trigueiro, 2006).

Efforts have been made in some cases to promote the active participation of estate residents. Policies such as those encouraging the 'management groups' in the Bijlmer estate in Amsterdam aim at enhancing the role of participants in creating and achieving a better living environment. In some cases groups of residents have taken direct action themselves, while in others they have been actively organised by the city district and brought together in 'theme groups' where topics such as 'traffic and safety' or 'public space' are discussed (Aalbers et al., 2004). These groups can be involved during the renewal process to provide feedback on the progress achieved. In the Kanaleneiland estate in Utrecht, a project initiated by social workers for the purpose of achieving the social integration of non-Dutch women resulted, among other things, in interventions in the public space that included pruning trees and providing better lighting for previously dark footpaths (Aalbers et al., 2003). Another positive example comes from the Marzahn estate in Berlin where a girls' workshop identified the need for a playground, which was subsequently designed and constructed (Knorr-Siedow and Droste, 2003).

In the Jósaváros estate in Nyíregyháza, the management company provides free soil with plants and flowers for residents to plant around their buildings. Usually five to ten per cent of the inhabitants of each building participate in this work, and it has been observed that the number of participants is increasing. These small gardens around the buildings, trimmed and cultivated with simple tools such as stakes and string, can be seen everywhere (Erdösi et al., 2003). Similar activities have taken place in the Havanna estate in Budapest where the municipality organises various public space maintenance programmes. Among these, it distributes shrubs and grass seed to the residents and gives advice on how to take care of them. The two companies that maintain the parks employ residents who are temporarily out of work, thereby giving them the 'added bonus of feeling they are contributing to the upkeep of their neighbourhood' (Erdösi et al., 2003, p. 49). Resident participation in the planning and improvement of the living environment is also quite developed in the Comasina estate in Italy. The residents actively participate in both large-scale issues such as neighbourhood care and environment and traffic management and micro-level issues such as reclaiming green spaces near their homes (Zajczyk et al., 2005). In other estates, resident involvement is focussed on issues concerning the sustainability of the neighbourhood, for example, the participation of inhabitants in the development programmes of the Orcasitas estate in Madrid. Residents participate, among other things, in the implementation of environmental measures such as the improvement of parks and green areas and the reduction of the level of noise and atmospheric pollution (Pareja Eastaway et al., 2003).

In these cases, resident participation in the planning of improvements and the actual implementation of specific renewal projects and activities has had a very positive influence on the attitude of neighbourhood residents and has contributed considerably to the enhancement of the feeling of neighbourliness. Resident involvement in the management, maintenance, and improvement of social space must be seen as one of the important mechanisms for encouraging social interaction and facilitating greater social cohesion in large housing estates.

Safety

Housing estates are often considered unsafe places, and when people are asked what is so unsafe about these residential areas, they often refer to public and semi-public places in the housing estate. Two issues are important here. First, are large housing estates really unsafe places?; and second, why do people feel unsafe in large housing estates? The second question is largely beyond the scope of the subject of this chapter (see Aalbers and Rancati, 2008). The fact that housing estates are considered unsafe does not necessarily mean that they are actually unsafe. While, for example, many residents expressed a fear of crime in the Bow Hat estate (UK), these fears are not necessarily reflected in the crime figures (Hall et al., 2004). The investigation of the safety situation in the Husby and Tensta estates (Sweden) showed that crime rates were not considered higher than in other parts of Stockholm. It was, however, observed that 'media representations often tend to spread the message that the estates are unsafe, and that they are dangerous places to visit and live in. Therefore, much work has been done of a more cosmetic character, with the explicit idea to try to establish a more positive image of the estates' (Öresjö et al., 2004, p. 41).

Nonetheless, safety is not always just an imaginary problem. Indeed, there are safety problems in several of the estates, and different countries have implemented different measures to deal with these problems. The 'Buurtvaders' [Neighbourhood Fathers] project initiated in Amsterdam New West was intended to deal with safety problems, particularly in areas where young male Moroccans were causing a lot of nuisance and trouble. The project not only makes neighbourhoods safer but also promotes social cohesion within groups, between groups, and between generations. While many indigenous Dutch people were very sceptical in the beginning, they also came to appreciate this initiative. The programme has now been copied in other neighbourhoods and cities, including Utrecht, and organisations in other countries have also shown interest in it (see Aalbers et al., 2005). In the city of Jönköping (Sweden), the municipal housing company has developed a project to promote safety and security in response to a survey which revealed that one-quarter of the residents in the Öxnehaga estate does not feel safe in their area during evenings and nights. The residential areas are being redesigned in order to increase security and safety in addition to the enhancement of cooperation between key local actors for the purpose of preventing crime and feelings of insecurity (Öresjö et al., 2004).

The Polish housing estates were found to experience more serious safety problems than most other estates covered by the research. The situation is particularly worrying in the Wrzeciono estate where feelings of insecurity have a considerable negative influence on the overall perception of the estate. More than half of the respondents from the Wrzeciono estate and more than a third of the respondents from the Ursynów estate do not feel safe in their neighbourhoods. Respondents perceived as a danger the groups of young people who hang around and vandalise public places such as staircases, benches, cellars, playgrounds, etc. Young people were also reported drinking alcohol in public spaces and leaving bottles under the benches and in the children's sandpits (Węcławowicz et al., 2004). This has resulted in social spaces such as green areas and playgrounds, that were designed for recreational purposes for all the residents, being taken over by youths behaving in a socially unacceptable manner and frightening away other user groups. Instead of integrating residents in their living environment, these places have thus turned into hot spots contributing to conflicts between younger and older generations. This is similar to the situation described by Madanipour (2004) in which domination and intimidation by a particular user group leads to a lack of safety and forces the withdrawal of more vulnerable groups from public areas and from engagement with others. It is, however, necessary to point out that many of the problems often referred to in this regard (such as drug abuse and graffiti) do not necessarily have a direct impact on the level of safety in a residential neighbourhood. They are primarily problems concerning deviant conduct and delinquency that may consequently influence people's feelings of safety while not necessarily presenting any actual safety threat. They may, however, negatively impact on the opportunities for social interaction and social cohesion.

In any event, it must be realised that the planning and organisation of public space certainly plays a role. The way public space is designed determines its nature and therefore its attractiveness for different uses, positive or negative. Inappropriate design often leads to these places being described as 'anonymous' and consequently considered less safe. This is why design techniques have often favoured facilitating 'eyes on the street'. But as has already been stated, insecure places do not cause but merely facilitate deviant behaviour. The argument here is that design alone cannot entirely eliminate feelings of insecurity. For example, adding functions to the ground floors of apartment buildings may in theory bring back 'eyes on the street', but research does not show that areas where the urban form allows 'eyes on the street' are safer (Musterd et al., 2004). Design alone is not enough to guarantee safety. In addition to being properly designed, public space must also be appropriately maintained and efficiently managed in order to ensure that it is not converted into undesirable uses that may lead to feelings of insecurity. Resident participation in the maintenance and management of public space may, once again, be one of the most effective ways of guaranteeing a greater feeling of safety in large housing estates that will encourage the use of social space and promote greater social interaction.

Conclusions

In order to achieve greater social interaction and social cohesion in housing estates, it is imperative that we have a better understanding of the complex nature and various uses of social space as well as the important roles it plays in these residential neighbourhoods. We have shown in this chapter that residents attach great value to social spaces (especially green areas) and generally consider them to be the most positive aspects of their residential environment in neighbourhoods where such spaces are appropriately planned, equipped, managed, and maintained. The sociability of public space is undoubtedly a major factor in establishing good environmental quality for a community in large housing estates. There is, however, not much evidence of the intergenerational interaction that (according to social theory) could be expected to take place in public spaces. On the contrary, many estates experience intergenerational conflicts that in most cases appear to arise from the failure to provide appropriately for the various activities that take place in social spaces, and the failure to take into account the specific public space requirements of specific categories of users. As described above, settings that force interaction are less successful than those that offer a sufficient level of autonomy between the various user groups. Intergenerational interaction may indeed be desirable, but the underlying aim in planning public space should be to create a well-balanced system of social spaces that offers a great variety of recreation activities and provides a wide range of recreation opportunities for the various categories of users.The emphasis is, also in this case, on differentiation.

It may generally be observed that public spaces in most large housing estates have been badly designed and/or badly maintained and managed, causing serious problems for the estates and their residents with respect to image, the use of public space, and the residents' sense of safety. Different countries have adopted different approaches and designed different projects and programmes aimed at improving the quality of social spaces and creating a better neighbourhood image. The problems concerning the management, maintenance, and improvement of public space, especially in CEE countries, have been linked either to disputes over land ownership or to 'imaginary' organisational and management ambiguities resulting mainly from unaccomplished privatisation procedures. It may be hoped that significant improvements will be achieved in this area after the conclusion of the land register modernisation projects and the processes of registering land titles that are currently underway in these countries.

While, in the majority of the research estates, current policies and programmes focus mainly on the physical renewal of residential buildings, it is important to realise that physical solutions alone may not always be sufficient since many of the problems are often social in nature (see Aalbers et al., 2004). This observation calls for the recognition of the mantra: 'Solve social problems with social solutions'. Depending on the particular circumstances, equal consideration should be given to programmes or activities intended to solve social problems as is given to programmes or refurbishment projects aiming at solving physical problems. From this perspective, the appropriate design, management, and maintenance of public and social space in a manner that fosters social interaction is just as important as the design and maintenance of the residential buildings. We once again raise the argument that deficient public space design may accelerate its appropriation for socially undesirable activity. In this case, bad design is a significant contributing factor to the development of a social problem. The point we wish to stress here is that appropriately designed public and social space provides people with a place to socialise, while inappropriately designed public and social space hinders socialising or encourages undesirable forms of socialising. The implementation of appropriate physical measures in solving social space problems must therefore constitute an essential part of all renewal and improvement programmes and projects in addition to the relevant socio-economic programmes. Redesigning bad public space as good social space will not solve unemployment but may foster greater sociability and legibility. This in turn may facilitate social networks among residents and improve the estate's image and reputation.

Which, of course, brings us back to the question of 'what is appropriate or good public space?' We have provided in the body of this discussion some indications of what constitutes a good public space. It is important to remind the reader of the need to ensure the sociability and legibility of public spaces. Good public space is embodied in the notion of a social space that adequately satisfies the needs of a variety of user groups, reflects an attractive and pleasant environment, promotes a feeling of belonging among inhabitants, and encourages social contact and interaction among residents.

References

Aalbers, M., Van Beckhoven, E., Van Kempen, R., Musterd, S. and Ostendorf, W. (2003) *Large Housing Estates in the Netherlands: Overview of Developments and Problems in Amsterdam and Utrecht.* Utrecht: Faculty of Geosciences, Utrecht University.
Aalbers, M., Van Beckhoven, E., Van Kempen, R., Musterd, S. and Ostendorf, W. (2004) *Large Housing Estates in the Netherlands: Policies and Practices.* Utrecht: Faculty of Geosciences, Utrecht University.

Aalbers, M., Bielewska, A., Chignier-Riboulon, F. and Guszcza (2005) Feelings of Insecurity and Young People in Housing Estates. In: R. Van Kempen, K. Dekker, S. Hall and I. Tosics (Eds), *Restructuring Large Housing Estates in Europe*, pp. 275–98. Bristol: Policy Press.

Aalbers, M. B. and Rancati, S. (2008) Feeling Insecure in Large Housing Estates: Tackling *Unsicherheit* in the Risk Society. *Urban Studies*, 45 (13), pp. 2735–57.

Allen, J. and Cars, G. (2001) Multi-Culturalism and Governing Neighbourhoods. *Urban Studies*, 38 (12), pp. 2195–209.

Andersen, H. S. and Leather, P. (Eds) (1999) *Housing Renewal in Europe.* Bristol: The Policy Press

Atkinson, R. (2003) Domestication by Cappuccino or a Revenge on Urban Space? Control and Empowerment in the Management of Public Spaces: A Review. *Urban Studies*, 40 (9), pp. 1829–43.

Burgers, J. (2000) Urban Landscapes: On Public Space in the Post-Industrial City. *Journal of Housing and the Built Environment*, 15, pp. 145–64.

Burrows, R. and Rhodes, D. (1999) *Unpopular Places: Area Disadvantage and the Geography of Misery in England.* Bristol: Policy Press.

Butler, G. D. (1968) *Introduction to Community Recreation.* New York: Mcgraw-Hill.

Carr, S., Francis, M., Rivlin, L. G. and Stone, A. M. (1992) *Public Space.* Cambridge: Cambridge University Press.

Clapham, D., Hegedus, J., Kintrea, K. and Tosics, I. (Eds) (1996) *Housing Privatisation in Eastern Europe.* London: Greenwood Press.

Coleman, A. (1985) *Utopia on Trial: Vision and Reality in Planned Housing.* London: Shipman.

Cooper, C. and Hawtin, M. (Eds) (1997) *Housing, Community and Conflict: Understanding Resident 'Involvement'.* Aldershot: Ashgate.

Černič Mali, B., Sendi, R., Boškić, R., Filipović, M. and Goršič, N. (2005) *Large Housing Estates in Ljubljana and Koper, Slovenia: Opinions of Residents on Recent Developments.* Utrecht: Faculty of Geosciences, Utrecht University.

De Chiara, J., Panero, J. and Zelnik, M. (Ed.) (1995) *Time-Saver Standards for Housing and Residential Development.* New York: Mcgraw Hill.

Diacon, D. (1991) *Deterioration of the Public Sector Housing Stock.* Aldershot: Avebury.

Dimitrovska Andrews, K. and Sendi, R. (2001) Large Housing Estates in Slovenia: A Framework for Renewal. *European Journal of Housing Policy*, 1 (2), pp. 233–55.

Elsley, S. (2004) *Outsiders! Children and Young People and their Use of Public Space.* Paper presented at the Conference 'Open Space–People Space' in Edinburgh.

Emms, P. (1990) *Social Housing. A European Dilemma.* Bristol: School For Advanced Urban Studies.

Erdősi, S., Gerőházi, É., Teller, N., Tosics, I., Ekés, A., Dancza, I., Popovics, L. and Szemző, H. (2003) *Large Housing Estates in Hungary: Overview of Developments and Problems in Budapest and Nyíregyháza.* Utrecht: Faculty of Geosciences, Utrecht University.

Gehl, J. (2004) *Public Spaces for a Changing Public Life.* Paper presented at the Conference 'Open Space–People Space' in Edinburgh.

Haider, J. and Kaplan, M. (2004) *Reclaiming Open Space for the Young: An International Perspective on Design.* Paper presented at the Conference 'Open Space–People Space' in Edinburgh.

Hall, S., Lee, P., Murie, A., Rowlands, R. and Sankey, S. (2003) *Large Housing Estates in United Kingdom: Overview of Developments and Problems in London and Birmingham.* Utrecht: Faculty of Geosciences, Utrecht University.

Hall, S., Murie, A., Rowlands, R. and Sankey, S. (2004) *Large Housing Estates in United Kingdom: Policies and Practices.* Utrecht: Faculty of Geosciences, Utrecht University.

Jacobs, J. (1961) *The Death and Life of Great American Cities.* New York: Random House.

Knorr-Siedow, T. and Droste, C. (2003) *Large Housing Estates in Germany: Overview of Developments and Problems in Berlin.* Utrecht: Faculty of Geosciences, Utrecht University.

Laé, J. F. (1991) Crise Des Banlieues, Le Béton N'est Pas En Cause. *Regards Sur L'actualité*, 3, July, pp. 23–34.

Lawson, B. (2001) *The Language of Space.* Oxford: Architectural Press.

Lowe, S. and Tsenkova, S. (Eds) (2003) *Housing Change in East and Central Europe: Integration or Fragmentation?* Aldershot: Ashgate.

Lynch, K. (1960) *The Image of the City.* Cambridge (MA): The Joint Centre for Urban Studies, MIT.

Madanipour, A. (2004) Marginal Public Spaces in European Cities. *Journal of Urban Design*, 9 (3), pp. 267–86.

Mandic, S. (1994) Housing Tenures in Times of Change: Conversion Debates in Slovenia. *Housing Studies*, 9 (1), pp. 27–38.

Murie, A., Knorr-Siedow, T., Van Kempen, R. (Eds) (2003) *Large Housing Estates in Europe. General Developments and Theoretical Backgrounds.* Utrecht: Faculty of Geosciences, Utrecht University.

Musterd, S., Ostendorf, W. and Deurloo, M. C. (2004) Stedelijke Context En Onveiligheid; Gelegenheid En Criminaliteit. *Beleid En Maatschappij*, 31 (3), pp. 163–72.

Newman, O. (1973) *Defensible Space. Crime Prevention through Urban Design.* New York: Macmillan.

Öresjö, E., Andersson, R., Holmqvist, E., Pettersson, L. and Siwertsson, C. (2004) *Large Housing Estates in Sweden: Policies and Practices.* Utrecht: Faculty of Geosciences, Utrecht University.

Pareja Eastaway, M., Tapada Bertelli, T., Van Boxmeer, B. and Garcia Ferrando, L. (2003) *Large Housing Estates in Spain: Overview of Developments and Problems in Madrid and Barcelona.* Utrecht: Faculty of Geosciences, Utrecht University.

Pearl, M. (1997) *Social Housing Management. A Critical Appraisal of Housing Practice.* London: Macmillan.

Pipard, O. (1995) *Etude De L'usage Des Espaces Extérieurs Du Quartier De La Darnaise Après Requalification: Minguettes, Vénissieux.* Lyon: Communauté Urbaine De Lyon.

Ploštajner, Z., Černič Mali, B., Sendi, R., Boškić, R., Filipović, M., Goršič, N., Ravnikar, D. and Tomšič, B. (2004) *Large Housing Estates in Slovenia: Policies and Practices.* Utrecht: Faculty of Geosciences, Utrecht University.

Power, A. (1997) *Estates on the Edge.* London: Macmillan.

Priemus, H. and Mandic, S. (2000) Rental Housing in Central and Eastern Europe as No Man's Land, Special Issue: Rented Housing in Eastern and Central Europe. *Journal of Housing and the Built Environment*, 15 (3), pp. 205–15.

Schwab, E. and Standler, K. (2004) *Youth Behaviour and Young People's Demands for Open Space: Teens Open Space.* Paper presented at the Conference 'Open Space–People Space' in Edinburgh.

Schwedler, H.-U. (Ed.) (1996) *Environmental Improvements in Pre-Fabricated Housing Estates.* Berlin, European Academy of the Urban Environment.

Sendi, R. (1995) Housing Reform and Housing Conflict: The Privatisation and Denationalisation of Public Housing in the Republic of Slovenia in Practice. *International Journal of Urban and Regional Research*, 19 (3), pp. 435–46.

Sendi, R., Dimitrovska Andrews, K., Kos, D., Trček, F., Cirman, A., Šuklje Erjavec, I., and Cotič, B. (2004) *Prenova Stanovanjskih Sosesk V Ljubljani. Končno Poročilo.* Ljubljana: Urbanistični Inštitut Republike Slovenije.

Struyk, R. J. (Ed.) (1996) *Economic Restructuring of the Former Soviet Block. The Case of Housing.* Washington DC: The Urban Institute Press.

Tanninen, T., Ambrose, I. and Siksiö, O. (Eds) (1994) *Transitional Housing Systems. East–West Dialogue on the New Roles of Actors in Changing Housing Policies.* Dessau: Bauhaus.

Trigueiro, M. (2006) *Les Rôles Attribués Aux Espaces Publics Et À Leurs Constituants Dans Les Stratégies De Renouvellement Urbain.* Lyon: Insa (unpublished Ph.D. thesis).

Turkington, R., Van Kempen, R., Wassenberg, F. (Eds) (2004) *High-Rise Housing in Europe: Current Trends and Future Prospects.* Delft: Delft University Press.

Turner, B., Hegedüs, J. and Tosics, I. (Eds) (1992) *The Reform of Housing in Eastern Europe and the Soviet Union.* New York: Routledge.

Van Kempen, E. (1994) High-Rise Living: The Social Limits to Design. In: B. Danermark and I. Elander (Eds), *Social Rented Housing In Europe: Policy, Tenure and Design*, pp. 159–80. Delft: Delft University Press.

Van Kempen, R., Dekker, K., Hall, S., and Tosics, I. (Eds) (2005) *Restructuring Large Housing Estates in Europe.* Bristol: The Policy Press.

Wassenberg, F. (2002) De Openbare Bijlmer. *Rooilijn*, 35, pp. 267–72.

Węcławowicz, G., Kozłowski, S. and Bajek, R. (2003) *Large Housing Estates in Poland: Overview of Developments and Problems in Warsaw.* Utrecht: Faculty of Geosciences, Utrecht University.

Węcławowicz, G., Guszcza, A. and Kozłowski, S. (2004) *Large Housing Estates in Poland: Policies and Practices.* Utrecht: Faculty of Geosciences, Utrecht University.

Węcławowicz, G., Guszcza, A., Kozłowski, S., Bielewska, A., Adamiak, A., Krasowska, M., Fader, A. and Bierzyński, A. (2005) *Large Housing Estates in Warsaw, Poland: Opinions of Residents on Recent Developments.* Utrecht: Faculty of Geosciences, Utrecht University.

Zajczyk, F., Mugnano, S. and Palvarini, P. (2005) *Large Housing Estates in Milan, Italy: Opinions of Residents on Recent Developments.* Utrecht: Faculty of Geosciences, Utrecht University.

7

Effects of Physical Measures on Social Cohesion: Case Studies in the Netherlands and Slovenia

Karien Dekker and Maša Filipovič

Introduction

Earlier chapters and earlier research have indicated that large post-WWII housing estates can suffer from serious social and economic problems, such as the concentration of poverty and high crime-rates, and physical problems such as the lack of maintenance and deterioration (see, e.g., Dekker and Van Kempen, 2004). These problems can be related to the low level of social cohesion, which is reflected in a higher proportion of conflicts, crime rates and vandalism, and problems related to the maintenance of public space. These are common problems in some large housing estates all over Europe (see Černič Mali et al., 2005; Van Beckhoven and Van Kempen, 2005; Belmessous et al., 2005; Knorr-Siedow and Droste, 2005).

Especially in several Western European countries, social cohesion has reached the top of the urban policy agenda (Home Office, 2001; 2004; Tweede Kamer, 2001). This is less the case in Eastern Europe (Weclawowicz et al., 2004; Szemzö and Tosics, 2004; Ploštajner et al., 2004). Partly, this difference could be due to variations in the levels of social cohesion. Although the layout and the buildings seem similar, the population and housing structure, and several of the problems in the estates, are different.

In this chapter we explore the possible effect of experienced policies on social cohesion. The starting point is that not the policies themselves, but mostly the extent to which the residents experience these policies, will impact on the attitude of residents towards their neighbourhood. If it is clear which policies in which fields have a positive effect on social cohesion then this might be helpful in designing more effective policies. This chapter therefore discusses the current relationship between experienced policy action and social cohesion. We aim to answer the following question: to what extent does the experience of policy action explain the level of social cohesion in large housing estates? We will compare a Central-Eastern European case (two estates in Slovenia) with a Western European case (two estates in the Netherlands). We refer to these cases because they present very different historical and cultural circumstances and also a different situation regarding policy efforts: a situation in which little policy effort is made (Slovenia) compared to one in which policy effort is extensive (the Netherlands). The cross-national comparison allows us to make some observations about the effect of policies on the dimensions of social cohesion.

In this chapter we will first briefly consider the literature on social cohesion and related factors which are important influences on it (e.g. the socio-economic and ethnic characteristics of the population of the estates). We will identify three dimensions of social cohesion: social networks in the neighbourhood, tolerance of difference, and neighbourhood attachment. Then we will review previous research on the explanatory value of other variables for social cohesion, especially policy measures. This short review is followed by a description of the case studies, the data collection and methods used. Then, drawing on the material from the case study areas, we illustrate which effective policy actions in the physical field, ranging from upkeep of public space to introducing a social mix and improving services, are related to social cohesion in the research areas. Finally, the conclusions point out how physical policy measures are helpful in explaining variances in the scores of the social cohesion indicators.

Defining social cohesion

Before variations in the level of social cohesion can be explained, the concept itself needs clarification because the academic discussion of the concept of social cohesion has been extensive and clouded with assumptions (Forrest and Kearns, 2001), and the definition of the concept has been rather ambiguous. Most definitions see social cohesion as *the answer to* individualisation (Pahl, 1991; Forrest and Kearns, 2001) *and a goal to be reached* to ensure sustainability, good relations, progress and also peace (both at the macro level of society as well as at the micro levels of cities and neighbourhoods). But what is it? Researchers (e.g. Amin, 2002), but also policymakers in the UK, use the definition of social cohesion given by Forrest and Kearns.

> a cohesive society 'hangs together'; all the component parts fit in and attribute to society's collective project and well being; and

conflict between societal goals and groups, and disruptive behaviour, are largely absent or minimal.

(Kearns and Forrest, 2000, p. 996)

Kearns and Forrest based their definition on the work of many others, but it seems to be a useful definition in relation to research on the effects of neighbourhood policies. We will therefore explore their construct in more detail here. Kearns and Forrest (2000) distinguish five dimensions of social cohesion:

- Social networks and social capital
- Common values and civic culture
- Place attachment and identity
- Social order and social control
- Social solidarity and reductions in wealth disparities.

With respect to the first dimension of social cohesion, *social networks and social capital* at the level of an estate would entail that there is a high degree of social interaction either between family members or within other social structures in the estate. The second dimension, *common values*, is linked to a common set of moral principles and codes of behaviour according to which people conduct their relations, and this implies engagement in public and collective affairs and a high level of social cooperation. *Place attachment* is the next dimension of social cohesion that Kearns and Forrest discern. This refers to notions of belonging and spatial mobility; it is related to the interlinking of personal and place identity. At the level of estates this means that the inhabitants feel part of the estate and are attached to it.

The framework set out by Kearns and Forrest (2000) outlines what social cohesion is and can be applied at the estate level. However, the last two dimensions are less applicable at the neighbourhood scale. *Social order and control* refer to the absence of general conflict and absence of serious challenge to the existing (democratic) order and system. This is highly influenced by processes that take place at higher spatial levels, for example, the increased gap between Muslims and Christians in society. We will therefore not take this dimension into account in this neighbourhood-level study. The last dimension, *social solidarity and reductions in wealth disparities,* is linked to a fair redistribution of finances and opportunities between groups and places (i.e. reduced disparities in income, employment, competitiveness, open access to welfare services). This dimension is clearly a state concern.[1] Consequently in the analysis we will concentrate on the first three dimensions in describing social cohesion at the estate level: social networks, common values, and place attachment.

Variations in the level of social cohesion

Now that we know what social cohesion is, how can variations in the level of social cohesion be explained? We will describe how the experience of policies probably influences social cohesion. However, since individual and household characteristics also influence social cohesion, these characteristics need to be controlled for in the analyses further on. We will therefore explain the impact of these variables first.

Individual and household characteristics in different types of neighbourhoods

The first dimension of social cohesion, *social networks*, refers essentially to the ties between persons within society, or within a spatial entity such as a neighbourhood (Friedrichs and Vranken, 2001). Earlier research found that social networks are stronger between people with similar characteristics. At the neighbourhood level, social networks are stronger between people who have a similarly strong focus on the neighbourhood, such as people with a low level of education, the unemployed, low-income groups, the elderly, women, and people with children (see Gerson et al., 1977; Fischer, 1982; Guest and Wierzbicki, 1999, Campbell and Lee, 1992).

Social networks of ethnic minorities, who can be strongly oriented towards their own group, may focus on the area where most of their co-immigrants live (Bolt, 2001). Campbell and Lee (1992) indicated in their research that, when comparing blacks and whites, blacks have stronger and larger neighbourhood networks. Dutch research has shown that immigrants from the first generation are especially strongly focused on their own groups for their social contacts (Bolt, 2001). In areas with large numbers of ethnic minorities of a particular group (such as in the Netherlands) immigrants will thus have a stronger focus on the neighbourhood for their social contacts than Slovene/Dutch majority populations.

The second dimension of social cohesion, *common values*, refers to the situation in which a group of people has a common set of values on how to behave and how to live their life. This also implies that people will have communal interests. Some researchers state that residents who do not regularly leave the neighbourhood, such as the unemployed or those on a low income, are more susceptible to developing a set of norms and values that does not match that of the wider community (Gowricharn, 2002).

In neighbourhoods with a large diversity of groups, cohesion within the group may lead to a lack of tolerance for 'others'. Those with a high level of education and a job, and thus probably a slightly higher income, are more likely to leave the neighbourhood on a regular basis. As a consequence they will less easily accept behaviour that bothers them or others, because they do not adapt so easily to what is considered 'normal' in deprived areas (Wilson, 1987). Indeed, Rosenbaum and colleagues (2002) found in Chicago that those with higher incomes do not so easily accept 'different' behaviour. Also homeowners tend to experience more problems with 'other' behaviour (Gerson et al., 1977) because they wish to protect the value of their property.

Ethnicity is an important indicator for the degree of acceptance of differences. As ethnic minorities tend to have stronger ties, this may indicate they are less tolerant of behaviour that threatens their networks. On the other hand, as the pluralist model of inclusion of migrants in Western societies assumes (Castles, 1995), immigrant populations are accepted and accept themselves as ethnic communities, which remain distinguishable from the majority population with regard to language, culture, social behaviour and associations. This would point towards mutual acceptance of difference between Slovene/Dutch majority populations and ethnic minorities.

The last dimension of social cohesion, *neighbourhood attachment*, means that people identify with the people that live around them and their physical living environment (Blokland, 2000). Neighbourhood attachment has many positive spin-offs such as a feeling of security, improved self-esteem, and it bonds people of different cultures and backgrounds. Socio-economic factors have an effect on neighbourhood attachment. Higher-income groups as well as homeowners tend to feel more attached to their neighbourhood than those with a lower income (Gerson et al., 1977; Woolever, 1992). Majority populations seem to prefer a homogeneous native neighbourhood, while non-native groups prefer mixed neighbourhoods, albeit with a substantial share of co-ethnics (Charles, 2003). In cases of urban restructuring this would be expected to lead to a lower level of attachment among the new middle class residents than among the original residents. Also, a shorter length of residence (Gerson et al., 1997; Lee and Campbell, 1999) and in-migration of younger people (Woolever, 1992) is expected to lead to less neighbourhood attachment.

The hypothesis that homeowners tend to feel more attached to their neighbourhood is based mostly on findings in the US. The history of housing and the housing market structure of the US is vastly different from the Netherlands and Slovenia, so we may expect some differences in these contexts. It can be assumed that the meaning of homeownership in Slovenia is strongly influenced by recent developments such as the sale of previously state-owned housing to the owners. Likewise the small amount of available housing in the social (and private) rented sector will have an impact on the value that people attach to having their own home.

In conclusion, the short overview of the literature indicates that individual and household characteristics do not always have the same kind of impact on each of the dimensions of social cohesion.

How policies influence social cohesion

In large housing estates the early policy answers to the problems in the neighbourhoods have been of a purely physical nature (Murie et al., 2003), despite the fact that most policymakers realise that the main problem is of a socio(-economic) nature. Often physical measures are designed to solve social problems. We will indicate for each dimension of social cohesion which measures may explain variations in the dimension.

First, *social networks*, can be positively influenced by physical improvements to the public space, for example by the creation of meeting places in the area, which may facilitate contacts between people. This corresponds with the findings that networks are less strong in places where there is little pedestrian culture and where primary services cannot easily be reached, as these both lead to fewer opportunities to meet (Leyden, 2003). Places such as playgrounds, for example, offer parents the opportunity to meet. The children are an easy 'intermediary' (Gerson et al., 1977; Campbell and Lee, 1992; Fischer, 1982; Guest and Wierzbicki, 1999). Recent research in the UK suggests that public space, if well maintained and co-created by the people themselves, does indeed support contact between people. Parks and markets are important, but so are car boot sales, allotments and supermarket cafés (Mean and Tims, 2005).

The second dimension of social cohesion, *common values*, can be enhanced by social-mix strategies, as explained earlier in this chapter. These strategies are expected to have a positive effect on the values and norms of the residents of the neighbourhood. As the concentration of people with a similar low socio-economic status is believed to be one of the causes of the problems in different values and lower civic involvement (Friedrichs, 1998), the low-income families are replaced with middle class families in the neighbourhoods through urban restructuring policies. The middle class households are expected to be a good example to the households with a lower socio-economic position.

Social-mixing strategies often come with the improvement of public space as well as the construction of better commercial and public facilities to attract higher incomes to the neighbourhood. These spaces function as places for people to share common interests, thereby creating common values about desirable behaviour (Mean and Tims, 2005).

The third dimension of social cohesion, *neighbourhood attachment*, is often emphasised in literature. City and neighbourhood authorities regularly try to foster a greater sense of emotional attachment to place, because it is assumed that this will lead to more commitment and care about what happens, eventually leading to political engagement. Various authors emphasise the physical aspects of the neighbourhood and its 'image' in the city as a whole as an important source of neighbourhood identity and attachment (Valera and Guardia, 2002; Kim and Kaplan, 2004). Also the creation of a social mix is believed to enhance positively the image of a neighbourhood. Place attachment can be boosted by improving the visual attractiveness of the place and giving it a middle class 'feel', for example, redesigning squares and shopping centres (Kearns and Forrest, 2000). Also safety-policies can enhance the feeling of attachment. If people feel safe in the neighbourhood they will be more satisfied and have less reason to move out of the neighbourhood, as was indicated in earlier research (Lindström et al., 2003; Brown et al., 2004). Relatively simple policies such as removing graffiti, enhancing safety and keeping the streets clean are a great incentive for neighbourhood attachment.

Concluding, there is a generally positive effect to be expected of physical policies on the three dimensions of social cohesion. Our hypothesis is that the positive effect of physical policies or actions is positively related to each dimension of social cohesion in large housing estates.

The case study neighbourhoods

The empirical part of this chapter draws on four case studies, two in Slovenia and two in the Netherlands. The estates illustrate the diversity of the large housing estates among countries, as well as within each country. As this section will show, there are significant differences among the estates in their position in the housing market, structure of population and housing, etc. In addition, the policy measures differ greatly: Slovenia presents a case in which little policy action is undertaken, while in the Dutch cases the Big Cities Policy is in full swing.

The Dutch cases

In the Netherlands two estates in Utrecht were chosen. One of them is New Hoograven. This estate was built between 1954 and 1965 and originally consisted of about 2251 dwellings. The estate is wedged in between canals and motorways and touches the city centre to the north of the estate. More than half of the housing stock consists of three- or four-storey, multi-family blocks in the social rented sector. The public areas are mainly green areas without a clear use. The estate ranks low on the urban ranking list due to problems related to social cohesion, unemployment, criminality, and a decrease in services (Aalbers et al., 2003).

The other estate, Kanaleneiland North, is slightly larger in size consisting of 2674 dwellings. The estate was built between 1956 and 1965. Four-fifths of the housing stock is in the social rented sector, and consists of multi-family dwellings with three to four floors (Aalbers et al., 2003). The estate has many problems and scores lowest on the urban ranking list; often mentioned are the high crime rates, problematic youth and the population composition (www.utrecht.nl).

The problems in the estates are tackled in an area-based fashion, under the heading of the Big Cities Policy. The major objectives are to increase the number of people in employment, to increase the number of middle- and high-income households and reduce out-migration of people aged 30–45 to surrounding municipalities. The 'Onze Buurt aan Zet' (Our Neighbourhood's Turn) project aims to enhance the quality of life, safety and social cohesion through stimulating community initiatives. Community groups are stimulated by offering subsidies and support from social work.

The two neighbourhoods are different with respect to physical restructuring. While in Hoograven the Big Cities Policy is in full swing, in Kanaleneiland the restructuring policies are still in the planning phase (Aalbers et al., 2004). Further activities entail:

- Public space is improved through small-scale gardening projects, redesign of squares between the houses, pollution prevention projects, improved lighting and more intensive maintenance schemes.
- Many projects are directed at enhancing safety, especially by involving young people in all types of activities and through better maintenance of public spaces.
- Education projects are aimed at involving more children from a younger age, to improve the command of the Dutch language, and to reduce the number of dropouts. An important focus is on the parents; they should get more involved with their children.
- There is no clear drug-related policy at neighbourhood level, although 'hostels' are to be set up for drug-users.

The Slovenian cases

In Slovenia two neighbourhoods were studied in two different towns: Fužine in Ljubljana and Žusterna-Semedela in Koper. The Fužine estate is situated in the eastern part of Ljubljana, approximately three kilometres from the city centre. The construction of Fužine estate started in 1977, with 1640 dwellings built, and ended with the second phase in 1981, when 2778 dwellings were built. At the time of construction over 70 per cent of the dwellings were social rental housing, however now, after privatization, the majority are privately owned. The quality of the environment is quite high, due to the proximity of green areas, but there are the playgrounds and other public spaces that are suffering from lack of maintenance. The Fužine estate has a rather negative status in the city, in public perception the name of the estate is linked to high crime levels. It is the largest and most densely populated estate in Ljubljana, and has the highest share of people from non-Slovenian ethnic backgrounds, mainly ex-Yugoslavian nationalities (Černič Mali et al., 2003).

The other case study is the Žusterna-Semedela estate, which can be found in the south-western part of the city of Koper. Construction of Žusterna began in 1981, but only one quarter of the original development plan was actually built. For the purpose of this research it has therefore been linked with the previously existing Semedela housing area (built in 1973–81). The change in ownership structure is similar to that on the Fužine estate. The quality of the environment in the estate is relatively low due to poor maintenance, and the infrastructure and services are limited. The status of the area in the town is neither negative nor positive (Černič Mali et al., 2003).

Even though there are no integrated area-based policy efforts comparable to those in the Netherlands, there are several community initiatives that influence the quality of life in the neighbourhoods (e.g. there is a strong involvement of various parties in the area, ranging from public services such as schools, to voluntary and private parties). Due to unresolved ownership issues the public space in Žusterna-Semedela is poorly and irregularly maintained. In Fužine the upkeep of green areas varies from neglect to regular care, depending on the initiative of the residents and housing managers (Černič Mali et al., 2003).

Differences between the estates

The four estates are comparable with respect to size and building type, but otherwise they are quite different. Not only were the Dutch estates built decades before the Slovenian ones, but also the quality of the public space, crime rates, problems with youngsters and quality of the public environment is much worse in the Netherlands than in Slovenia. The government in the Netherlands is very actively improving the quality of the estates through social-mixing strategies and improvements of the public space. In Slovenia such a policy is lacking, but the communities themselves are actively involved in neighbourhood maintenance.

There are some significant differences between residents of the case study estates. In the Dutch case studies, of the residents sampled, only a minority of the respondents were educated to a medium or high level, or had an average or high income when compared to the national level. According to the aims of the restructuring policy, these are the people who should bring about societal effects and achieve the important objective of creating more heterogeneous populations (Kleinhans, 2005). The residents in the Slovene estates, especially in Nove Fužine, are better educated, but the levels of education are similar to the Dutch respondents. The proportion of ethnic minorities is relatively high in the Dutch Kanaleneiland, at over 50 per cent. This shows that Kanaleneiland, more than any of the other neighbourhoods, is a concentration area of ethnic minorities. In the Slovene estates and the Dutch Hoograven the proportion of ethnic minorities is 23–7 per cent. In the Dutch estates, a higher proportion of respondents was younger (31–45 -years-old), childless, tenant, and had moved in less than three years ago, compared to the respondents from the Slovene estates. The differences can be understood by the position of the estates on the housing market. In the Netherlands, the estates are at the bottom of the housing market and most residents will move again to another neighbourhood as soon as they have the chance. In Slovenia, however, the position of the estates is declining but still relatively positive.

Data and analysis

Multivariate analyses were performed on data derived from a survey held in the research neighbourhoods in April and May 2004. In Slovenia a total of 407 questionnaires were filled in from a sample of about 700 adresses: 236 in Fužine, and 171 in Žusterna-Semedela. The response rate in Slovenia was quite high (in both estates 60 per cent). The portion of those who could not be reached was 15 per cent in Fužine (59 addressees) and 27 per cent (75 addressees) in Žusterna-Semedela. The reason for a higher portion of the unavailable addressees in the case of Žusterna-Semedela was due to the relatively high proportion of secondary dwellings, whose owners are not permanent residents and are therefore more difficult to reach.

In Utrecht a total of 523 questionnaires was collected: 270 in Nieuw Hoograven (sample 700) and 253 (sample 800) in Kanaleneiland.

The response rate in the Dutch estates was quite low (38.6 per cent in Nieuw-Hoograven and 31.6 per cent in Kanaleneiland). The non-responses in Kanaleneiland were mainly due to refusals (51.5 per cent) because people were not in the mood, were tired of the questionnaires, etc. In Nieuw-Hoograven 32.7 per cent of the non-responses were due to refusals which can attributed to one of the reasons mentioned before. The rest of the non-responses were caused by a high proportion of respondents who were not at home at the time of the questionnaire.

Measuring social cohesion: dependent variables

Social cohesion is represented in three dimensions: social networks, common values, and place attachment. We measure social cohesion as a quantitative representation of the feelings and actions of individuals. The three dimensions of social cohesion are represented through five indicators.

The first dimension of social cohesion, *social networks* is measured using two indicators:

- The importance of the neighbourhood for social contacts. For the analysis, people with many friends and relatives in neighbourhood are considered to have a strong social focus on the neighbourhood.
- A qualitative evaluation of the contacts between residents. When an individual recognises this contact to be good or moderate, this is seen as an indication of good social contacts. This is the second indicator of social networks.

The *common values* dimension of social cohesion is measured using one indicator:

- Attitude towards the behaviour of others: 'Do you personally experience problems in the neighbourhood with respect to different values/norms/lifestyles?'. Those who answer that they do not experience problems with other behaviours are considered more tolerant and open than those who do experience problems.

The last indicator of social cohesion, *neighbourhood attachment,* is measured using two indicators:

- Satisfaction with the neighbourhood. Respondents were asked to indicate on a scale between one (very low) and ten (very high)

how satisfied they are with their neighbourhood. People who indicate six or higher are considered to be reasonably or very satisfied with their neighbourhood.
- Respondents were asked, 'Do you feel weakly or strongly attached to the neighbourhood?'. Those respondents who answer strong or neutral are considered to feel attached to their neighbourhood.

Independent variables

The level of effective policy or action was measured from the respondent's point of view in two fields: the improvement of upkeep of public space and the improvement of public and commercial services. To measure the effect of improvements in public space and service improvements, respondents were asked if they personally experience serious problems in the neighbourhood with respect to these issues. Then the respondent was asked if the mentioned aspects have been improved by any policy or action. The effect of policies and actions was thus related to the experience of problems.

In the survey the opinion of the residents on eight issues relating to the maintenance of the neighbourhood and the service provision were measured. The physical issues indeed measure the same thing and are thus co-related (Cronbach's alpha = .76). They are: dirt on the streets, upkeep of public spaces, condition of the roads, playgrounds for children, and maintenance of the buildings. Also the service-related issues to measure the same topics (Cronbach's alpha = .81). They are: quality of the schools, quality of the commercial services and quality of the public services. The 'upkeep of public spaces' and 'quality of commercial services' variables have the highest scores on the factor analysis (not shown) and were thus chosen to represent the other variables.

The third indicator of the effect of physical policy on social cohesion is the degree of social mix in the neighbourhood from the residents' point of view. The question 'Do you regard the estate you are living in to be socially mixed (households with very different incomes) or socially homogeneous (mostly households with approximately similar incomes)?' provides an indication of the degree of social mix in the estate. Table 7.1 provides an overview of the indicators of physical policy per estate.

As we aim to show to what extent an experience of physical policy action has a positive effect on social cohesion, a series of logistic regression equations are estimated, each using a different indicator of social cohesion as the dependent variable, and the indicators of physical improvement as the independent variables. In the models, we control

Table 7.1   Perception of physical policies (percentage of the respondents per estate)

	Kanaleneiland	Nw. Hoograven	Nove Fuzine	Zusterna
Perception of degree of social mix				
% Homogeneous	41.0	18.5	5.1	11.6
% Moderately or more mixed	39.8	65.9	89.4	84.3
% Unknown	19.1	15.6	5.5	4.1
Perception of upkeep of public space: experienced problems and effect of policies or actions				
% *No*, I don't have problems with this	39.4	40.7	53.0	38.4
% *Yes*, I do have problems with this and				
I see no improvement due to policy cr action	6.4	7.8	8.1	3.5
% *Yes*, I do have problems with this and				
I do see improvement due to policy or action	22.3	19.6	25.4	52.9
% *Yes*, I do have problems with this, but *I don't know*				
if there is improvement due to policy or action	10.8	7.0	10.2	4.1
% Unknown opinion on the upkeep of public space	21.1	24.8	3.4	1.2
Perception of the commercial services: experienced problems and effect of policies or actions				
% *No*, I don't have problems with this	56.2	53.7	91.1	83.1
% *Yes*, I do have problems with this and				
I see no improvement due to policy or action	2.8	3.7	1.7	.6
% *Yes*, I do have problems with this and				
I do see improvement due to policy or action	6.4	8.1	2.1	12.2
% *Yes*, I do have problems with this, but *I don't know*				
if there is improvement due to policy or action	6.4	4.8	2.1	1.2
% Unknown opinion on the upkeep of public space	28.3	29.6	3.0	2.9
Total number of cases (= N)	251	270	236	172

Source: RESTATE Database, 2004.

for individual, household and neighbourhood characteristics. Using this method, the relative explanatory power of the evaluation of policies and actions for social cohesion can be estimated. As all dependent variables are measured on a binary scale, a logistic regression is chosen here.

For each indicator of social cohesion, two logistic regression models are estimated. In the logistic model, first only the control variables are entered into the logistic regression equation: age, household composition (1 = household without children), education (1 = higher education), income (1 = below average income; 2 = unknown), ethnicity (1 = ethnic minorities), tenure (1 = tenants), year first moved into the neighbourhood (1 = 2001 or more recent). Also the four neighbourhoods are entered into the model (Kanaleneiland is the reference category). Then a second model is estimated for each indicator of social cohesion, this time also entering the experienced effect of better upkeep of public spaces, and improvements in commercial services. Five categories of answers are included in the analyses: (0) does not experience any problems with respect to this topic[2] (reference category); (1) does experience problems, but sees no improvements due to policy or action; (2) does experience problems, and does notice positive effects due to policy or action; (3) does experience problems, but is not certain about the effect of policies; (4) unknown. By classing the cases in this manner, there are no missing cases on this variable. The reference category represents those people who do not experience problems, compared to the other categories that do experience problems.

The variable indicating the degree of social mix is also entered into the analyses. Three categories of answers are included: (0) I live in a socially homogeneous estate (reference category); (1) I live in a (moderately) socially mixed estate; (2) unknown. Again, by classing the cases in these categories there are no missing cases on this variable. Table 7.2 illustrates the variables included in the logistic regression models and provides descriptive statistics on each variable.

Are physical policies linked to higher levels of social cohesion in the research areas?

Social cohesion in the research areas

Our hypothesis is that the experienced positive effect of physical policies or actions is positively related to each dimension of social cohesion in large housing estates. But, as explained in the theoretical part of this chapter, social cohesion is also influenced by individual and household

Table 7.2 Descriptive statistics for variables used in logistic regressions models

	Mean	SD
Dependent variables		
% Positive rating of social contacts in the neighbourhood	16.7	
% Negative rating of social contacts in the neighbourhood	83.3	
% Many friends and/or family within the neighbourhood	49.0	
% Not many friends and/or family within the neighbourhood	51.0	
% No experience of problems due to different values, norms, or lifestyles	71.0	
% Does experience problems due to different values, norms, or lifestyles	29.0	
% High neighbourhood satisfaction	64.8	
% Low–medium neighbourhood satisfaction	35.2	
% Feels (strongly) attached to the neighbourhood	20.3	
% Does not feel attached to the neighbourhood	79.7	
Independent variables: Individual and household characteristics		
Age in years	45.88	15.8
Household composition		
% Household with children	47.0	
% Household without children	53.0	
Education		
%Lower-average education	56.8	
%Higher education	43.2	
Income		
% Below average	60.3	
% Average or higher	30.9	
% Unknown	8.8	
Tenure		
% Tenant	51.6	
% Homeowner	48.4	
Year first moved into the neighbourhood		
< 2001	79.1	
≥ 2001	20.1	
Ethnicity		
% Native	69.0	
% Non-native	31.0	
Neighbourhood of interview		
% Kanaleneiland	27.0	
% Nieuw Hoograven	29.1	
% Nove Fuzine	25.4	
% Zusterna	18.5	

(*Continued*)

Table 7.2 (Continued)

	Mean	SD
Social mix		
% that lives in a homogeneous population composition neighbourhood	19.9	
% that lives in a moderately or very mixed population composition neighbourhood	68.2	
% unknown opinion on social mix	11.8	
Maintenance of public space		
% *No*, I don't have problems with this	43.1	
% *Yes*, I do have problems with this and *I see no* improvement due to policy or action	6.7	
% *Yes*, I do have problems with this and *I do see* improvement due to policy or action	28.0	
% *Yes*, I do have problems with this, but *I don't know* if there is improvement due to policy or action	8.3	
% Unknown opinion on the maintenance of public space	14.0	
Commercial services		
% *No*, I don't have problems with this	69.3	
% *Yes*, I do have problems with this and *I see no* improvement due to policy or action	2.4	
% *Yes*, I do have problems with this and *I do see* improvement due to policy or action	6.9	
% *Yes*, I do have problems with this, but *I don't know* if there is improvement due to policy or action	3.9	
% Unknown opinion on the upkeep of public space	17.5	
Total number of cases (= N)	929	

Notes:
Lower-average education: 0–12 years school education since the age of six.

Income classifications are a response to the question: 'Would you classify the monthly household income as high, medium high, average, medium low, or low, compared to national levels?'

Division native-non native is a response to the question: 'In terms of ethnicity, how would you call yourself?' (self categorisation).

Source: RESTATE Database, 2004.

characteristics of the population. On the basis of these characteristics, we expect that the Dutch estates (especially Kanaleneiland) have much lower scores on the indicators of social cohesion than the two Slovenian estates (see Table 7.3). In the Slovenian estates the long time that people have lived in the estate (which is closely related to age), combined with high homeownership rates, promises higher rates of social networks, higher scores on common values, as well as more neighbourhood attachment than in the Dutch estates. However, taking ethnicity into account, the high proportion of ethnic minorities in Kanaleneiland might indicate stronger social networks within the neighbourhood, higher levels of neighbourhood attachment and problems related to common values.

Table 7.3 Characteristics of the respondents in the survey (percentage of the respondents per estate)

	Kanaleneiland	Nw. Hoograven	Nove Fuzine	Zusterna
Age***				
18–30 years	12.4	15.9	19.1	15.1
31–45 years	39.4	40.4	16.9	22.7
46–60 years	29.5	22.2	51.7	39.5
60+ years	18.3	20.7	10.6	22.1
Unknown	.4	.7	1.7	.6
Years of education***				
≤ 12 years	61.0	50.0	48.3	61.6
> 12 years	32.3	44.4	50.8	37.8
Unknown	6.8	5.6	.8	.6
Income class				
Low-medium	53.4	59.6	66.5	62.8
Average-high	33.9	29.6	30.1	29.7
Unknown	12.7	10.7	3.4	7.6
Ethnicity***				
Majority populations	45.8	72.2	72.9	79.1
Ethnic minorities	51.8	23.7	22.9	17.4
Unknown	2.4	4.1	4.2	3.5
Household composition***				
With children	44.6	37.4	54.7	55.8
Without children	55.4	60.0	55.9	44.2
Unknown	4.0	2.6	.5	0
Tenure***				
Home owner	14.3	11.9	94.1	89.5
Tenant	84.5	86.7	5.1	9.3
Unknown	1.2	98.5	.8	1.2
Year first moved into the nbh				
< 2001	75.70	67.04	88.98	93.60
≥ 2001	24.30	32.96	11.02	6.40
Unknown	0	0	0	0
Total abs in all groups (100%)	251	270	236	172

Source: RESTATE Database 2005.
*** p < 0.01

Indeed, in line with the expectations based on the individual and household characteristics of the population, the empirical findings show higher scores on the indicators of social cohesion in the Slovenian estates when compared to the Dutch estates (Table 7.4). Kanaleneiland in particular has very low overall scores in comparison to the other estates.

Table 7.4 clearly shows that the four neighbourhoods have different 'strong cohesion dimensions' according to their residents. Part of the differences between the estates may also be the result of local circumstances. In the logistic regression analysis below, we therefore include a neighbourhood variable to control for this, as well as socio-demographic variables.

The question that we need to consider next is the extent to which policies or actions that are evaluated positively by the residents lead to higher scores on the indicators of social cohesion, while controlling for the individual, household and neighbourhood characteristics. This will generate insight into the relationship between physical policies and social cohesion.

The impact of policies on social networks

Earlier research has shown that weak ties provide support (Granovetter, 1973), and that they give the feeling of home, a sense of identity, security (Henning and Lieberg, 1996) and can generate communal action

Table 7.4 Dimensions of social cohesion per neighbourhood (percentage of the respondents per estate)

	Kanaleneiland	Nieuw Hoograven	Nove Fuzine	Zusterna
Positive rating of social contacts in the neighbourhood***	81.1	89.8	90.5	94.0
Yes, many friends and or family in the neighbourhood	55.4	48.1	48.3	54.7
No experience of problems due to different values/ norms/lifestyles***	54.3	62.6	71.1	74.5
High neighbourhood satisfaction***	50.8	75.8	73.6	64.3
Feels strongly attached to the neighbourhood	20.3	20.1	22.1	21.1

***p < 0.01; **p < 0.05; *p < 0.10

Source: RESTATE Database 2005.

(Kearns and Forrest, 2000). Certainly in deprived urban areas such as the case studies in this chapter, these weak ties are worth stimulating.

The findings show that most residents (around 90 per cent) in the estates value their social contacts in the neighbourhood positively. In Hoograven and Žusterna-Semedela people are much more positive compared to Nove Fužine and Kanaleneiland (Table 7.4). When it comes to real contact, about half of the residents state they have family, many friends, or both in the neighbourhood (Table 7.4). The Slovenians have slightly more friends and family in the neighbourhood than the Dutch.

These differences between the estates can perhaps partially be explained by the individual and household characteristics of the respondents. In line with the expectations formulated in the theoretical section, it was found that households with children, people with lower education, those who have lived in the estate for more than five years, and ethnic minorities, more often have positive scores on the indicators of social networks (Table 7.5).

The question that can now be addressed is what is the impact of physical policies on the social networks' dimension of social cohesion. First of all, it is expected that a social mix helps to enrich the social networks. The findings here confirm the hypothesis partially: residents who believe that they live in a socially mixed estate rate the social contacts in the neighbourhood more positively, although they do not actually have more friends and family in the neighbourhood. This shows that people may not actually have strong ties with each other, but feel more comfortable in a neighbourhood where different kinds of people live together. The concept that social mixing will enrich the social networks in the neighbourhood thus partially holds true.

The literature review suggested that the positive experience of places to meet such as public spaces or shopping centres could be positively related to social networks. The analysis shows that this expectation holds true: people who experience problems with the public spaces or commercial services, are generally significantly less positive about their social contacts, and have less friends and family in the neighbourhood than people who feel satisfied with the upkeep of public spaces and the commercial facilities. The positive impact of services may be explained by the fact that schools, public facilities, or commercial services function as meeting places. Here people chat, feel connected, maybe only have eye contact, but at least know who else lives in the neighbourhood (Mean and Tims, 2005). Services are of great importance for the social network dimension of social cohesion.

176

Table 7.5 Logistic regression-analysis of social contacts in the neighbourhood (a) rating of social contacts (b) friends and family in the neighbourhood[3]

	Social contacts (1 = positive rating)				Friends and family in the neighbourhood (1 = yes, many)			
	B	Sig.	B	Sig.	B	Sig.	B	Sig.
Age	0.003	0.675	0.003	0.645	−0.018	0.000 ***	−0.020	0.000 ***
Household without children	−0.370	0.092	−0.430	0.057 *	0.089	0.568	0.093	0.560
Higher education	−0.587	0.006 ***	−0.638	0.004 ***	−0.637	0.000 ***	−0.617	0.000 ***
Below average income	0.687	0.075 *	0.536	0.186	0.066	0.836	−0.092	0.782
Income not mentioned	0.253	0.518	0.177	0.664	−0.303	0.352	−0.415	0.218
Ethnic minority	0.701	0.008	0.848	0.002 ***	0.609	0.001 ***	0.645	0.000 ***
Tenant	−0.412	0.204	−0.447	0.178	0.332	0.176	0.351	0.163
Moved in ≥ 2001	−0.067	0.789	−0.034	0.896	−0.387	0.045 **	−0.396	0.047 **
Kanaleneiland (= ref cat)		0.001 ***		0.001 ***		0.292		0.264
Hoograven	0.818	0.002 ***	0.762	0.007 ***	−0.079	0.693	−0.202	0.341
Nove Fuzine	−0.027	0.940	−0.272	0.487	0.207	0.463	−0.068	0.824
Zusterna	0.878	0.034 **	0.775	0.080 **	0.462	0.110	0.287	0.358
Social mix			0.872	0.019 **			−0.109	0.724
Opinion on social mix unknown			1.104	0.001 ***			0.435	0.116
Upkeep of public space: yes problems, no improvements			−0.395	0.320			−0.145	0.627
Upkeep of public space: yes problems, yes improvements			−0.517	0.046 **			−0.341	0.062 *

	B	Sig.	B	Sig.	B	Sig.	B	Sig.
Upkeep of public space: yes problems, unsure about improvements			−1.030	0.003 ***			−0.267	0.341
Opinion on upkeep of public space unknown			−0.319	0.401			−0.812	0.006 ***
Commercial services: yes problems, no improvements			−0.374	0.513			0.056	0.909
Commercial services: yes problems, yes improvements			−0.656	0.073 *			−0.052	0.858
Commercial services: yes problems,? Improvements			0.287	0.598			0.789	0.052 *
Opinion on commercial services unknown			0.016	0.963			0.179	0.488
Constant	1.254	0.051	0.941	0.203	0.741	0.133	0.960	0.095
N	846		846		846		846	
minus 2 LL	694.7		670.2		1113.6		1095.4	
model chi−square	44.7		69.1		59.0		81.2	
Df	10		20		10		20	
P	.000		.000		.000		.000	
Nagelkerke R square	.088		.135		.090		.122	

*= p < 0.10; ** = p < 0.05; *** = p <0.001

Source: RESTATE Database, 2004.

However, improvements of public spaces or in commercial facilities do not lead to better scores in this dimension of social cohesion. In Hoograven the policy efforts to improve safety through better maintenance of public space, as well as the opening of a new shopping centre, cannot be related directly to more positive ratings of, and higher density social networks within, the neighbourhood.

The impact of policies on common values

From the theoretical framework it has become apparent that feelings of communality flourish when people know each other, and discussion on differences and how to cope with differences is stimulated (Forrest and Kearns, 2001). A socially cohesive neighbourhood is not necessarily a homogeneous neighbourhood, but in a cohesive neighbourhood the differences between people are respected.

The indicator of this dimension of social cohesion is the tolerance of difference. When people have no problems with differences in lifestyles this may be interpreted as a sign of cohesion. In Slovenia only a quarter of the people experience problems that result from differences in lifestyles, norms and values. In the Dutch cases, especially in Kanaleneiland, this proportion of the residents is significantly greater. Here nearly half of the residents claim to experience problems related to different values, norms or lifestyles (Table 7.4). The (in socio-economic and ethnic terms) more diverse population in the Dutch estates does lead to problems with different values and norms between the residents. As Gerson and collegues stated (1977), people identify more easily with others who have similar income, education, ethnicity, and lifestyle. Interestingly, ethnic minorities are more tolerant towards different lifestyles than majority populations. This may be due to the fact that they still feel the ones who are 'different' from the rest, in contrast to majority populations who feel that their lifestyle is the predominant lifestyle, making the latter group less tolerant.

Looking at the effect of physical policies on the tolerance of difference, it is rather striking that those respondents who feel they live in a socially mixed estate do not experience more problems than those in homogeneous estates. The social mix itself is thus not the cause of problems related to differences in lifestyles (Table 7.6). An explanation may be found in the experience of other problems, besides those connected to the different lifestyles. The analysis does indeed show that those who experience problems with the upkeep of public spaces and commercial services also experience significantly more problems related to differences in lifestyles, values and norms. Clearly a problem does not come alone.

Table 7.6 Logistic regression-analysis of common values and a civic culture in the neighbourhood: tolerance of difference

	Tolerance of difference (1=no problems due to different values, norms, lifestyles)			
	B	Sig.	B	Sig.
Age	0.006	0.235	0.002	0.788
household without children	0.062	0.723	−0.012	0.948
higher education	−0.356	0.037**	−0.298	0.097*
below average income	−0.197	0.594	−0.133	0.731
income not mentioned	−0.717	0.057	−0.659	0.093*
ethnic minority	0.980	0.000***	1.053	0.000***
tenant	0.608	0.019**	0.589	0.029
Moved in >= 2001	0.419	0.052*	0.305	0.176
Kanaleneiland		0.000***		0.000***
Hoograven	0.550	0.011**	0.566	0.015**
Nove Fuzine	1.307	0.000***	1.157	0.001***
Zusterna	1.495	0.000***	1.683	0.000***
social mix			−0.296	0.402
Opinion on social mix unknown			−0.142	0.662
Upkeep of public space: yes problems, no improvements			−0.732	0.021**
Upkeep of public space: yes problems, yes improvements			−0.965	0.000***
Upkeep of public space: yes problems, unsure improvements			−0.462	0.138
Opinion on upkeep of public space unknown			−0.419	0.187
Commercial services: yes problems, no improvement			−0.887	0.077*
Commercial services: yes problems, yes improvement			−0.945	0.002***
Commercial services: yes problems, unsure improvements			−1.004	0.010**
Opinion on commercial services unknown			0.139	0.619
Constant	−0.337	0.543	0.595	0.365
N	846		846	
minus 2 LL	969.6		918.9	
model chi-square	53.9		104.6	
df	10		20	
p	.000		.000	
Nagelkerke R square	.088		.166	

*=p < 0.10; **=p < 0.05; ***=p < 0.001
Source: RESTATE Database, 2004.

As with the previous dimension of social cohesion, there is no significant impact of the successfulness of a policy in the field of public spaces or services on the common values dimension of social cohesion.

Neighbourhood attachment

It is expected that neighbourhood attachment can be enhanced through improving the quality of the physical space: by keeping the streets clean, enhancing safety, removing graffiti (Kearns and Forrest, 2000). Also the provision of public and commercial services such as shopping centres is considered important. We expect that neighbourhood attachment is positively influenced by physical measures (Valera and Guardia 2002, Kim and Kaplan 2004) and better services (e.g. Lupton 2003).

Kanaleneiland has lower scores than the other estates on this dimension, and Nieuw Hoograven and Nove Fužine do better than the others (Table 7.4). In Kanaleneiland about half of the population is satisfied with the estate, in Žusterna-Semedela this is 64.3 per cent and in Nieuw Hoograven and Nove Fužine about three quarters of the people are satisfied. Surprisingly the feeling of attachment is very low in all estates, with only about a fifth of the residents saying they feel attached to the neighbourhood.

Earlier research has shown that socio-economic status is positively associated with neighbourhood attachment (see literature review). Those with higher incomes tend to feel more attached to their neighbourhood than those with lower incomes (Gerson et al., 1977; Woolever, 1992). Surprisingly, we found the opposite in our estates: lower income earners feel more attached to the neighbourhood than higher income earners (Table 7.7). Those with higher incomes are probably more inclined to think that they will find another dwelling in a more suitable neighbourhood in the future.

Furthermore, the analyses point out that ethnic minorities feel more attached to the neighbourhood, and are more satisfied with it, than majority populations. The difference may be due to a different point of reference, as the housing circumstances of other immigrants are probably similar to those of ethnic minorities in the research areas (Bolt and van Kempen, 2002). For the majority populations, comparison with other majority populations in the city probably leads to a less positively coloured conclusion on their own situation. They will therefore feel less satisfied with the neighbourhood.

As expected, elderly people feel more attached to the neighbourhood than younger people. This is strongly related to the time that people have lived in the neighbourhood.

The differences in neighbourhood satisfaction and attachment may be explained by the degree to which people experience problems with the upkeep of public spaces. In line with other research, we found that removing graffiti and clean streets are positively related to neighbourhood satisfaction (Table 7.7). However, a relationship with policy action to improve the upkeep of public spaces was not found in our case studies.

The impact of the experienced quality of commercial services on neighbourhood attachment is rather ambiguous. Based on the literature review, we expected a positive relationship between policy action that improves the neighbourhood and neighbourhood attachment. However, we found that people who experience problems related to the quality of commercial services, but see no policy action to improve them, feel more attached than all other categories, including those that experience problems, and do see improvements.

As the analysis above has shown, there was no straightforward conclusion on the positive effect of the experience of physical policies on social cohesion in the neighbourhood. Our analysis showed that indeed there is a strong relationship between physical problems (e.g. the poor upkeep of public spaces and low quality of services) and social cohesion. However, the fact that residents notice policies or actions aimed at improving the problematic situation was found to be of no significance for social cohesion. Clearly, the physical environment has its impact on people's mindsets about the neighbourhood, whereas the actions by governmental organisations are of less importance. As other research has shown, the success of urban regeneration depends largely on the participation of the residents and their levels of involvement (Taylor, 2000; Brown et al, 2004). Perhaps this explains the importance of involving citizens in the improvement of public spaces and services, as only in this manner can social cohesion also be improved while improving the physical characteristics of the neighbourhood.

Conclusions

In this chapter we aimed to answer the question: To what extent does the experience of policy action explain the level of social cohesion in large housing estates? We distinguished three dimensions of social cohesion: social networks, common values, and neighbourhood attachment. We hypothesised that an effective policy approach (measured as a policy that has been effective in the eyes of the respondents) has a positive effect on these three dimensions of social cohesion. In order to answer the research question, we compared the effects of policies on social cohesion in large housing estates in the Netherlands and Slovenia

Table 7.7 Logistic regression-analysis of neighbourhood attachment (a) neighbourhood satisfaction; (b) neighbourhood attachment

	Neighbourhood satisfaction (1=high)				Neighbourhood attachment (1=high)			
	B	Sig.	B	Sig.	B	Sig.	B	Sig.
Age	0.000	0.995	−0.003	0.605	0.026	0.000***	0.023	0.000***
household without children	0.073	0.659	0.064	0.706	0.035	0.859	0.067	0.740
higher education	−0.225	0.172	−0.223	0.193	−0.250	0.205	−0.283	0.163
below average income	0.677	0.031**	0.502	0.131	0.352	0.402	0.270	0.540
income not mentioned	0.414	0.198	0.323	0.340	0.411	0.333	0.369	0.405
ethnic minority	0.164	0.385	0.188	0.335	0.954	0.000***	1.022	0.000***
tenant	0.018	0.943	0.014	0.958	0.021	0.948	0.118	0.726
moved in >= 2001	0.009	0.964	0.020	0.926	−0.479	0.081	−0.534	0.059*
Kanaleneiland		0.000***		0.000***		0.535		0.805
Hoograven	1.226	0.000***	1.242	0.000***	0.286	0.257	0.193	0.467
Nove Fuzine	1.126	0.000***	0.855	0.006***	0.461	0.209	0.354	0.374
Zusterna	0.743	0.011**	0.673	0.033**	0.375	0.311	0.281	0.483
social mix			0.283	0.361			−0.424	0.282
Opinion on social mix unknown			0.592	0.034**			0.235	0.476
Upkeep of public space: yes problems, no improvements			−0.486	0.122			−0.185	0.636
Upkeep of public space: yes problems, yes improvements			−0.546	0.004***			0.109	0.623
Upkeep of public space: yes problems, unsure improvements			0.115	0.712			−0.533	0.153
Opinion on upkeep of public space unknown			−0.588	0.051*			−1.031	0.010**
Commercial services: yes problems, no improvement			−0.707	0.151			0.499	0.417

	Model 1		Model 2		Model 3		Model 4	
Commercial services: yes problems, yes improvement			−0.865	0.003 ***			−0.712	0.105 *
Commercial services: yes problems, unsure improvements			−0.528	0.174			−0.036	0.946
Opinion on commercial services unknown			−0.020	0.940			0.749	0.017 *
Constant	−0.652	0.194	−0.402	0.495	−3.394	0.000	−3.262	0.000
N	846		846		846		846	
minus 2 LL	1038.3		1004.3		800.4		779.5	
model chi-square	50.7		84.7		53.9		47.8	
df	10		20		10		20	
p	.000		.000		.000		.000	
Nagelkerke R square	.080		.132		.097		.133	

*=p < 0.10; **=p < 0.05; ***=p < 0.001
Source: RESTATE Database, 2004.

on the basis of a quantitative dataset. The rationale behind comparing the Dutch situation to the Slovenian one, was that in Slovenia few policies have been implemented while in the Dutch cases the Big Cities Policy entails both physical, social and economic measures.

The analyses showed that not only are the characteristics of policies different in Slovenia and the Netherlands, but the level of social cohesion is also very different. We found that the four estates have clear differences in the dimensions of social cohesion, which again demonstrates the diversity among large housing estates in Europe. Generalising it can be stated that Kanaleneiland in the Netherlands has the lowest scores on the indicators of cohesion and both estates in Slovenia have the highest scores on these indicators. The differences in social cohesion can partially be related to the individual and household characteristics of the population in the neighbourhoods.

Ethnicity in particular has an important influence on the level of social cohesion in all dimensions. Ethnic minorities have more ties than majority populations to the neighbourhood, experience fewer problems due to different lifestyles, values and norms, and are more satisfied with their neighbourhood. Thus, ethnic minorities have a higher level of social cohesion within the neighbourhood. This holds true for both countries. There is however an important difference between the Dutch and the Slovenian estates: the ethnic minorities in the Dutch cases are mainly of Northern African origin, while the ethnic minorities in Slovenia largely originate from countries of former Yugoslavia. The cultural difference between majority populations and ethnic minorities is thus not so big in Slovenia. In the Dutch cases the proportion of ethnic minorities is so large that ethnic minorities feel comfortable with this, whereas the native Dutch find these concentrations too high and complain about the large proportion of ethnic minorities in their neighbourhood (Dekker and Bolt, 2005).

Surprisingly age, income, having children and tenure did not have a significant impact on the levels of social cohesion, which is quite opposite to findings of other authors. The differences in the level of social cohesion between the estates can therefore only partially be explained by the different characteristics of the population. We think that the general contextual differences between the estates and countries are more important in explaining the differences in the levels of social cohesion. Also the importance that is attached to homeownership may account for part of the variance.

One of these context variables is related to the residents' experience of policies in the estate. The central question of this chapter, the extent to which the experience of policy action explains the level of social cohesion, has an ambiguous answer. In the field of the improvement of public spaces and services, we found no relationship between the extent to which people notice policy action and their scores on the indicators of social cohesion. However, although it was found that the *physical policy action* was not related to social cohesion, the analyses show that the experience of *physical problems* was related to social cohesion. In the case where respondents mentioned few problems in the field of physical space and services, high scores on the indicators of social cohesion were also found. This implies that the public space and service facilities in the estate indeed function as meeting places, allowing residents to build new networks, create a common set of values on how to behave, and leading to more neighbourhood attachment.

Why do the policies, if they are experienced positively, not have a positive impact on social cohesion? It could be that there exists a time lag between the improvement effort of policies and their positive influence on social cohesion dimensions. Perhaps the negative experiences and evaluations of residents take a significant time to change and are therefore of a more enduring quality (in positive as well as negative ways). This would best be measured by a longitudinal survey. On the other hand, perhaps physical improvements should not be delegated by the state only (from above), but coordinated and executed together with the residents. These more participatory policies might improve social cohesion in the neighbourhoods more.

The next variable, the experience of a socially mixed neighbourhood, has very limited positive effects on the indicators of social cohesion. In areas that are perceived as mixed, people rate their contacts more positively, but this does not influence the number of contacts they actually have. Strikingly, in areas that are perceived as mixed, there are not more problems related to the difference in lifestyles and people do not feel more or less attached to the neighbourhood. This research thus does not provide empirical evidence for the hypothesis of policymakers that in estates where the residents experience a social mix, middle class households build weak ties with people with a lower socio-economic status, thereby involving people in mainstream society value patterns and enhancing neighbourhood attachment.

The policy implications of the findings here are not straightforward. We cannot simply argue that to solve problems that result from a lack of social cohesion all one has to do is make physical improvements in the public spaces and in the level of services, in the expectation that this will also improve the level of social cohesion in the estate. Clearly the policy action itself does not lead to a more cohesive community in the estate. Nor is the creation of a social mix a solution to strengthen social cohesion, as this would entail more majority populations inhabiting the neighbourhood and probably lead to even less social cohesion in the estate. In order to enhance social cohesion in large housing estates, it is probably best to facilitate and accommodate the diversity of groups in the estate, while at the same time the physical environment must also be well-maintained and give ample opportunity to meet others and identify with the people and the built environment.

Notes

1. See Dekker and Bolt (2005) for a more elaborate discussion.
2. Undefined if this means respondent doesn't care or is satisfied with the situation.

References

Aalbers, M., Van Beckhoven, E., Van Kempen, R., Musterd, S. and Ostendorf, W. (2003) *Large Housing Estates in the Netherlands: Overview of Developments and Problems in Amsterdam and Utrecht.* Utrecht: Urban and Regional Research Centre.

Aalbers, M., Van Beckhoven, E., Van Kempen, R., Musterd, S. and Ostendorf, W. (2004) *Large Housing Estates in the Netherlands: Policies and Practices.* Utrecht: Urban and Regional Research Centre.

Amin, A. (2002) Ethnicity and the Multicultural City. *Environment and Planning A*, 34 (6), pp. 959–81.

Belmessous F., Chernin, C., Chignier-Riboulon, F., Commerçon, N., Trigueiro M. and Zepf, M. (2005) *Large Housing Estates in France. Opinions of Residents on Recent Developments.* Utrecht: Urban and Regional Research Centre.

Blokland, T. (2000) Unravelling Three of a Kind: Cohesion, Community and Solidarity. *Netherlands Journal of Social Sciences*, 36 (1), pp. 56–70.

Bolt, G. (2001) *Wooncarrières van Turken en Marokkanen in ruimtelijk perspectief.* Utrecht: Faculteit Ruimtelijke Wetenschappen.

Bolt, G. and Van Kempen, R. (2002) Moving up or Moving down? Housing Careers of Turks and Moroccans in the Netherlands. *Housing Studies*, 17 (3), pp. 401–22.

Brown, G., Brown, B. and Perkins, D. (2004) New Housing as Neighbourhood Revitalisation: Place Attachment and Confidence among Residents. *Environment and Behaviour*, 36, (6), pp. 749–75.

Campbell, K. E. and B. A. Lee (1992) Sources of Personal Neighbor Networks: Social Integration, Need or Time? *Social Forces*, 70 (4), pp. 1077–100.

Castles, S. (1995) How Nation-States Respond to Immigration and Ethnic Diversity. *New Community*, 21 (3), pp. 293–308.

Černič Mali, B., Sendi, R., Boškić, R., Filipović, M., Goršič, N. and Zaviršek Hudnik, D. (2003) *Large Housing Estates in Slovenia: Overview of Developments and Problems in Ljubljana and Koper.* Utrecht: Urban and Regional Research Centre.

Černič Mali, B., Sendi, R., Boškič, M. and Goršič, N. (2005) *Large Housing Estates in Ljubljana and Koper, Slovenia. Opinions of Residents on Recent Developments*. Utrecht: Urban and Regional Research Centre.

Charles, C. A. (2003) Dynamics of Residential Segregation. *Annual Review of Sociology*, 29, pp. 167–207.

Dekker, K. and Van Kempen, R. (2004) Urban Governance within the Big Cities Policy. *Cities*, 21 (2), pp. 109–17.

Dekker, K. and Bolt, G. (2005) Social Cohesion in Post War Estates in the Netherlands: Differences between Socio-Economic and Ethnic Groups. *Urban Studies*, 42 (12), pp. 2447–70.

Fischer, C. S. (1982) *To Dwell Among Friends: Personal Networks in Town and City*. Chicago: The University of Chicago Press.

Forrest, R. and Kearns, A. (2001) Social Cohesion, Social Capital and the Neighbourhood. *Urban Studies*, 38 (12), pp. 2125–43.

Friedrichs, J. (1998) Do Poor Neighbourhoods Make Their Residents Poorer? Context Effects of Poverty Neighbourhoods on Residents. In: H. J. Andress (Ed.) *Do Poor Neighbourhoods Make Their Residents Poorer? Context Effects of Poverty Neighbourhoods on Residents*, pp. 77–99. Aldershot: Ashgate.

Friedrichs, J. and Vranken, J. (2001) European Urban Governance in Fragmented Societies. In: H. T. Andersen and R. Van Kempen (Eds), *European Urban Governance in Fragmented Societies*, pp. 19–40. Aldershot: Ashgate.

Gerson, K., Stueve, C. A. and Fischer, C. S. (1977) Attachment to Place. In: C. S. Fischer, R. M. Jackson, K. Gerson, L. McCallister Jones and M. Baldasarre (Eds) *Attachment to Place*, pp. 13–161. New York: The Free Press.

Gowricharn, R. (2002) Integration and Social Cohesion: The Case of the Netherlands. *Journal of Ethnic and Migration Studies*, 28 (2), pp. 259–73.

Granovetter, M. S. (1973) The Strength of Weak Ties. *American Journal of Sociology*, 78 (6), pp. 1360–80.

Guest, A. M. and Wierzbicki, S. K. (1999) Social Ties at the Neighbourhood Level. Two Decades of GSS Evidence. *Urban Affairs Review*, 35 (1), pp. 92–111.

Henning, C. and Lieberg, M. (1996) Strong or Weak Ties? Neighbourhood Networks in a New Perspective. *Scandinavian Housing and Planning Research*, 13, pp. 3–26.

Home Office (2001) *Community Cohesion: A Report of the Independent Review*. London: Home Office.

Home Office (2004) *Community and Race: Community Cohesion*. Retrieved: 14 September 2004, from www.homeoffice.gov.uk.

Kearns, A. and Forrest, R. (2000) Social Cohesion and Multilevel Urban Governance. *Urban Studies*, 37 (5–6), pp. 995–1017.

Kim, J. and Kaplan, R. (2004) Physical and Psychological Factors in a Sense of Community: New Urbanist Kentlands and Nearby Orchard Village. *Environment and Behaviour*, 36 (3), pp. 313–40.

Kleinhans (2005) *Sociale implicaties van herhuisvesting en herstructurering*. Delft: TU Delft.

Knorr-Siedow, T. and Droste, C. (2005) *Large Housing Estates in Germany. Opinions of Residents on Recent Developments*. Utrecht: Urban and Regional Research Centre.

Lee, B. A. and Campbell, K. E. (1999) Neighbor Networks of Black and White Americans. In: B. Wellman (Ed) *Networks in the Global Village: Life in Contemporary Communities*, pp. 119–46. Boulder: Westview Press.

Leyden, K. M. (2003) Social Capital and the Built Environment: The Importance of Walkable Neighbourhoods. *American Journal of Public Health*, 93 (9), pp. 1546–51.

Lindström, M., Merlo, J. and Östergren, P. (2003) Social Capital and Sense of Insecurity in the Neighbourhood: A Population-Based Multilevel Analysis in Malmö, Sweden. *Social Science and Medicine*, 56, pp. 1111–20.

Lupton, R. (2003) *Poverty Street: The Dynamics of Neighbourhood Decline and Renewal.* Bristol: The Policy Press.

Massey, D. and Denton, N. (1993) *American Apartheid: Segregation and the Making of the Underclass.* Cambridge: Harvard University Press.

Mean, M. and Tims, C. (2005) *People Make Places: Growing the Public Life of Cities.* York: Joseph Rowntree Foundation.

Murie, A., Knorr—Siedow, T. and Van Kempen, R. (2003) *Large Scale Housing Estates in Europe: General Developments and Theoretical Backgrounds.* Utrecht: Urban and Regional Research Centre.

Pahl, R. E. (1991), The Search for Social Cohesion: From Durkheim to the European Commission. *European Journal of Sociology*, XXXII, pp. 345–60.

Ploštajner, Z., Černič Mali, B. and Sendi, R. (2004) *Large Housing Estates in Slovenia. Policies and Practices.* Utrecht: Urban and Regional Research Centre.

Rosenbaum, J. E., Reynolds, L. and Deluca, S. (2002) How Do Places Matter? The Geography of Opportunity, Self-Efficiency and a Look Inside the Black Box of Residential Mobility. *Housing Studies*, 17 (1), pp. 71–82.

Szemzö, H. and Tosics, I. (2004) *Large Housing Estates in Hungary. Policies and Practices.* Utrecht: Urban and Regional Research Centre.

Taylor, M. (2000) Communities in the Lead: Power, Organisational Capacity and Social Capital. *Urban Studies*, 37 (5), pp. 1019–35.

Tweede Kamer der Staten Generaal (2001) *Grotestedenbeleid.* Den Haag: SDU Uitgevers.

Valera, S. and Guardia, J. (2002) Urban Social Identity and Sustainability: Barcelona's Olympic village. *Environment and Behaviour*, 34 (1), pp. 54–66.

Van Beckhoven, E. and Van Kempen, R. (2005) *Large Housing Estates in Utrecht, the Netherlands. Opinions of Residents on Recent Developments.* Utrecht: Urban and Regional Research Centre.

Weclawowicz, G., Guszcza, A. and Kozlowski, S. (2004) *Large Housing Estates in Poland. Policies and Practices.* Utrecht: Urban and Regional Research Centre.

Wilson, W. J. (1987) *The Truly Disadvantaged.* Chicago: Chicago University Press.

Woolever, C. (1992) A Contextual Approach to Neighbourhood Attachment. *Urban Studies*, 29 (1), pp. 99–116.

Part III Difference in Policy and Approach

8
Large Housing Estates, Policy Interventions and the Implications for Policy Transfer

Alan Murie and Ronald van Kempen

Introduction

To a considerable extent the pattern and nature of the post-WWII large planned housing estates were influenced by a common professional and technological view about what would make a successful estate (see, e.g., Turkington et al., 2005 and Chapter 1 of this book). A coalition of interests between national and local governments, the architectural profession, planners and the construction industry favoured particular types of standard developments. Images of mass housing estates across Europe are remarkably similar, and they are also familiar in North America. Superficially then, there is a phase of mass housing associated with a particular historical conjuncture, reflecting the common challenges facing different economies (Murie et al., 2003).

Some 30 or more years later, the neighbourhoods that were built to be the solution to urban problems are very often seen as symbolising the problems of urban housing. They now often no longer match the housing aspirations of households. In addition to the quality of the housing stock, the quality of open space and the maintenance and management of the estates within which dwellings are located has become a source of concern among policymakers.

When describing the basic features of post-WWII large housing estates in Europe, there is a clear tendency in the literature to look at these estates as if they have common characteristics and the same problems. Hence, the same kind of policy solutions could be applied. Although researchers generally refer to case studies and sometimes even make comparisons between estates in different countries, the idea of convergence dominates many analyses and conclusions. For some authors it seems to be clear that the influx of low-income households in an estate is a major cause of neighbourhood decline (Grigsby et al., 1987; see also Megbolugbe et al., 1996). In other cases the increasing concentration of minority ethnic groups seems to be the cause of decline (Skifter Andersen, 2003). The idea of a common spiral of decline associated with the design of dwellings and estates (Coleman, 1985) or with a wider set of factors has also been popular (Prak and Priemus, 1985; Power and Tunstall, 1995; Taylor, 1995; see also Chapter 2 of this book). Sometimes it is concluded that all problems could be solved in a managerial way (Power, 1997), and in an increasing number of countries terms like tenure mix, residential mix and social mix are seen as the solution for the decline of neighbourhoods (see, e.g., Jupp, 1999; Tunstall, 2003; Uitermark, 2003; Berube, 2005; Van Beckhoven, 2006; Musterd, 2008).

In this chapter we challenge this idea of convergence. We challenge the view that the problems faced on large estates and the solutions being adopted for them fall into one category. We suggest three contexts and patterns of policy intervention which characterise the large post-WWII estates in Europe and discuss the implications for policy transfer. The underlying question in this chapter is thus: 'Why are there different patterns of policy intervention and what are the implications of these differences for the scope for policy transfer?' Our main conclusion is that we need to be extremely careful when talking about the possibility of policy transfer. A successful policy in one spatial or political context will not necessarily be successful in another context and, in any case, may only be able to be transferred if there are comparable legal, organisational and financial arrangements in place. Success is always at least partially determined by contextual factors and by the ownership, financial and organisational features associated with estates in different countries and cities.

Policy intervention and convergence

Two distinctive approaches to explain the similarities and differences relating to large housing estates are evident in the existing literature. They present two alternative starting points for the discussion of how estates built in the same era develop. The first one emphasises convergence based on a common built form, common spirals of decline or common pressures of gentrification. We can call this an inward-looking approach. The second starting point emphasises path dependency and embeddedness within policy and social organisation which perpetuate differences. Rather than being preoccupied with the similarities associated with built form, this more outward-looking approach tends to emphasise the differences associated with welfare state and policy traditions. It is these different perspectives that we can reflect upon through recent research.

Looking inwards

The similarity in the surface characteristics and circumstances of estates built in the post-WWII era in different countries has encouraged a tendency to refer to them as if they form a common group with common problems irrespective of where they are. Some of the research-based accounts explicitly present comparisons between different countries that emphasise the continuity and similarity of problems and suggest that there are similar solutions in different cases. These contributions adopt a framework associated with common dynamics in neighbourhoods of similar vintage, construction and design and the convergence of policy and problems between countries. Common social and economic pressures in a global economy and common features of the built environment are seen as generating common problems associated with urban change and policy and with housing provision. In the literature referring specifically to large post-WWII housing estates, this convergence thesis is apparent in a number of contributions.

As early as 1985, the Dutch housing researchers Niels Prak and Hugo Priemus suggested a common dynamic affecting large estates, although their work was based essentially on the Netherlands, a country with a relatively large number of social rented dwellings (see Chapter 2 for a more elaborate account of their contribution). At about the same time, Alice Coleman (1985) in the UK presented what was widely regarded as an environmentally deterministic view of the reasons for the failure of large public-sector estates. In 1997, Anne Power's study of high-rise housing estates presented material related to the UK, Ireland, Denmark, Germany and France and again suggested continuities associated with construction, design and management (Power, 1997). This literature presents accounts of common spirals of decline affecting these neighbourhoods irrespective of where they were, implying an inevitability associated with the passage of time, and with little room for residents or others to impact on the process (Power and Tunstall, 1995; Taylor, 1995; 1998).

Looking outwards

The alternative starting point for international comparison of change affecting large estates is the literature concerned with international comparison of urban change and urban policy systems. Within this literature the most influential contributions have often built on Esping-Andersen's (1990) discussion of the *The Three Worlds of Welfare Capitalism*. Esping-Andersen argued that the development of welfare state regimes owed more to the specific historical and political circumstances of different countries than it does to stages in economic development or global processes. The fact that countries all develop welfare states of some kind does not demonstrate that they develop because of some logic of industrialisation or economic development. He rejected views that welfare states emerged as a result of universal physiological forces, technological determinism, or as a consequence of industrialisation. He also rejected the view that they were a necessary and inevitable consequence of political development and the growth of democracies. Consequently, welfare-state systems had distinctive attributes in terms of underlying objectives and principles, the scope and generosity of benefits, entitlement and redistribution. From this, Esping-Andersen developed a discussion of three welfare-state regime types and suggested that the policy choices open were affected by regime type – a representation of path dependency that has had considerable influence.

The literature on welfare regimes has had a considerable influence on comparative housing studies. While Esping-Andersen's consideration of the welfare state placed little emphasis on local welfare state provision and on services provided in kind – including housing – many of the discussions of different national approaches to housing provision show a similar pattern.

Some authors have, however, produced classifications of welfare state provision that include housing or even put it at the forefront. Doling (1997, p. 213; 1999, p. 230) argues that other contributions by Kemeny (1981) and Barlow and Duncan (1994) further extend the Esping-Andersen typology to housing policy and focus on understanding housing-policy differences in terms of the particular course and nature of economic and political developments which have characterised older industrial countries. Harloe's more historical account of social and public or de-commodified housing in Europe also draws on this approach and emphasises path dependency as well as a common economic pressure from the mid-1970s for convergence on a residual model (Harloe, 1995).

Taken together, these and other contributions (such as Donnison, 1967; McGuire, 1981; Boelhouwer and Van der Heijden, 1992) indicate that there are different traditions or regime types in relation to housing-policy development in Europe. These do not always coincide neatly with Esping-Andersen's welfare regime types, but path dependency is emphasised. Housing policy leaves a legacy which affects the next stage of policy development. There is a legacy in terms of the built environment but also in terms of financial and organisational systems, and professional culture and practice. The countries with large, not-for-profit or state housing systems have very different organisational arrangements and capacity, and the careers of professionals are embedded within these arrangements with different assumptions about process and practice. All of these features, established in one period, affect what happens in the next. Path dependency, in other words, is an important concept when we want to explain the current situation and future developments of large housing estates.

Similarity and difference

The research carried out in the RESTATE project highlights differences associated with dwellings built in large housing estates constructed across Europe in the same era and under some similar influences in the post-war period. The large estates included in the study nevertheless have common features: they have very important roles in the housing market and also have a common set of problems emerging. These common problems include physical problems associated with poor materials, poor construction, poor insulation, poor estate layout and small rooms; and, especially in Eastern Europe, there are parking problems associated with these neighbourhoods. They have social problems associated with a decline in the income mix (especially in North-Western Europe), with new population groups involving a new mix of cultures and lifestyles, problems of criminality and drug abuse and a relative isolation and lack of social contacts. They are also all under pressure as competition from new housing has highlighted the less attractive features of these estates (see also Chapter 2). There are management problems: both management of the dwelling (including repairs and maintenance) but also of the estate as a whole including public spaces (see Dekker and Van Kempen, 2005; Musterd and Van Kempen, 2005). Because owners of estates often have limited finances to invest, there is always a competition going on between and within estates: which parts will be improved, which ones demolished and which parts will be left on their own?

The similar problems mentioned above, combined with the surface appearance of these estates (see also Chapter 3), pulls the analysis into the inward-looking account just referred to. However, closer interrogation of evidence about the estates begins to expose dimensions of difference that are better able to explain why there is not a convergence of policy responses: similar estates work differently; policy interventions impact on dynamic situations, and the direction and drivers of change on estates operate in different organisational, ownership and market contexts. The problems and opportunities associated with the estates differ. Policy interventions reflect wider factors and policy resources. There are no common causal factors and the similarity of surface appearances, both in the built form and in problems, is misleading (see Chapter 2). The implication that there are simple common solutions is inaccurate.

The most effective way to understand both similarities and differences is initially to recognise three distinctive contexts within which large estates operate in Europe. These three groupings reflect different histories and political contexts but also differences in ownership, organisational and policy frameworks and the financial arrangements associated with these. In the remainder of this chapter we highlight these differences initially by referring to examples associated with three different groupings of estates (Southern Europe; Central and Eastern Europe; Northern and Western Europe) and then by summarising the wider conclusions from research.

Southern Europe

The large housing estates in Southern Europe[1] operate within welfare state regimes in which the family and other traditional social institutions are enormously important. The emphasis in public policy has not been on major redistribution but rather on support for the family and traditional organisations including the church and charitable organisations connected with the church.

In Esping-Andersen's terms, the state in these countries is corporatist rather than redistributive. It has a more active programme to maintain the social order than liberal welfare states but the scope and generosity of benefits is relatively limited. In housing, the role of the state has been less significant than elsewhere. The size of the de-commodified or public-sector housing provision is more comparable with liberal welfare states, and patterns of ownership on large mass housing estates are less dominated by the non-profit sector. Large housing estates were often built explicitly as part of agendas to house particular sections of the population working in particular parts of the economy, rather than for general housing needs. For example, in Spain two estates in Barcelona (Trinitat Nova and Sant Roc), provide a different insight into the process of social change and gentrification.

Trinitat Nova was developed in the 1950s to house immigrants from rural areas and other parts of Spain. It has some 3200 dwellings and more than 70 per cent of these are owner-occupied. All of the dwellings are in multi-family buildings, constructed with poor materials and a considerable number suffer from structural defects, which means that they are scheduled for demolition. The intention is to replace them with new dwellings. Trinitat Nova experienced significant demographic changes with an ageing and declining population between 1981 and 1996. This was caused mainly by a strong movement of second-generation inhabitants away from the area as no dwellings were available at that time. Unemployment was relatively high, especially among young inhabitants, and educational levels were low (Pareja Eastaway et al., 2003).

Sant Roc was built between 1962 and 1965 and comprises 3395 dwellings in six blocks, varying from 5 to 14 storeys high. The quality of the dwellings has always been poor and, again, a significant number of dwellings are being demolished to be replaced by new dwellings. Throughout the estate, owner-occupation is the dominant tenure. Around 40 per cent of the inhabitants of Sant Roc are gypsies. The area has become increasingly associated with lower income households and foreign immigrants, especially from outside the EU, with few financial resources (Pareja Eastaway et al., 2003).

The changes planned for these two estates are to improve the quality of the dwellings, but also to break the concentration and separation of the gypsy population from the non-gypsy population, and to improve the overall status of the estate. There is an explicit aim to mix gypsies and other households. In effect this means dispersing those households (re-housing them in other neighbourhoods when their present dwellings are demolished). Some gypsy families feel discriminated against in this process, although the precise dwelling allocated to households is determined by a lottery (Pareja Eastaway et al., 2003).

Central and Eastern Europe

The large housing estates built in Central and Eastern Europe were constructed at a slightly later stage than those in the rest of Europe. They were constructed under state socialist governments which dominated in the post-WWII period up until the end of the 1980s. These governments initially invested in establishing the economy. Turning their attention to the social infrastructure, including housing, tended to come at a slightly later stage. While, especially in Western Europe, the construction of high-rise housing more or less stopped in the middle of the 1970s, new high-rise buildings in the Central and Eastern European countries were built until well into the 1990s (see Turkington et al., 2005). Estates in Central and Eastern Europe have very similar physical characteristics compared to Western European estates, although, for example, provision for parking space was more limited, green areas were less abundant and provision for communal activities was in some cases more considerable.

The role of these estates in the housing market was very different to elsewhere. For decades, these were the modern, highest quality houses being built at a considerable distance from the city centres and the alternatives were often overcrowded, dilapidated, older private sector housing in the heart of cities. Consequently the large estates were often those that were most attractive to the middle- and higher-income groups. There is however an evident gradation between estates. Some were built with better facilities than others and were associated with professional workers and the political elite. Accounts of the process of access and allocation of housing under state socialism highlight the extent to which party members and the key sections of the workforce had priority over the population in general. The more attractive estates were populated by those who had more bargaining power within this framework and so it was often middle- and higher-income groups who lived in these estates, with lower-income groups remaining in the older parts of the city, or in less attractive estates.

Housing has been an important element in the change in political and economic structure of these societies since 1989. Renaud (1995) for example refers to housing as a shock absorber and privatisation of housing has had a major impact on estates across Central and Eastern Europe. Again the evidence suggests that privatisation advanced further in the better estates with the higher-income groups in them (Murie et al., 2005).

Despite some variation between different estates, at present the large housing estates built in Central European urban areas in the post-WWII period are very rarely at the bottom of the housing hierarchy. Compared to other parts of the cities, they are still better estates in terms of quality and condition of properties and design, and they still house middle- and even higher-income groups rather than the lowest-income groups. Because of privatisation at the beginning of the 1990s, owner-occupiers predominate, under different legal arrangements for condominiums and cooperatives. Because these estates are still relatively new and some of them were very well built, they do not conform in most cases to the image of run-down, poor neighbourhoods. While they have problems associated with design and construction, the lack of parking space and the lack of funds to maintain and improve estates, their role in the market is distinctively different from other parts of Europe and the pattern of ownership and population is also very different.

Two estates in Hungary illustrate the differences from the previous examples from Spain. The Jósaváros estate in Nyiregyhaza is situated close to the city centre and was built between 1970 and 1979. It contains 3600 dwellings in two distinct zones of high-rise buildings and lower-rise apartments. The Havanna estate in Budapest was built between 1977 and 1983 as a large estate investment project using prefabricated construction methods. There are 6200 dwellings on the estate in high-rise buildings of 11 storeys. Both of these estates initially provided housing for rent owned by the state (Erdősi et al., 2003).

Jósaváros has always been considered to be a fairly average segment of the housing market. It did not house either the lowest or the highest sections of society and ethnic minorities were never a significant element in the estate. While Jósaváros underwent a demographic transition in the two decades after the 1980s, with a significant decline in population, especially in households with children, and a growth in single-person households, the impact of privatisation was to narrow the social base of the estate. Before 1989, many of the residents in the estate were already owners of flats (in housing cooperatives or owners of condominium flats). Both of these types of property had been funded by the national savings bank, which offered very favourable loans to relatively affluent households. After the political and economic changes in 1989, families, especially with rising incomes after the transformation, often moved to single-family houses or to newly built condominiums, and in many cases located elsewhere in the city. At the same time an economic crisis caused a decrease in demand for housing. Students, young couples and lower middle class families moved into the estate, replacing more affluent older households (Erdősi et al., 2003).

This picture is very different from the one in Havanna in Budapest. From the outset Havanna had a poor reputation and a high level of poverty with socially underprivileged and gypsy families overrepresented. The opportunities to purchase housing under privatisation programmes were taken advantage of by lower-income households who saw an opportunity to sell on and make some financial gain from buying and then selling. The households buying these dwellings at full value did not come from low-income sections of the community, but rather from those who had sufficient resources to buy at full market value. The consequence of this has been a widening of the social base in a way more compatible with some notions of gentrification. The Havanna estate continues to have lower prices than other estates in Budapest and continues to have a poorer reputation than elsewhere. It has not seen significant regeneration in terms of improvements of the physical infrastructure, the maintenance of buildings or other elements, and yet it has seen a change in the social base with an increasing number of middle- and lower-income households moving in (Erdősi et al., 2003).

In both of these estates there remain enormous problems to do with the buildings, the heating systems, the maintenance and management of estates. There are enormous difficulties in generating funding for effective renovation and renewal of heating systems, or other elements, in the structure of buildings. Fragmented ownership underlies these problems and inhibits renovation and renewal. In the long run, this may weaken the market position of these estates and contribute to a narrowing of the social base as they are seen to be less attractive than new developments. However, the experience of these two estates demonstrates the different kinds of market responses to privatisation and to changes in public policy.

Northern and Western Europe

The third type of context relates to Northern and Western Europe. In this section we focus on the UK, the Netherlands and Sweden. These are the clearest cases where strong organisational and financial capacity has imparted a different approach to estates. These are not countries with the same welfare states. The Netherlands and Sweden have, in Esping-Andersen's terms, a more social democratic, redistributive regime. The UK is closer to a liberal regime, or is a hybrid with a mixed economy of welfare with some strong redistributive elements alongside some much less well developed elements. Another major difference is the considerable diversity in the housing stock, with the highest levels of de-commodified or social rented housing apparent in the Netherlands and, until 1980, in the UK. The common feature of the UK, the Netherlands and Sweden can be found in a tradition of a highly active state-led housing and planning policy in the 50 years after WWII.

The large housing estates in these countries have one thing in common: their position in the housing market has shifted enormously. While they started off, in the decades when they were built, as very popular and attractive housing estates, they have gradually become the places where only those with low incomes and no other alternatives on the housing market want to live. Various factors have contributed to this: the declining attraction and residualisation of state and social rented housing in general, uneven economic, demographic and social development, and failures of management and policy. (see, e.g., Murie et al., 2003). Many estates have also been affected by tenure transfers, although in the UK the Right-to-Buy and privatisation has had less impact on these large estates than on the more traditional property types that characterise older estates in the UK. Compared with the UK, privatisation has been much more limited in the Netherlands and Sweden.

In Sweden and the Netherlands the process of change on these estates has been particularly associated with increasing concentrations of black and minority ethnic groups. In Western Europe examples exist of estates in which already over 80 per cent of the total population belongs to minority ethnic groups. Their low incomes and large families often lead to limited opportunities in the urban housing market; the affordable and relatively large houses in the post-WWII housing estates are a logical option, when those who can afford it move out. Simultaneously the share of original residents diminishes through death (Dekker and Van Kempen, 2005). The way in which this has come about is very similar to the process of residualisation in the UK. It relates to the structure of the housing market as a whole and the structure of social incomes and social inequality. It also relates to processes of access and allocation to different parts of the housing market.

The current role of estates is different from the past. In all cases it has been affected by the growth of homeownership, the supply of newer dwellings elsewhere, and by the consequent movement of middle- and higher-income groups from the flats in the large housing estates to these new developments. In the UK, as well as in the Netherlands, this process involved a considerable narrowing of the social base of social rented housing (see, e.g., Meusen and Van Kempen, 1994; Murie, 1997).

Because some owner-occupied property exists within the same areas as a result of the Right-to-Buy (Jones and Murie, 2006), there is more social mix than is implied by the tenure statistics. However, where estates are located within unattractive areas, the market price of former council housing is relatively low and the social mix is more limited.

Contexts and policy approaches

Table 8.1 summarises the material presented in the previous section relating to the different contexts for large housing estates in different parts of Europe. It also refers to the different policy approaches being adopted.

There is a major contrast between the approaches adopted in *Northern and Western Europe* and those operating elsewhere. In recent years there has been a variety of management and community initiatives designed to make estates more attractive to live in. Attention has been given to

Table 8.1   Large housing estates in Europe: Different contexts for similar dwellings

	South Europe	East/Central Europe	North/West Europe
Size of public housing legacy	Small (<10%) (40%+)	Very large	Large (>20%)
Vintage of public housing	Post 1945	Post 1960	Post 1919 but mainly post 1945
Original target for building in large post-war estates	Specific need groups	Key workers and party members	Mixed: affluent working class and slum clearance households
Current social standing of housing in large post-war estates	Low status	Middle/high status	Mixed but increasingly low
Welfare regime type	Corporate	Transition from state socialist	Mixed/redistributive
Current ownership of dwellings in large post-war estates	Mainly home ownership	Fragmented following privatisation	Mixed but mainly rented from state or not-for-profit organisations
Current means of access to housing in large post-war estates	Market	Bureaucratic systems replaced by market	Market operating alongside bureaucratic systems addressing housing need
Financial and organisational capacity associated with owners and policy community	Weak Fragmented ownership and limited policy interventions	Weak Fragmented ownerships. Some cooperatives and condominiums but low income of owners and lack of public funds prevents action	Strong Local authorities and housing associations with strong traditions, resources and political support to develop interventions
Current public policy initiatives	Limited number of community initiatives	Minimal and restricted to more affluent areas	Major continuing programmes with shift to integrated regeneration involving substantial demolition and refurbishment

access and allocation. For example in England government has promoted choice-based letting schemes based on experiences in the Netherlands. More recently, further initiatives have included significant investment in redesigning estates. Notwithstanding the differences, these three countries have all adopted active policies to address the problems they perceive in their large housing estates. In the UK, a series of policies from the Priority Estates Programme through Estate Action and the Estate Renewal Challenge Fund have added to the use of main funding programmes to improve these estates. In the UK, the Netherlands and Sweden there are major renewal and regeneration programmes involving very substantial sums of public expenditure, often designed to leverage private finance as well. They involve substantial refurbishment, and often demolition, of parts of estates, and then attempt to alter the physical appearance of estates to make them more attractive neighbourhoods to live in, by introducing mixed tenure and aiming at a more mixed population. These approaches have often been principally property led – with purchase involving the sale of land and property and the improvements to the physical structure of dwellings and estates.

Increasingly these policies are more holistic, with property regeneration being located within a broader programme of social and economic regeneration. The Dutch Big Cities Policy and the Strong Neighbourhoods Policy are examples of such a policy, as are approaches to sustainable communities and neighbourhood management in England (see, e.g., Van Kempen, 2000; Mullins and Murie, 2006; Van Kempen, 2008). Policies are designed to improve skills and increase access to the labour market, to improve transport links and to improve the public services available: schools, leisure facilities, and social services. At the same time there are attempts to introduce more commercial and retail activities into neighbourhoods which were once wholly residential, and to change neighbourhoods from being simple dormitory areas to ones with a greater variety of activities. In these policies the lead is often taken by the public sector, by local authorities or not-for-profit housing organisations. But there is a strong practice of joint venture companies and working with different agencies in the public, private and not-for-profit sectors. The distinguishing feature of many of these approaches is the high level of resource input, both in financial terms and in organisational and management resources, and the extended timescale for regeneration projects. Periods of ten or more years are not unusual in major regeneration schemes affecting large housing estates. Governments have continued to accept a policy responsibility for these estates and have been willing to allocate public funds – as well as to try to leverage private finance.

In contrast, in *Southern Europe* the approach is very different. Here most of the estates are dominated by owner-occupiers, albeit often lower-income households. There is not a strong tradition of public policy nor significant organisational capacity within local government. The development of more holistic approaches is also not very common. Agendas for refurbishment and renewal are modest. Partly as a consequence of the weakness of public policy, residents on estates are used to arranging things for themselves. Nevertheless, significant demolition and rebuilding does take place in some areas, for example, in Sant Roc in Barcelona. Again, this is partly because of the nature of the welfare state and the organisational capacity in different parts of the public sector. It would appear that approaches are less ambitious, but the political tradition also means that active tenants and residents' organisations are often involved in these initiatives. It may, indeed, be that the organisational strength and capacity of the Northern and Western European systems have the effect of crowding out some of the grassroots and resident-led activity associated with Southern Europe.

Finally, in *Central and Eastern Europe*, the pattern is different again. The privatisations of the early 1990s were designed partly to shift the burden of repair and maintenance costs from the state to the individual. Funds are not available for regeneration to the extent that they are in Northern and Western Europe – nor does the organisational capacity exist. Here, estates are not generally the worst estates. Therefore the priority given to wholesale regeneration or renewal is not high.

However, there are neighbourhoods with major problems associated with construction and design. They are often affected by heating systems which were installed at original construction and which now generate very high costs that cannot be controlled by the individual households. Replacement of these heating systems or dealing with failing parts of the structure of buildings is extremely expensive but, in many estates, the private owners living in them do not have the resources to deal with them. The ability to borrow private finance to fund physical improvements is damaged by the fragmentation of ownership in the estates, and the low incomes of many residents mean that significant investment is not possible. In some of the better estates there are mechanisms that have been developed to enable improvement: sales of parcels of land may generate funds which can be invested elsewhere; open space or run-down commercial premises can be redeveloped in a way that generates such surpluses for reinvestment in residential property. The slightly more affluent estates might also be able to bear some higher costs. What is happening then is a more modest pattern of investment and responses by households, in some cases the more affluent households moving out, in other cases the lower-income households moving out to escape high costs. Over time this will change the possibilities for renewal, but in the short and medium term the picture is one of relative inactivity and, certainly, without the major investments associated with Northern and Western Europe.

These policy accounts indicate that there are divergent patterns of intervention associated with Southern Europe and Central and Eastern Europe, and with Northern and Western and Europe. The overall research results indicate that major contextual and policy differences lie behind the superficially common characteristics (built form, architectural and engineering features) of public-sector housing built in the post-WWII period. These differences mean that there is an increasing divergence between estates: in Northern and Western Europe estates are being radically redesigned and transformed through demolition and substantial new investment; elsewhere fragmented ownership and weak financial and organisational resources result in considerable inertia and policy responses are both more limited and different in type.

These different contexts have affected the current social standing of the large estates. Many, but not all, of the estates in Eastern and Central Europe retain a relatively high status. They have better equipped and more modern dwellings than those available in much of the rest of the private housing market. They remain more desirable than the alternatives that exist in many cases. In Northern and Western Europe there has been a pattern of declining attractiveness and these estates have become less aspirational: but there continues to be important differences between the worst estates and the best estates. In Southern Europe these estates more commonly have a low social standing.

The results from this research highlight important national and contextual differences including differences in patterns of intervention. There are a number of alternative perspectives of why different approaches to intervention have been adopted. The reasons why there is not a convergence of policy responses involve a variety of factors but this research has suggested four key dimensions: the changing welfare state, political behaviour, ownership and resources.

The welfare state

One starting point for grouping different national experience relates to the nature and structure of the welfare state, and to political coalitions which have developed around the provision of welfare and housing. This kind of approach fits the view that there is significant path dependency affecting neighbourhoods and service delivery systems. The way the different estates operate and the behaviour dynamics of inhabitants are affected by wider social, economic and political systems and are mediated and moderated by embeddedness within wider processes. We have elaborated on this earlier in the chapter.

Political behaviour

A second perspective relates to the nature of politics and political participation and cross agency working. This perspective emerges most strongly from consideration of 'best practice' in regeneration and highlights the emphasis placed on participation in different parts of Europe. Not all countries attempt integrated approaches or are equally involved in partnerships or participative approaches. Van Beckhoven (2006) concludes:

> that tendencies to work with the single sector are still strongly embedded in the organisation of many governments. Administrative cultures and organisational divisions and practices tend to foster the maintenance of a sectoral status quo and, in many cases, the continuation of authority at central government level. This inertia prevents the integration of different policy sectors.
>
> (p. 152).

She goes on to say:

> In various European countries, the integrated approach to policymaking remains a philosophy that is not easily implemented in practice. The philosophy – that dealing with the physical, economic and social aspects simultaneously leads to the most effective solutions – ignores the complexity and the path-dependency of administrative organisations and cultures. It takes more than a philosophy to achieve the integration of different policies and their related policy cultures and practices.
>
> (p. 153)

This discussion begins to move towards an explanation of policy differences that refers to external factors rather than the more common features associated with the appearance and internal dynamics of estates. In general there is a contrast between countries that are more inclined towards integrative approaches, partnerships and participation, than those which are not. In relation to partnerships, Van Boxmeer et al. (2005) contrast these strong partnerships in the Netherlands with weak partnerships in Spain, and Van Beckhoven (2006) explains this difference largely in terms of the strong consensual tradition, the structure of the welfare state, tradition of democracy, the legitimacy attributed to democratic institutions in the Netherlands and the urban regeneration context. The relatively young democracy of Spain has little experience in the formation of partnerships. In the more developed democracy of the Netherlands the involvement of private actors has been a central characteristic of urban policy for several years. Since the 1990s, as a result of deregulation processes, many of the Dutch government's responsibilities have been transferred to other public and private actors as can be seen in the increased responsibility of housing associations. The Dutch urban regeneration context therefore consists of a wide range of actors, and power has been shared more equally than it has in this context in the younger democracy of Spain. These sentiments could equally be extended to the UK although the possibility that the centralising tendency of government is much greater, affects the emerging pattern.

When discussing the role of residents in regeneration policy, a similar pattern emerges. The development of integrated policies, public/private partnerships and the growing involvement of residents in urban policy are seen as characteristic of the Netherlands in contrast, say, to Spain and Hungary. The fact that Spain and Hungary are younger democracies than the Netherlands accounts for the differences in the importance attached to participation (see also Van Beckhoven, 2006). There is still room to analyse how these things operate in practice and how effective they are in re-balancing power, but there is undoubtedly a different starting point.

Ownership of property

The ownership of properties in the post-WWII large estates is much less uniform than the physical character of the dwellings. In Southern Europe dwellings are predominantly owner-occupied. Because of a large-scale privatisation process, this has also become true in Eastern and Central Europe but with different forms of organisation, through cooperatives and condominiums as well as individual ownership. In Northern and Western Europe, patterns vary between countries but in general there is a higher proportion of property that is still owned by a single landlord – a local authority or, more commonly, a not-for-profit housing association. Even in the UK, where privatisation has been adopted more enthusiastically than in other parts of Northern and Western Europe, individual home ownership has expanded more slowly in the large post-war estates than elsewhere. Consequently the dominance of municipal ownership or housing association ownership remains.

With the change in patterns of ownership, the means of accessing housing in the large estates has also changed and is very different between the three different patterns of intervention identified. In Central and Eastern Europe, market systems have increasingly replaced the bureaucratic systems as privatisation has had an impact. The market also dominates in Southern Europe and has a strong impact on access in Northern and Western Europe. However, because of the continuing high levels of ownership by housing associations and local authorities, which allocate housing through bureaucratic processes associated with housing need, the direct market process is less evident in Northern and Western Europe where de-commodification remains higher. This difference in ownership is one of the major differences between the Northern and Western European estates on the one hand and the Southern and Central/Eastern European estates on the other hand. Clearly, this difference influences the possibility to take action: when the estates are owned by only one owner, it is easier to carry out a large improvement plan. When ownership is fragmented it is much more difficult to carry out such a plan. Moreover owner-occupiers usually have to pay for improvements themselves, while in a situation of ownership by one public owner, the financial burden usually does not fall on the shoulders of the inhabitants themselves.

Organisational and financial resources

This leads us towards a final explanation of why there are substantial differences in the policies and programmes being adopted for these estates. In Northern and Western Europe, patterns of ownership, as well as the organisational and financial resources of the owners, mean that there is very considerable professional, managerial and financial capacity and capability to intervene: to redesign, restructure and reshape estates. In Southern, Central and Eastern Europe, there is nothing like such a strong capacity. Current public policy initiatives in these cases are very limited. Initiatives are smaller in scale, involve fewer resources and are less ambitious in redesigning estates. Although there are examples of major interventions, they are the exception rather than the rule. In Northern and Western Europe, there has been a growing emphasis on developing new initiatives targeted at problem estates, with a shift away from policies that simply involve improved management or refurbishment of properties towards ones that adopt a more integrated or holistic approach to regeneration. These newer approaches are more likely to involve substantial demolition and refurbishment, and significant social and economic programmes, to change the dynamics of the neighbourhood and the estate in general. Integrated area-based approaches tend to be welcomed more and more, but these strategies are also criticised because, for example, of the unavoidable displacement effects that are a logical consequence of these targeted policies (see, e.g., Slob et al., 2007; Van Kempen et al., 2008).

Conclusions

This chapter has described key differences associated with what are superficially similar large post-WWII housing areas in different European cities. It has argued that the distinctive characteristics and contexts relating to these housing areas outweigh their apparently similar physical design and appearance. Rather than a convergence related to common built form, internal dynamics, spirals of decline or global gentrification pressures, there are different outcomes and processes associated with contextual and organisational differences and distinctive patterns of policy flow from these. As well as having different dynamics, the estates are currently subjected to different kinds of policy interventions. This perspective runs counter to some of the earlier literature which emphasises similarities and common spirals of decline and is over reliant on inward-looking accounts of the influences on estates.

The differences between the three European types identified in this chapter cast doubt on some of the earlier literature but also cast doubt on the possibility of effective direct policy transfer. We should be cautious about the potential for policy transfer involving other cities and countries. The difficulties associated with policy transfer as well as other key factors associated with the process and pattern of policy intervention mean that the large estates built in the post-WWII period in Europe are likely to follow divergent paths in the future.

Note

1. In the RESTATE research project Italy and Spain were investigated.

References

Barlow, J. and Duncan S. (1994) *Success and Failure in Housing Provision: European Systems Compared*. Oxford: Pergamon Press.
Berube, A. (2005) *Mixed Communities in England: A US Perspective on Evidence and Policy Prospects*. York: Joseph Rowntree Foundation.
Bickford, A. and Massey, D. S. (1991) Segregation in the Second Ghetto: Racial and Ethnic Segregation in American Public Housing. *Social Forces*, 69, pp. 1011–36.
Boelhouwer, P. and Van der Heijden, H. (1992) *Housing Systems in Europe, Part 1: A Comparative Study of Housing Policy*. Delft: Delft University Press

Cameron, S. (2003) Gentrification, Housing Redifferentiation and Urban Regeneration: 'Going for Growth' in Newcastle upon Tyne. *Urban Studies*, 40 (12), pp. 2367–82.

Coleman, A. (1985) *Utopia on Trial*. London: Hilary Shipman.

Dekker, K. and Van Kempen, R. (2005) Large Housing Estates in Europe: A Contemporary Overview. In: R. Van Kempen, K. Dekker, S. Hall and I. Tosics (Eds), *Restructuring Large Housing Estates in European Cities*, pp. 19–45. Bristol: Policy Press.

Doling, J. (1997) *Comparative Housing Policy. Government and Housing in Advanced Capitalist Countries*. London: Macmillan.

Doling J. (1999) Housing Policies and the Little Tigers. How Do They Compare with Other Industrialized Countries? *Housing Studies* 14 (2), pp. 229–50.

Donnison, D. (1967) *The Government of Housing*. Harmondsworth: Penguin.

Erdősi, S., Gerőházi, É., Teller, N. and Tosics, I. (2003) *Large Housing Estates in Hungary. Overview of Developments and Problems in Budapest and Nyíregyháza*. Utrecht: Faculty of Geosciences, Utrecht University.

Esping-Andersen, G. (1990) *The Three Worlds of Welfare Capitalism*. Cambridge: Polity Press.

Fuerst, J. S. (1974) Public Housing in the United States. In: J. S. Fuerst (Ed.), *Public Housing in Europe and America*. London: Croom Helm.

Grigsby, W., Baratz, M, Galster, G. and MacLennan, D. (1987) The Dynamics of Neighborhood Change and Decline. *Progress in Planning*, 28 (1), pp. 1–76.

Harloe, M. (1995) *The People's Home?* Oxford: Blackwell.

Kemeny, J. (1981) *The Myth of Home Ownership: Public versus Private Choices in Housing Tenure*. London: Routledge

Jones, C. and Murie, A. (2006) *The Right to Buy*. Oxford: Blackwell.

Jupp, B. (1999) *Living Together: Community Life on Mixed Housing Estates*. London: Demos.

Lees, L. (2000) A Reappraisal of Gentrification: Towards a Geography of Gentrification. *Progress in Human Geography*, 24 (3), pp. 389–408.

McGuire, C. C. (1981) *International Housing Policies: A Comparative Analysis*. Lexington (MA): Lexington Books.

Megbolugbe, I. F., Hoek-Smit, M. C. and Linnenman, P. D. (1996) Understanding Neighbourhood Dynamics: A Review of the Contributions of William G. Grigsby. *Urban Studies*, 33, pp. 1779–95.

Meusen, H. and Van Kempen, R. (1994) *Dutch Social Rented Housing: A British Experience?* Bristol: University of Bristol, School for Advanced Urban Studies.

Mullins, D. and Murie, A. (2006) *Housing Policy in the UK*. Basingstoke: Palgrave Macmillan.

Murie, A. (1997) The Social Rented Sector, Housing and the Welfare State in the UK. *Housing Studies*, 12 (4), pp. 437–62.

Murie, A., Knorr-Siedow, T. and Van Kempen, R. (2003) *Large Housing Estates in Europe: General Developments and Theoretical Backgrounds*. Utrecht: Faculty of Geosciences, Utrecht University.

Murie, A., Tosics, I., Aalbers, M., Sendi, R. and Cernic-Mali, B. (2005) Privatisation and After. In: R. Van Kempen, K. Dekker, S. Hall and I. Tosics (Eds), *Restructuring Large Housing Estates in European Cities*, pp. 83–103. Bristol: Policy Press.

Musterd, S. (2008) Residents Views on Social Mix: Social Mix, Social Networks and Stigmatisation in Post-War Housing Estates. *Urban Studies*, 45 (4), pp. 897–915.

Musterd, S. and Van Kempen, R. (2005) *Large Housing Estates in European Cities. Opinions of Residents on Recent Developments*. Utrecht: Faculty of Geosciences, Utrecht University.

Pareja Eastaway, M., Tapada Berteli T., Van Boxmeer, B. and Garcia Ferrando, L. (2003) *Large Housing Estates in Spain. Overview of Developments and Problems in Madrid and Barcelona*. Utrecht: Faculty of Geosciences, Utrecht University.

Popkin, S., Katz, B., Cunningham, M. K., Brown, K. D., Gustafson, J. and Turner, M. A. (2004) *A Decade of HOPE VI: Research Findings and Policy Challenges*. Washington: The Urban Institute.

Power, A. (1997) *Estates on the Edge: The Social Consequences of Mass Housing in Europe*. London: Macmillan.

Power, A. and Tunstall, R. (1995) *Swimming against the Tide. Polarisation or Progress on 20 Unpopular Council Estates, 1980–1995*. York: Joseph Rowntree Foundation.

Prak, N. L. and Priemus, H. (1985) A Model for the Analysis of the Decline of Post War Housing. *The International Journal of Urban and Regional Research*, 10, pp. 1–7.

Renaud, B. (1995) The Real Estate Economy and the Design of Russian Housing Reforms, Part 2. *Urban Studies*, 32 (9), pp. 1437–51.

Sendi, R. (2006) Improving Public Spaces. In: R. Van Kempen, A. Murie, T. Knorr–Siedow and I. Tosics (Eds), *Regenerating Large Housing Estates in Europe: A Guide to Better Practice*, pp. 109–19. Utrecht: Faculty of Geosciences.

Skifter Andersen, H. (2003) *Urban Sores. On the Interaction between Segregation, Urban Decay and Deprived Neighbourhoods*. Aldershot: Ashgate.

Slob, A., Bolt, G. and Van Kempen, R. (2007) Dispersal Patterns of Households who are Forced to Move: Where do They Move to and Why? Paper for the EUGEO–conference, Amsterdam, 20–23 August 2007.

Smith, N. (1996) *The New Urban Frontier: Gentrification and the Revanchist City*. London and New York: Routledge.

Taylor, M. (1995) *Unleashing the Potential*. London: Joseph Rowntree Foundation.

Taylor, M. (1998) Combating the Social Exclusion of Housing Estates. *Housing Studies*, 13 (6), pp. 819–32.

Tunstall, R. (2003) 'Mixed Tenure' Policy in the UK: Privatisation, Pluralism or Euphemism? In: *Housing, Theory and Society*, 20, pp. 153–9.

Turkington, R., Van Kempen R. and Wassenberg, F. (2004) *High-Rise Housing in Europe. Current Trends and Future Prospects*. Delft: DUP Science.

Van Beckhoven, E. (2006) *Decline and Regeneration: Policy Responses to Processes of Change in Post-WWII Urban Neighbourhoods*. Utrecht: Faculty of Geosciences, Utrecht University.

Van Boxmeer, B. and Van Beckhoven, E. (2005) Public–Private Partnerships in Urban Regeneration: A Comparison of Dutch and Spanish PPPs. *European Journal of Housing Policy*, 5 (1), pp. 1–16.

Van Kempen, R. (2000) Big Cities Policy in the Netherlands. *Tijdschrift voor Economische en Sociale Geografie*, 91, pp. 197–203.

Van Kempen, R. (2008) Social Cohesion, Social Mix, and Urban Policies in the Netherlands. Paper for the Housing Studies Spring Conference in York, 2–4 April 2008.

Van Kempen, R., Bolt, G. and Slob, A. (2008) Displacement Effects of Urban Restructuring: A Case Study of Three Dutch Cities. Paper for the UAA-Conference in Baltimore (MA), US, 23–26 April 2008.

Uitermark, J. (2003) 'Social Mixing' and the Management of Disadvantaged Neighbourhoods: The Dutch Policy of Urban Restructuring Revisited. *Urban Studies*, 40 (3), pp. 531–49.

Wright, G. (1981) *Building the Dream: A Social History of Housing in America.* New York: Pantheon.

9
Local Participation in Large Housing Estates: A Comparison of the Netherlands, Spain and Hungary

Ellen van Beckhoven, Brechtje van Boxmeer and Hanna Szemző

Introduction

In Europe, (local) government has traditionally been the main actor in urban regeneration projects. However, in the 1990s, in parallel with major social changes such as the shift from a welfare to a post-welfare 'mode of regulation', an economic shift from a Fordist to a post-Fordist 'mode of accumulation', and the shift from a 'providing' state to an 'enabling' state, urban government authorities encountered a movement leading towards more differentiated forms of governance. More partners, such as housing associations, different local institutions and the private sector, became involved in governing activities and decision-making. As a result, the role of urban government authorities within urban regeneration projects changed: local government became urban governance (see e.g. Healey et al., 1995; Elander and Blanc, 2001; Vranken et al., 2003; Dekker, 2006).

Andersen and Van Kempen (2003, p. 80) list four developments that accompany this policy transition: (1) the replacement of universalistic by targeted policies; (2) an attempt to integrate policy fields from various departments into a unitary project organisation; (3) a growing use of covenants as policy regulation; (4) a concentration on the empowerment of the inhabitants of cities and specific neighbourhoods. This increased awareness of the contribution of residents is exemplified by an increase in the interest in resident participation.

Resident participation occurs on different scales and in different fields. In this chapter, the focus is on participation in urban regeneration processes, predominantly on large post-war housing estates. The chapter reports on a comparative analysis concerning local participation in the regeneration processes of post-WWII large housing estates, in three European countries with distinct regional and historic backgrounds: The Netherlands, Spain, and Hungary. The juxtaposition of these cases facilitates the examination of three countries from different European regions: Western, Southern, and Eastern Europe. The central focus is to assess to what extent national dimensions influence the organisation of local participation within post-WWII large housing estates; why is participation at the neighbourhood level organised differently in the Netherlands, Spain, and Hungary? Differences within the national frameworks are expected to result in different forms of involving residents at the neighbourhood level. Given its political traditions (to be explained later) we expect the Netherlands to show a wider variety in local participation than Spain and Hungary.

Most recent writing about international comparative research suggests that there are two general reasons for undertaking this kind of research in the social science: (1) the furtherance of explanatory and predictive theory, and (2) the understanding and transfer of policy from one country to another (Counch et al., 2003). The comparison in this chapter is mainly related to the first reason.

In the next section, local participation is placed in a broader context and is related, among others, to the concept of democracy. Other aspects of participation are discussed and defined in this section as well. In the third section, an analysis is presented of the practice of local participation in regeneration policies in the three selected countries. The situation on three large housing estates is described: one in Utrecht (the Netherlands); one in Barcelona (Spain); and one in Budapest (Hungary). The selected case studies were chosen to present interesting cases of residential involvement, where the interaction between the national legislative context and the local residential involvement can be highlighted. The chapter ends with some conclusions.

Local participation in a broader context

All over Europe, democracy is now put forward as an important reason for involving residents in policymaking. This development is a response to a decline in the number of voters, resulting in problems with traditional representation, traditional local government practices (bottom-up instead of top-down) and obscurity about the accountability of both elected and non-elected officials.

This is not to say that local participation is a completely new concept; it has featured in more traditional policies as well. During the last decade, however, related to the increased emphasis on governance arrangements, its extent and importance has increased. For local governments, the shift from government to governance implies that responsibilities are delegated to lower levels, such as the neighbourhood, and to other parties, among them citizens. 'Sounding-board groups', partnerships, expert teams, and community groups are just a few of the new organisational forms that shape policymaking processes. This section focuses among others on these aspects of local government.

Democracy and local participation

The complexity of modern society is often said to ask for a more engaging form of democracy. According to Stoker (2004), for example, representative democracy – a form of democracy in which citizens exercise their right of participation in making political decisions through elected representatives – should be supplemented by a participative form of democracy. In his view, the representative character of democracy needs to be strengthened, and policymakers require more direct influence from the citizen to reduce the distance between the voters and the elected. Residents often think that their ideas are not adequately reflected in government policies; indifference can be the result. Linking civil society more closely to policymaking processes implies a general concept of participative democracy – a form of democracy, which stresses the citizen's participation as its most important quality (Stoker, 2004).

Achieving functional and fruitful participation is difficult, however. In a historical perspective even de Tocqueville, one of the greatest theoreticians of modern democracy, stressed that one of its utmost problems lies in the tension between quantity and quality (Reeves, 1982). The number of participants (quantity) should be a tool, a control instrument. In many cases, however, participation seems to be a goal; a large number of participants is considered more important than the ensuing result. In a well-functioning democracy there should be a balance between authority and participation: between the elected and the voters. This balance is, however, variable and difficult to attain.

Pointing to the importance of local participation, it is also argued that the core institution of democracy is not the national state; according to Hirst (2000) and Stoker (2004), democracy must have a strong local dimension. At the local level, the balance between authority and participation may lean more to the side of participation than is the case at the national level.

Local participation: Why and why not?

From a micro-level point of view, local participation is concerned with the belief of policymakers that involving residents produces more effective policy outcomes; it can improve policy, since residents can bring significant knowledge resources to the table. A simple example is their knowledge about what will and what will not work in a specific neighbourhood: what facilities would be used and what would rapidly be daubed with graffiti and be abandoned (Taylor, 2000). Residents can be crucial in both the diagnosis of the systematic causes of problems and in who should be engaged in resolving them (Wilkinson and Applebee, 1999).

Another important objective encouraging policymakers to involve residents in drawing up policy is to develop more democratic policies in which citizens are heard and are empowered (Font, 2003). Related to this, local participation is also expected to bridge the gap between the electors and the elected (creating political trust). In some cases, having politicians with an open attitude and citizen-centred policies can be a marketing strategy to 'sell' policy to the electorate. Local participation also often encourages the acceptance of policy implemented within an area.

Furthermore, local participation can be developed in order to create or increase human and social capital. Local involvement is collective action – involvement in influencing, planning, managing, and working in local activities and services; it develops the skills and confidence needed if social exclusion is to be dealt with effectively (Taylor, 2000).

Apparently, the increasing involvement of residents is often presented as a panacea for estate regeneration. It is commonly assumed that it is a good thing when many people participate – as they have the potential to bring the positive qualities of grass-root movements and direct democracy into the formalised political life. Moreover, they increase the capacity of policymaking; the results created by local participation are expected to be longer standing, better, and cheaper than those generated by 'traditional' programmes (Andersen and Van Kempen, 2001; 2003).

However, involving residents in policymaking can also include significant traps, such as questions with regard to accountability, the exclusion of specific groups and the losing of transparency in many political processes. Two reasons can be identified for opposing the involvement of residents from the policymakers' point of view. The first is related to the possibly undemocratic representation within the participation process. Many forms of urban governance (including local participation) are not open to all stakeholders (that is, the entire neighbourhood population); governance can be closed to those who are not involved (Elander and Blanc, 2001). The question of whether participating residents represent the whole neighbourhood has become a classic debate (Font, 2003). In addition and related to this, it is interesting to consider why potential

residents (that is, residents from elsewhere who will move to the neighbourhood) are hardly ever involved in urban regeneration projects.

The second reason for policymakers to oppose local participation
is related to their expectation that the demands of participants will
be unrealistic. Participants may have no appreciation of the technical
difficulties and might not take the arguments of other sectors into consideration. Involving citizens then takes too much time and may delay
policymaking. Related to this, policymakers may be unwilling to give
residents a voice. As we will see below, the government's motives for
involving residents and the political willingness to share power result
in different forms of local participation.

Organising local participation

Local participation can take many forms, depending on the political
and institutional culture of a given locality, and the requirements of the
specific project. The organisation can be categorised by the level of citizens' power, and top-down or bottom-up orientation. These forms may
coexist in each particular participation process and help us analyse local
participation in practice. Below, some ways of organising participation
are described and are discussed later in the context of the case studies.

Share of power

Within the various local democracies, local participation is organised in
different ways. These differences become visible, among others, in the
division of power in the policymaking process. Power determines who
participates and in what ways. One of the obstacles to participation is
the reluctance of local politicians to share power with local people. The
political will to share power is therefore important for the form of local
participation that is embedded in the policymaking process (Del Pino
and Colino, 2003).

Residents can be involved in estate regeneration to a greater or lesser
degree. A number of academic commentators have sought to provide
analytical tools to assess this activity. The most well known of these
is the 'Ladder of Participation' set out by Sherry Arnstein in 1969 (see
Figure 9.1). She developed a framework for outlining the key stages leading towards citizen control, by ranking eight stages of participation on
a participation ladder. The stages vary from a low level of citizen power
to the highest level, where citizens are in control ('citizen control').
On the lowest two rungs of the ladder, those with power are simply
manipulative and one cannot speak of local participation (these forms

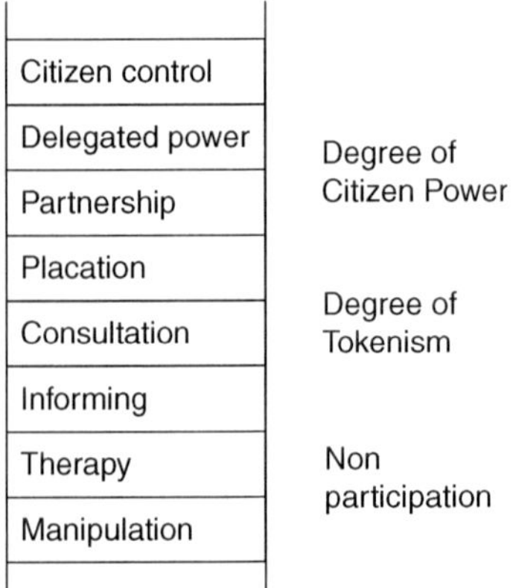

Figure 9.1 Arnstein's ladder of participation.

are referred to as 'manipulation' or 'therapy'). Further up the ladder, residents are informed, or asked for their opinions ('informing' and 'consulting' respectively). On the top four rungs, residents are involved in the decision-making process increasingly as equal partners: they acquire an advisory role ('placation'), are involved in 'partnerships', acquire 'delegated power', and finally are in control. On the top rungs of the ladder, decisions match increasingly closely the wishes of the whole community.

More opportunities to participate do not automatically result in more effective or more democratic policy. Without specific resources, residents' power may not give the expected desired results. Participation should be organised differently in different circumstances to meet the expectations of different interests (Wilcox, 1998). In a democracy, residents' responsibility also has limits; the elected politicians take ultimate responsibility. In this context the question arises of how much power is appropriate; although in many cases power with respect to the management of an estate may be limited, residents may have more power regarding other issues, such as the design of public spaces.

Top-down versus bottom-up, informal versus formal

In the case of *top-down* local participation, local, regional, or national government authorities make available formalised instruments such as sounding-board and steering groups. In a *bottom-up* form of local participation, on the other hand, residents put themselves forward to make their voices heard. They ask the policymakers for more power in decision-making processes. In practice, these two forms of local participation (top-down and bottom-up) can result in different numbers of participating residents.

Related to some extent to the top-down and bottom-up forms of participation, there is a distinction between informal and formal participation (see e.g. Walliser, 2003). *Informal* participation takes place around different types of interaction between actors or as a result of protests and demonstrations that result in negotiations. *Formal* participation, on the other hand, is organised via formal government instruments.

Local participation in large housing estates in Utrecht, Barcelona, and Budapest

In the previous section, it was stated that the local level is often seen as the core institution of democracy. Van Beckhoven and colleagues (2005) have shown that local participation can be stimulated most effectively at this level. This section gives an overview of how local participation is regulated with regard to urban policy and urban regeneration in the three countries we have put central in this chapter: the Netherlands, Spain and Hungary.

The three countries have distinct regional and historic backgrounds. In order to find out to what extent national dimensions influence the organisation of local participation within post-WWII large housing estates and whether residents actually want to participate, we used interviews and discussions with stakeholders and end-users, such as local officials, social workers, employees of housing associations and members of residential organisations. Also, we analysed policy reports and memoranda of the different case studies. Before discussing the case studies separately, we briefly describe the tradition of local participation in each country (see Table 9.1 for a summary), and then briefly refer to the large housing estates that are central in this chapter.

The tradition of local participation in the three countries

In *the Netherlands*, formal instruments have always been important for fostering local participation. The concept of participation was introduced in the 1950s. At that time, information and consultation were the main forms used to involve residents. In the 1960s and 1970s, in relation to the general process of democratisation, residents increasingly wanted to have a say in the content and implementation of policies (Engbersen, 2004; Van der Ham and Van der Meij, 1974). As a result, more and more meetings and discussions were organised at which residents could let

Table 9.1 Overview of forms of and tools for participation in housing policies in the Netherlands, Spain and Hungary

	The Netherlands	**Spain**	**Hungary**
Informal participation	Weak	Has been very strong, especially residents' associations	Important, mainly in the form of demonstrations
Formal participation	Strong policies stimulate participation; many tools available	Tools are being created	Strengthening, tools are being created
Individual/ association participation	Associations are becoming important	Associations have been important for some time	Individual, but with the strengthening of the NGOs they are expected to become more involved

their voices be heard. It was also in this period that particular forms of informal participation existed; various urban social movements, among them squatters, let their voices be heard. These movements had a similar ambition, namely defending urban living space for young people by trying to influence urban policy (Mamadouh, 1992). Against a background of the declining legitimacy of local politics in the 1990s, policymaking and planning processes have been characterised by interactivity and openness; instead of considering each other as opponents, citizens and government were thought of as partners (Vranken et al., 2003). In the case of urban regeneration processes, residents are supposed to be involved in the process at an early stage (Engbersen, 2004). In order to realise this, such actors as housing associations, interest groups, or welfare organisations, have to approach residents more.

Despite these changes, participation in the Netherlands still seems to be an instrument of government and stakeholders; these parties decide to what extent and at what times residents will be involved in the process. Policymaking processes in this country can therefore be characterised by a top-down approach.

Unlike the Netherlands, *Spain* has only a short political tradition of formal local participation. Informal participation, however, has a much longer history. In Spain, between the late 1960s and the early 1980s, urban crises and political change resulted in the most significant urban mobilisation in Europe since 1945 (Castells, 1986). Residents' associations played a major part in these large social movements. Although nowadays the residents' associations are less important within the neighbourhood, local government authorities still use these associations as their principal partners to work with (Pindado, 2000). In addition to these associations, local government is currently developing tools for other types of formal participation. At the local level, several institutions have been developed that concentrate on increasing the extent of participation.

Hungary represents a case where formal local participation is in the phase of formation, and – given the country's history as a member of the Socialist block – there has been limited space for the development of informal participation as well. This latter form of participation became important after 1990: from the mid-1990s, when the opinion of the residents and that of the NGOs was purposefully not listened to, or they were not informed properly, demonstrations often ensued.

In recent years, the use of formal local participation in Hungary, has witnessed a change: consultation with residents in urban development programmes has become more normal. Within a number of urban development programmes – partly as a consequence of the requirements of the European Union, partly as a result of a strengthening civil society – residents, NGOs and other members of civil society are now actively involved, even in the planning phase of the programme. Furthermore, what gives residents a special status in Hungary is the fact that most of them are owners. So, despite the relatively underdevelopment of the formal tools, as a consequence of the massive giveaway type of privatisation of the 1990s, residents can enjoy a fair share of power; with regard to their apartment and their building, the ultimate decision rests with them. Some problems still exist. For example, residential participation is often restricted to office hours of local representatives and the local authority, which can be seen as an inefficient means of communication between residents on the one hand and politicians and policymakers on the other hand (Szemző and Tosics, 2005).

The case studies: Their history and present situation

The Dutch case we discuss here is *Nieuw-Hoograven* in *Utrecht*. The estate was constructed in the 1950s and 1960s and is located relatively near the city centre. The estate was built as part of an extensive national programme designed to resolve the post-WWII housing shortage in the Netherlands. In many cities a large number of dwellings had to be built as quickly as possible, so 'efficiency' became the keyword. In this post-WWII neighbourhood, multi-family dwellings (medium-rise) – primarily belonging to the social-rented sector – are over-represented.

Trinitat Nova, the Spanish case, is situated in the peripheral neighbourhoods of *Barcelona*. The estate was built in the 1950s and 1960s to accommodate households moving to Barcelona from rural areas in other parts of Spain. With respect to ownership, most dwellings in the area are officially protected houses (that is, public dwellings with a deferred ownership).[1] Furthermore, the area is characterised by a mixture of medium-rise and high-rise apartment blocks.

Havanna, the Hungarian estate that is central in this chapter, was built in *Budapest* from the mid 1970s through the early 1980s – more than a decade later than the other estates featured in this chapter – and consists only of high-rise complexes. It is located on the outskirts of the city, and initially housed people coming from poor neighbourhoods. The poorest people left Havanna after the privatisation of the housing stock in the mid 1990s. They experienced difficulties with maintaining the apartments – the utility costs are usually very high in these buildings. Despite the relative unpopularity of these apartments, selling them assured some financial gain to the owners; the apartments were sold to them for a fraction of their value in the process of privatisation and could be sold the following day for their real value. Although the initial population composition has changed, the estate still struggles with its bad reputation and a financially weak population.

In addition to differences in ownership, there are some differences between the estates with respect to the composition of the neighbourhood population as well. Nieuw-Hoograven has changed from a homogeneous neighbourhood with a native population into a heterogeneous area with a range of different cultures. Trinitat Nova and Havanna, on the other hand, have always been characterised by a homogeneous population with a native background.

Another difference between the estates is related to participation. By the end of the 1960s, the residents in Trinitat Nova in Barcelona had started to organise themselves in order to campaign for better living conditions; many facilities were lacking and construction deficiencies had become apparent. The government responded to the protests by putting plans into effect to improve the neighbourhoods. In contrast with Trinitat Nova, the history of the Utrecht and the Budapest neighbourhoods shows no patterns of informal local participation; plans to improve the areas have mainly been initiated by the national and local government authorities.

At present, all three estates are confronted with physical, economical and social problems. Although initially these areas functioned well in the urban housing market, in all three cases some of the 'classic' problems of large housing estates have emerged: vandalism, drug abuse, the antisocial behaviour of gangs and groups of youths, unemployment, educational arrears, and the obsolescence of the housing stock (see Aalbers et al., 2003, for further information about the Utrecht neighbourhood; Pareja Eastaway et al., 2003, for the Barcelona case; Erdősi et al., 2003, for the Hungarian case). It must be stressed, however, that every neighbourhood is different. The social tensions on the problem estates of Hungary are generally of a lesser extent than those on the problem estates of the Netherlands or Spain. Despite the many problems they face, which are mostly of a physical nature, large housing estates in Hungarian cities are not the most seriously deprived urban neighbourhoods.[2]

The case of Nieuw-Hoograven (Utrecht): Policies and participation

Policies

Within the framework of the national Big Cities Policy, Dutch cities could designate specific neighbourhoods as needing extra attention. These neighbourhoods often belonged to the post-WWII parts of the urban housing stock and were characterised by a population that is weak in socio-economic terms. The city of Utrecht, among others, nominated Nieuw-Hoograven as such an estate.

In 2001, the plans for the physical regeneration of Utrecht within the framework of the national BCP were documented in the DUO agreement (*De Utrechtse Opgave*[3]). This agreement sets out the powers and responsibilities of all partners in the regeneration process, including the residents. The extent to which residents can influence plans (citizen power) depends on how they are organised. Referring to the ladder of participation (see earlier in this chapter) a residents' association is often involved in the form of 'placation': they can give advice to officials of the local government. The opinion of individual residents is gathered through surveys or interviews organised by the housing association or by the local government authority ('consulting').

At the same time, in common with other local authorities, Utrecht initiated the 'neighbourhood approach'; local authorities have become more active at the neighbourhood level (by organising evenings for the dissemination of information or discussions about planned policy interventions, for example). This approach is expected to increase the interest and involvement of citizens in policymaking (Van Brunschot et al., 2002).

Organisation of participation

Before the DUO agreement was set up, residents living in neighbourhoods where large-scale interventions were planned, were invited to work in focus groups on a plan of requirements. This procedure was also followed in Nieuw-Hoograven. All the people who were affected by the regeneration interventions (residents, entrepreneurs, for example) were invited by the local government to think about one particular aspect, such as safety. However, because several of the plans that came out of these meetings were unrealistic or unaffordable, the decision-makers considered them to be impracticable. As a result, the participating residents became disappointed; they thought their opinions were not taken seriously. To prevent such situations recurring, residents' power is now clearly defined in the DUO agreement. Depending on how residents are organised, in each regeneration project they have the right to: (1) give (unasked and qualified) advice; (2) signal bottlenecks; (3) test plans/visions; (4) influence decisions; (5) take part in discussions; (6) receive information. Furthermore, in the case of a demolition/new-building project, consensus of 60 per cent of the residents of the project is necessary.

In addition to the agreements bundled in the DUO agreement, since 2001 Nieuw-Hoograven, along with every other neighbourhood or district in the city of Utrecht (ten in total) has acquired a neighbourhood council (*wijkraad*). This council consists of a group of residents who represent the neighbourhood population. They can give the local government solicited as well as unsolicited advice on whatever is felt deserves more attention in the neighbourhood. Not long after their establishment, the method was considered to need improvement in several respects. For example, the position of these councils was not made sufficiently clear, which in some cases resulted in confusion; unlike other resident associations, neighbourhood councils have closer links with policymakers and are more directly involved in policymaking. Furthermore, members of the councils were of the opinion that their advice was not taken seriously.

Of course, not all residents always aspire to become involved, but they should be able to do so, if they wish (see e.g. Van Beckhoven and Van Boxmeer, 2006). The above shows that local politicians in Utrecht are willing to share some of their power with residents. Residents' power is clearly defined in the DUO agreement. Some difficulties have to be dealt with however. It can be seen, for example, that aspects such as information provision are capable of improvement. Also, the question of representativity arises: do the participating residents represent the neighbourhood population accurately? Although in the opinion of the local politicians they do, social workers and people working at the neighbourhood level often take the opposite view (see Aalbers et al., 2004).

The case of Trinitat Nova (Barcelona): Policies and participation

Policies

In Spain, there is no central policy or general integrated approach regarding the physical regeneration of neighbourhoods. Urban regeneration concerns mainly the demolition of the most dilapidated dwellings and their replacement with newly built dwellings. These processes only take place in areas where rehabilitation would be more expensive than new construction. In the second half of the 1990s, the local and regional government authorities directly responsible for the dwellings decided to implement certain urban regeneration and renewal projects in the neighbourhood of Trinitat Nova in Barcelona. These projects mainly focussed on the poor technical state of the dwellings.

When the public authorities developed these physical interventions, the residents' association in Trinitat Nova took the initiative of developing a programme focussing on social development and local participation, the so-called Community Development Plan (CDP: *Plan de Desenvolupament Comunitari*). This CDP aims to prevent social exclusion and improve the residents' quality of life (Direcció General de Serveis Comunitaris, 2002). In the CDP the involvement of residents is seen not as an aim but as a strategy to achieve the objectives.

The residents' association is the initiator and most responsible partner of this programme. They receive funding from the local and regional government. The Community Team is responsible for managing the programme. This team is paid by and is very closely related to the residents' association.

Unlike the CDP, in the physical regeneration programme local participation is not promoted. Nevertheless, the residents have intervened in the decision-making process of the physical regeneration to a certain extent. They have put forward some ideas, such as the orientation of the dwellings to the sun and other sustainable elements, that have been included in the Special Plan for Interior Reform: *Plan de Especial de Reforma Interior* (PERI). Apparently, the residents' association is an important player in both the CDP and the physical regeneration of the estate.

The set up of the CDP in Trinitat Nova was the reason for the regional government to develop a policy concerning these kinds of Plans. As a result, CDPs have been implemented in many more neighbourhoods in Barcelona and its region.

Organisation of participation

In Trinitat Nova, the residents' position on Arnstein's participation ladder is quite high, located on the step of 'placation' and maybe even 'partnership'. The CDP in Trinitat Nova has extended and reinforced social networks and created various projects. One of the factors contributing to the large number of participating residents and the positive results of the CDP is the bottom-up organisation of the programme. The CDP in Trinitat Nova has gone further than the formal policy set up by the regional government; the objectives and projects put forward by the administrative programme have been surpassed.

In Trinitat Nova, the strong social cohesion is a positive factor in the local participation. Although the residents' organisation was relatively weak at the start of the CDP, it has contributed to a strong association structure in the neighbourhood and has played an important part in establishing the CDP and the regeneration process.

The case of Havanna (Budapest): Policies and participation

Policies

The chances of a complex rehabilitation of the Havanna housing estate largely depend on the existence of a national programme. Any complex rehabilitation, which includes elements from social, physical and technical aspects, requires a financial contribution that exceeds the possibilities of both the local government and that of the residents (the majority of whom are owners). Such a national programme was first created in 2007 – with the first round of results in 2008/2009 – with the help of EU structural funds.

Prior to this, the only national policy – stemming from 2001 – that subsidised the renewal of housing estates concentrated quite exclusively on physical renewal, more precisely on energy efficiency: it has subsidised heavily the energy efficient renewal of the insulation system, the changing of the windows, and interventions concerning the engineering of a building. It offers a non-repayable loan, which is currently maximised at one-third of the costs (500.000 HUF/approximately 1900 EUR), financed by the state. The local government and the condominium either share the remaining two-thirds of the cost, or the condominium covers it alone. Starting on 1 August, 2005, a special loan programme was set up for those condominium owners and local government authorities unable to finance their own share for the reconstruction works. This state-subsidised fifteen-year loan has fixed interest rates of 5–6 per cent. For the socially deprived owners the state covers the costs of the interest rate. Although the role of the state is crucial through its financial support – as shown by the figures above – the inhabitants of condominiums have to take the initiative for the rehabilitation or renovation of an apartment complex.

This state-subsidised system has been positive in a sense that it turned the refurbishment of large housing estates into a national programme, and did a lot to focus public attention on the problems these estates face. Also, with a growing number of condominiums and local governments realising the importance of partly renewing the buildings on the estates, the programme has become really successful with large numbers of applicants every year. However, the programme, with its very technical approach, falls short of tackling some of the social challenges that many of these large housing estates encounter.

The first opportunity for an area-based programme targeting social deprivation and aimed at the development of a well-working residential participation in large housing estates came in 2007. With the help of the EU-funded strategic funds, a limited number of housing estates will be given the opportunity to carry out a socially sensitive, complex renewal. The due date for the first round of applications is May 2008. The amount of the resources suggest that it will be approximately seven to eight housing estates in the Central Hungarian Region where Budapest and, within that, the Havanna estate are located. Therefore, the estate will have the opportunity to carry out a complex renewal.

The problem of the Havanna estate is rather complex and it further highlights the fact that the execution of an integrated area-based policy requires national support. Although the local government has taken the problem of the estate seriously, only when the opportunity of the EU-funded integrated programme arose, have they prepared a complex rehabilitation plan for the estate. Before that the regeneration was conceptualised as a slow, step-by-step process, initiated and conducted by separate departments of the local government authority, with no coordinating body.

It was within this framework that a few elements of the renewal have already materialised: a CCTV system has been installed and the presence of the police has strengthened. Furthermore, attention has been paid to expand the presence of institutional diversity on the estate (besides schools, kindergartens and a medical centre, there is an educational advisory service and a well-functioning community centre among other things) and an annual, one-week-long festival was introduced to improve the reputation of the estate. Although these have been minor changes, they have been relatively successful, as they drew more positive attention to the Havanna estate and made the residents feel that they are important.

The new programme offers the advantages of an integrated approach, as it combines the elements of physical renewal – that of the central promenade area, the improvement of green areas and a solution to the parking problem – with aspects of specially designed youth policies – creating spaces of leisure for them – and criminal prevention. Also, a very positive new improvement is the fact that the development of the programme has involved extensive discussion with the residents, NGOs and churches present at the estate, creating a dialogue that was missing previously.

Organisation of participation

The intensity of residential participation on the Hungarian housing estates is difficult to assess. On the one hand, it can be said that residents – as owners – are very much involved in the life of the estate. As owners, they have the right to initiate rehabilitation works (both small and large) in their building; their decision is in fact necessary for any intervention. To reach a mutual decision, depending on the type of intervention they are planning, either a simple majority (50 per cent plus one vote) or the consensus of 80 per cent of the owners is necessary. As shown by the example of the Havanna estate, where the local government authority wanted to deal with security problems by installing a CCTV system, each and every building had to give permission to install the cameras. Using Arnstein's ladder, this situation indicates that the residents have control and delegated power in this respect.

An almost opposite situation can be observed when taking into account the residents' involvement in the affairs of the housing estates as a whole; this almost never matches the residents' involvement in the affairs of a condominium. On the Havanna estate, when a decision concerns not just one building but the entire estate, the responsibility lies with the local government. People tend to think only about their own property and their own building and disregard larger-scale issues. There are no residential organisations and – outside their own building – the residents have little opportunity to promote their interests.

Despite this generally low interest, a new trend can be observed on the Havanna estate. During the development of the new complex renewal

Table 9.2 Overview of the role of participation in regeneration policies and the instruments used

	Nieuw-Hoograven	Trinitat Nova	Havanna
Regeneration policy			
Role of participation in policy	Important item in national and urban regeneration policy Aim: – improving social structure – building political trust	No important item in urban regeneration policy; Important in CDP as a strategy to prevent social exclusion	After years of neglect, greater residential involvement and the encouragement of active participation can be observed. However, it still isn't the most important item in urban regeneration policy
Tools to participate	– Previously mainly through focus groups – Currently documented in the DUO agreement (advisory role for residents' associations, discussions, information meetings, neighbourhood councils, surveys, interviews)	– Workgroups in CDP – Residents contracted professionals as interlocutors with local government	Municipal office hours, residential forums present the opportunity for residents to express their opinion
Organisation of local participation			
Position on participation ladder	Placation Consulting Information	Partnership Placation Consulting Information	Information and consulting Partnership (in cases regarding condominiums)
Bottom-up vs. top-down	Top-down	Bottom-up	Top-down
Associative/individual participation	Associative	Both associations play an important role and individuals participate in workgroups	Individual
Number of participating residents	Low	High	Low

programme, the local government put more emphasis on active consultation: they paid attention to the opinion of residents and consulted the churches and different NGOs present on the estate. This signals a break with the past when, generally speaking, local government authorities in Hungary were not very enthusiastic about encouraging residential participation. Referring back to Arnstein's ladder, this situation characteristically equals what she defines as providing information. In addition, the newer developments suggest that there is also consultation.

Conclusions

The changing function of urban governments and the evolution of governance have led to considerable transformations of urban policies in contemporary Europe. As described in this chapter, this change has altered the way in which responsibilities are distributed, policies conceived, and decision-making processes operated. One aspect of this change has been the growing involvement of residents and NGOs in the field of urban policy, especially in the process of urban regeneration.

Although these changes are to be found all over Europe, their presence can vary from country to country and between cities in the same country, with specific elements being more important in one place than another. This chapter has concentrated on one element of the change from government to governance: the extent to which the participation of residents can now be regarded in Europe as a standard process. Through the analysis of three renewal projects it compared the situation in three different countries – the Netherlands, Spain, and Hungary – with distinct regional and historic backgrounds and explained why participation at the neighbourhood level is organised differently in these countries.

In analysing the cases, important differences between the three countries with respect to their national legislation were found: in the Netherlands, legislation and norms stimulate local participation; in Spain, there is less stimulation; and in Hungary, it can be seen that participation is being stimulated more and more. There are many factors responsible for bringing about these differences, but the fact that Spain and Hungary are younger democracies than the Netherlands is important in this respect. In relatively young democracies, the idea of involving residents in decision-making is less familiar than in older, more established democracies. So, in contrast with the Netherlands, regeneration policy in Spain and Hungary puts no emphasis on local participation; the right of residents to have a voice in the discussion and decision-making concerning their city or neighbourhood does not seem to be fully acknowledged. In turn, the longer tradition of local participation in Dutch policymaking results in the availability of more participation instruments in the Netherlands than in Spain or Hungary.

The availability of formal instruments at the local level does not, however, automatically lead to a situation in which many residents use these instruments. An instrument may be used more in one neighbourhood than another. In Trinitat Nova, for example, the residents themselves developed instruments (in the CDP) to enable themselves to participate. They used these instruments more than did the residents in Nieuw-Hoograven, whose instruments were offered by the policymakers. Taking this into account, it can be questioned whether formalising participation automatically leads to a large number of people participating, or whether it can be considered as a restriction for residents to develop their own instruments. Probably, some kind of adjustment needs to be found, leaving room for residents to develop their own ideas.

However, the lack of formal instruments does not automatically imply that residents develop their own. As the Hungarian case study demonstrates, residents – even as homeowners – often develop very little interest in engaging themselves in the affairs of the housing estates. They would rather take care of their own property (as it was pointed out above, it is up to the residents to undertake any kind of renovation, for example), and leave the responsibility for public good to the local government. On the other hand, it is through homeownership – and the rights associated with it – that even with the lack of any formalised instrument of participation, residents can have a decisive role in any process of urban renewal in Hungary.

In addition, the cases showed that where instruments to facilitate participation are available, local variables have an enormous influence on their use. A weak structure of residential organisations, no such organisations, or organisations lacking cooperation, form a barrier to the development of local participation (as is the case in Havanna). On the other hand, in neighbourhoods with a strong structure, the resident organisations can play an important part in the regeneration process (as in Trinitat Nova). Furthermore, a bottom-up process and a management model in which the project managers are directly connected with a residents' organisation have a positive effect on local participation (as in Nieuw-Hoograven).

As the comparison of the three cases demonstrates, the organisation of local participation can differ enormously between countries. Generally speaking, however, participation mostly reaches what Arnstein calls the degree of tokenism, with Hungary on its lower rank (information and sometimes consultation) and the Netherlands and Spain on the higher rank (consultation and placation). Generalisations are, however, difficult to make for any of the countries. This is shown by the Hungarian case, where residents sometimes become partners through the fact that they are homeowners. Finally, apart from the local factors, national legislation and tradition – which currently determine how the policy of residential participation functions in a country – the policies and norms of the European Union have to be mentioned. This raises the expectation that, despite the lack of participatory traditions in many of the new and some of the old member states, in the long run local participation and the idea of effective and valuable residential involvement will be promoted and accepted in most countries.

Of course this is not to say that local participation is a general panacea that will automatically lead to the improvement of urban development programmes. It is a tool that requires careful employment and consideration. However, a skilful use of residential participation – adapted to the different local traditions – can enhance the success of an urban development programme in the long run.

Notes

1. Residents pay a relatively small monthly sum for about 25 years before becoming owners of the dwellings. An officially protected dwelling (VPO: *Vivienda de Protección Oficial*) starts as a publicly owned dwelling and finally becomes a dwelling in the owner-occupied sector.
2. Large housing estates form a substantial segment of the Hungarian housing market – approximately 20 per cent of it. Their status depends largely on the position they occupy in their local housing market (Bányai et al., 1999). Despite the physical troubles they face, their population – among whom many poor people can be found – are generally not the most deprived people in Hungary; many solid middle-class and lower-middle class households can be found on Hungarian large housing estates.
3. In 2005, the term DUO agreement was changed into Utrecht Vernieuwt (*Utrecht Renews*).

References

Aalbers, M., Van Beckhoven, E., Van Kempen, R., Musterd, S. and Ostendorf, W. (2003) *Large Housing Estates in the Netherlands: Overview of Developments and Problems in Amsterdam and Utrecht*. Utrecht: Utrecht University.
Aalbers, M., Van Beckhoven, E., Van Kempen, R., Musterd, S. and Ostendorf, W. (2004) *Large Housing Estates in the Netherlands: Policies and Practices*. Utrecht: Utrecht University.
Andersen, H. T. and Van Kempen, R. (2001) *Governing European Cities: Social Fragmentation, Social Exclusion and Urban Governance*. Hampshire: Ashgate.

Andersen, H. T. and Van Kempen, R. (2003) New Trends in Urban Policies in Europe: Evidence from the Netherlands and Denmark. *Cities*, 20 (2), pp. 77–86.

Arnstein, S. (1969) A Ladder of Citizen Participation. In: P. LeGates and F. Stout (Eds) (1996), *The City Reader*, pp. 240–52. London: Routledge.

Bányai, J., Geröházi, É., Hegedüs, A. and Tosics, I. (1999) *Javaslat a paneles épületek felújítását elősegítő műszaki, pénzügyi, jogi és szervezési intézkedésekre* (Proposal for technical, financial, legal and organization steps preparing the rehabilitation of pre–fabricated buildings). Budapest: Metropolitan Research Institute.

Castells, M. (1986) *La Ciudad y Las Masas. Sociología de los Movimientos Sociales Urbanos*. Madrid: Alianza Editorial.

Dekker, K. K. (2006) *Governance as Glue. Urban Governance and Social Cohesion in Post–WWII Neighbourhoods in the Netherlands*. Utrecht: Faculty of Geosciences, Utrecht University.

Del Pino, E. and Colino, C. (2003) *Las nuevas formas de participación en los gobiernos locales*. http://www.enredalicante.org/documentos/estudi–_fundacio_alternativas.pdf, visited on 13 January 2003.

Direcció General de Serveis Comunitaris, Dervei de Plans i Programes [General Direction of Community Services, Plan and Programme Service] (2002) *Memòria 2002*. Barcelona: Generalitat.

Elander, I. and Blanc, M. (2001) Partnerships and Democracy: A Happy Couple in Urban Governance? In: H. T. Andersen and R. Van Kempen (Eds), *Governing European Cities. Social Fragmentation, Social Exclusion and Urban Governance*, pp. 93–124. Aldershot: Ashgate.

Engbersen, R. (2004) *Bottom up werken met top support. Handreiking of handleiding?* Discussion Paper for the Expert Meeting of the Netherlands Institute for Care and Well–being on Residents' Participation Post–WWII Restructuring Neighbourhoods.

Erdösi, S., Geröházi, É., Teller, N. and Tosics, I. (2003) *Large Housing Estates in Hungary: Overview of Developments and Problems in Budapest and Nyíregyjáza*. Utrecht: Utrecht University.

Font, J. (2003) *Public Participation and Local Governance*. Barcelona: Institut de Ciencies Polítiques i Socials (ICPS). Universitat Autonoma Barcelona.

Healey, P., Cameron, S., Davoudi, S., Graham, S. and Madanipour, A. (Eds) (1995), *Managing Cities: The New Urban Context*. Chichester: Wiley.

Hirst, P. (2000), Democracy and Governance. In: J. Pierre (Ed.), *Debating Governance*. Oxford: Oxford.

Mamadouh, V. D. (1992) De stad in eigen hand: Provo's, kabouters en krakers als stedelijke sociale bewegingen (Provos, Kabouters and Squatters as Urban Social Movements). Amsterdam: SUA.

Pareja Eastaway, M., Tapada Berteli, T., Van Boxmeer, B. and Garcia Ferrando, L. (2003) *Large Housing Estates in Spain: Overview of Developments and Problems in Madrid and Barcelona*. Utrecht: Utrecht University.

Pindado, F. (2000) *La participación ciudadana en la vida de las ciudades*. Barcelona: Ediciones del Serbal.

Reeves, R. (1982) *American Journey: Traveling with Tocqueville in Search of Democracy in America*. New York: Simon and Schuster.

Stoker, G. (2004) *Transforming Local Governance*. Basingstoke: Palgrave Macmillan.

Szemzö, H. and Tosics, I. (2005) Hungary. In: R. Van Kempen, M. Vermeulen, and A. Baan (Eds) *Urban Issues and Urban Policies in the New EU Countries*, pp. 37–61. Aldershot: Ashgate.

Taylor, M. (2000) Communities in the Lead: Power, Organizational Capacity and Social Capital. *Urban Studies*, 37 (5–6), pp. 1019–35.

Van Beckhoven, E. and Van Boxmeer, B. (2006) Resident Participation. In: R. Van Kempen, A. Murie, T. Knorr–Siedow and I. Tosics (Eds) *Regenerating Large Housing Estates in Europe: A Guide to Better Practice*, pp. 61–70. Utrecht: Faculty of Geosciences, Utrecht University.

Van Beckhoven, E., Van Boxmeer, B. and Garcia Ferrando, L. (2005) Local Participation in Spain and the Netherlands. In: R. Van Kempen, K. Dekker, S. Hall and I. Tosics (Eds) *Restructuring Large Housing Estates in Europe*, pp. 231–55. Bristol: The Policy Press.

Van Brunschot, A. G. M., Hulshof, M. E., de Wal, M. I. and Jansen, R. M. (2002) *Over wijken, bewoners en (sub)lokaal bestuur. Handreiking voor het instrumentarium van binnengemeentelijke decentralisatie.* Den Haag: Ministerie van Binnenlandse Zaken en Koninkrijksrelaties.

Van der Ham, T. and Van der Meij, G. (1974) *Gereedschap voor inspraak in de ruimtelijke ordening.* Baarn: Wereldvenster.

Vranken, J., de Decker, P. and Van Nieuwenhuyze, I. (2003) *Social Inclusion, Urban Governance and Sustainability. Towards a Conceptual Framework for the UGIS Research Project.* Antwerpen: Garant.

Walliser, A. (2003) *Participación y ciudad.* Madrid: Centro de Estudios Avanzados en Ciencias Socials.

Wilcox, D. (1998) *The Guide to Develop Trust and Partnerships.* http://www.partnerships.org.uk/pguide, accessed in March 2004.

Wilkinson, D. and Applebee, E. (1999) *Implementing Holistic Government: Joined-up Action on the Ground.* Bristol: The Policy Press.

10
Whose Regeneration? The Spectre of Revanchist Regeneration

Rob Rowlands and Alan Murie

Introduction

The earlier chapters of this book have established some of the key dimensions of large housing estates built in the post-WWII period in Europe, largely by public sector and 'not-for-profit' organisations. The social role and market position of all of these estates have changed over the years since they were first built and many, but not all of these estates, are now seen as problematic. Partly because of this problematic status regeneration has become an increasingly prominent element on the policy agenda for them. However regenerating poverty neighbourhoods raises questions about who benefits, about displacement because of demolition, and about gentrification. Some academic discussions of regeneration, especially in the USA and to a lesser extent the UK, have presented a critical view of such regeneration as exclusionary and even revanchist. However, many of these contributions are longer on assertion and deduction than evidence. In this chapter we draw on research carried out in five estates in three different countries to develop a fuller and more evidence-based view of regeneration. The analysis recognises the importance of critical questions about who benefits, but suggests that a differentiated and contextualised account of regeneration and its impacts is more convincing than an approach based on the assumption that gentrification and exclusion is a consistent attribute of regeneration, or indeed its most important feature.

The chapter engages with the existing literature on gentrification and regeneration and focuses on the changes that have taken place on large estates connected with ideas of revanchist gentrification. It provides evidence around these issues and develops a more robust account of social and market change associated with estate regeneration in Europe.

In particular it considers different contexts and trajectories of estates affected by regeneration, referring to changes affecting these large estates associated with residualisation and with privatisation of parts of the housing stock as well as regeneration. In so doing, we seek to complement the existing deductive, assertive approach with a more empirical approach. The conclusions of the chapter consider the implications of this for future policy development and implementation.

Regeneration, the market and gentrification

Processes of gentrification have been observed in major world cities since the 1960s, and similar trends have been recognised in other European and North American cities (Glass, 1964; Smith and Williams, 1986; Hamnett, 1991; Atkinson, 2000). Gentrification refers to the process of production and consumption of space for a more affluent and different incoming population (Slater et al., 2004). It emerged as a key feature of transformation in privately owned, working-class neighbourhoods of cities in the nineteenth- and early-twentieth-centuries where, until the point of change, a majority of housing had been privately rented. The portrait of gentrification was one of a transition of areas that had previously housed workers in manufacturing and industrial employment: these areas, for example in inner London, saw a major change in social composition and came to house young professionals and white-collar workers. In some cases this involved significant modernisation of homes that had been neglected by private landlords and, in others, a conversion of shared and subdivided properties back to large family homes or self-contained flats. The overriding features of gentrification identified in this earlier research were:

- A colonisation of cheaper residential neighbourhoods by more affluent households and a change in the social class composition;
- A reinvestment in the physical housing stock;
- A tenure transfer from private landlordism to owner occupation;
- Displacement of existing residents in some but not all cases.

These features are further summarised in Table 10.1 alongside the differing attributes of more recent gentrification.

While in the early 1990s there was a view that economic recession had signalled the end of gentrification (Bourne, 1993), the tide has shifted and there has been a more vigorous debate about post-recession gentrification (Lees, 2000; Lambert and Boddy, 2002). This suggested

Table 10.1   Old and new gentrifications

	Old gentrification	**New regeneration**
Main Features	19th/early 20th century property London/world cities Formerly private rented Stable low turnover market Single family houses/street properties Rehabilitation/conversion back to single family houses	Mid to late 20th century property All major urban areas Formerly public sector housing Unstable, high turnover market Mid- and high-rise flats and maisonettes Demolition (sometimes partial, sometimes large scale)
Previous Inhabitants	Established working class Elderly	Post industrial underclass Young and elderly
New Inhabitants	Younger affluent households	Younger affluent households
Short term Impact	Break-up of community Changing social capital	Further break-up of unstable 'community' Broadening social capital
Longer-term Impact	New stable middle class enclaves	New transitional housing a significant part of new mixed community
Driver	Investment by individuals to achieve housing goals and to build family assets	Investment initiated by state and supported by development industry
Lead Agents	Individual speculator households	Corporate interests involving developers in partnership with state and not-for-profit agencies

new phase of gentrification is the focus of this chapter. While it shares some parallels with the phases of gentrification identified in the 1960s, some clearly different dimensions are identified which are particularly pertinent to the large (former) public housing estates.

The new phase involves purposive action related to whole estates or neighbourhoods rather than the accumulation of a series of separate decisions about individual properties. This is partly because of the different nature of the properties themselves – larger blocks of flats present different investment challenges to individual family houses – but also reflects the explicit concern of public policy to address neighbourhood effects and break up concentrations of deprivation. For example, Uitermark et al. (2007) describe the increasing and changing role of the private sector in relation to the regeneration of residential neighbourhoods in Rotterdam. Therefore, this is no longer a process of individuals buying property and changing the tenure, but is based around large property companies working with the state to strategically remodel and remake entire neighbourhoods. Nor is tenure transfer a shift from private renting to owner occupation, but rather a complex pattern of shift from state or social renting to private ownership, both owner occupation but also, and significantly in the UK, to private landlordism. And although dilapidated properties may be refurbished, in many cases demolition is a favoured option. This means a more dramatic reshaping, redesigning and rebuilding of whole neighbourhoods, often involving densification through building on open spaces or on vacant sites within estates. While this does not automatically displace residents, it potentially contributes to changing the social profile of the area. What is important to highlight is the active role of the state in delivering the conditions, process and sometimes resources to facilitate this change.

The outcomes of these changes have been the focus of intense debate. One view of such market-led regeneration is that it reduces the options for lower-income and working-class households and increases the options of the more affluent. Where the aim of policy is more explicit in delivering such social change and assisting the free market, the process has been described as 'revanchist' (see Smith, 1996), an active aim to reverse previous gains achieved by working-class households. This notion is plausible where the initial state-support for public and not-for-profit housing was won through political processes and by coalitions including working-class interests (see, e.g., Harloe, 1995). Dismantling the gains achieved through such political processes is seen as part of a shift in power away from these groups, a shift in the aims of public policy, and as state-led gentrification which will benefit more affluent groups and economic elite. Neil Smith's 'revanchist' model of gentrification proposes that global pressures mean that urban change must be managed to ensure that cities remain competitive (Smith, 1996). To this extent the role of regeneration is to provide an environment in which the market can operate to its best ability rather than in effect be led by household strategies designed to achieve household aspirations. In so doing, it is suggested that gentrification has become a state-sponsored activity under the guise of regeneration and that this process necessitates the containment or displacement of certain populations in order to ameliorate urban areas and make them attractive to the middle classes. The focus is on the exclusionary aspects of policy either through the process of displacement or in physical segregation and elimination of 'undesirable' populations. In programmes such as the urban renaissance proposals in England (Urban Task Force, 1999) gentrification is ambitiously and scrupulously planned as a central goal of urban policy. It is carried out by corporate and governmental partnerships on a large scale and involves more than simply residential change. Other contributions also take a negative view of regeneration and contrast its planned and exclusionary pattern with a largely unplanned, earlier phase of market-led gentrification. For example, Atkinson (2003) and Cameron (2003) both refer to concerns that regeneration in the UK aims at the displacement and relocation of lower-income households and this connects with Smith's (1996) account of policy in New York as a punitive, revanchist response to the poor.

While this debate about the gentrification associated with urban renaissance has attracted considerable attention, and the importance of global pressures on regeneration is undeniable, the evidence base on which claims of displacement and regeneration are made is weak. Smith's argument evolves from the experience of urban policy in the USA and especially the HOPE VI programme and actions towards the homeless. The HOPE VI programme included high levels of demolition of public housing and replacement by a very strictly managed regime of newly built neighbourhoods with mixed communities. Taken to its extreme, some of the policies introduced in the USA to modernise and renew public housing estates were explicitly designed to move the poorest on and to eradicate social stigma by erasing the neighbourhood and the memory of it. Neil Smith's is an account of revanchist regeneration as an exclusionary process designed to displace the residents of public sector neighbourhoods and to relocate them to different neighbourhoods while recreating these neighbourhoods as attractive areas of privatised housing.

However, there are alternative representations of, and evidence from, the US experience which undermine this argument. Others have commented, through more empirical and comprehensive evaluation, that the outcome of HOPE VI programmes is largely dependent on the context and, most acutely, the management of each scheme (Galster, 2007a, 2007b; Galster et al., 2003; Popkin et al., 2006). While in some locations this has tended towards the revanchist conclusion, where the state has been more involved in managing the process of relocation and redevelopment, benefits have been derived for both the area and for the extant residents. Therefore the key to a more mature and enlightened regeneration policy is to consider the manner in which regeneration is undertaken, in particular the way in which the process is managed to ensure the delivery of more balanced outcomes.

We lack evidence-based accounts related to these developments in Europe. Some accounts are essentially deductive and analyse probable outcomes from certain broad principles. Within the existing literature, there is limited evidence of the scale and nature of displacement associated with the redevelopment of neighbourhoods with high concentrations of low-income households (see Kleinhans, 2003, and Musterd and Ostendorf, 2005, for an initial analysis). Furthermore, there are few accounts of resident involvement in regeneration initiatives and of the social relations in newly gentrified areas. And there remains an absence of evidence related to the provincial cities that have been at the forefront of developments related to city living and city centre regeneration (Atkinson, 2002) and the change in public housing estates where real estate assets are now being realised in the pursuit of urban change. While accepting Smith's initial proposition that regeneration is a response to global pressures, it is important to acknowledge the other pressures. Rather than gentrification as the predictable outcome from regeneration, arising as a consequence of the global pressures to be competitive, it seems likely that other factors will have a bearing on the impact of regeneration for the neighbourhood and its population, on the extent of displacement and change in the social profile and whether this is properly presented as gentrification. This is the central proposition addressed in this chapter.

The commodification of public housing estates before regeneration

The literature referring to gentrification in the context of the regeneration of large post-war public and social rented estates tends to be inexplicit about the previous patterns and trends in these estates. It tends to present them as stereotypes of working-class neighbourhoods or territories that have been the preserve of lower-income and working-class households. Earlier chapters of this book have highlighted the continuities between estates built in the same era and subject to similar professional, political and technical influences. But they also highlight the differences between estates – differences associated with their initial location and design and their relative attractiveness or position in the hierarchy of housing choice; and differences associated with local economic changes and changes in the alternatives available in the local housing market. In considering the impact of regeneration it is important to recognise these differences and the journey that the estates we have studied have taken. This journey is part of the picture to consider in addressing the questions for this chapter.

Some of the literature concerning regeneration comes dangerously close to painting a romantic picture of large public housing estates as products of working-class political action – being built by the state to provide better housing conditions for the working classes – and understating the erosion of rights associated with these estates in recent years. This provides the launch pad for a critique of regeneration. Any loss of both the housing and the space in which it is located is seen as eroding the gains achieved in the past. But this perspective requires considerable modification in view of the very significant progress of both residualisation and privatisation affecting these estates. These estates were initially insulated from the majority of market pressures because of the pattern of ownership by the state and its agencies. They were de-commodified and they redistributed housing opportunities on the basis of housing need rather than ability to pay. However before considering the impacts of regeneration, it is essential to recognise that the de-commodified status of these estates has often been seriously compromised in the period since they were built. They have often become less attractive to affluent working-class and middle-income households because of an adverse comparison with homeownership. At the same time poor management and maintenance have damaged these estates and they have drifted down the status and value hierarchy within the housing market. These effects differ between and within cities but the direction of change is the same across most of Europe. While the picture is most strongly painted in the UK and, as a result of differing origins and processes, is more complicated in the former state socialist countries of Central and Eastern Europe (as outlined in Chapter 1), the residualisation and de-valorisation of all or some of the housing built by and for the state in earlier eras is common (Harloe, 1995; Murie et al., 2002; Dekker and van Kempen, 2005; Hall et al., 2005).

In discussing change in these estates it is important to refer to the commodification that follows privatisation. Privatisation forms a separate, though connected, process of re-commodification that has further contributed to residualisation. Although privatisation of public sector housing has not been uniform across Europe, being most prolonged in the UK, most extensive in Eastern and Central Europe and evident, even to a small extent, everywhere, its impacts have tended to add to the differentiation between estates, with the best estates becoming more difficult to access.

The sale of state housing has transformed what were seen as political gains for local communities and workers into marketable assets for individuals – capturing the gains for individuals who were in the right place at the right time and eroding collective political gains and entitlements. The 'give away' privatisation of this housing in some Central and Eastern European countries has gone one step further and placed individual property ownership centre stage. Overall, these trends of privatisation have removed the insulation that these estates had from the market and, in some cases, have made gentrification possible where the conditions are conducive. Commodification is a slow process and may follow a considerable time after the initial privatisation when market-accessed succession signals that properties are fully absorbed into the market; and commodification only strictly involves gentrification, when new purchasers on the open market have higher incomes and replace the lower-income households who have traditionally lived on these estates.

In considering this as part of the 'revanchist gentrification' the picture is not as simple as others may contend. The process of privatisation through sale to sitting tenants does not initially involve any displacement of population because it is the existing residents that buy properties. There is, however, an indirect displacement at a later stage. When the sitting-tenant purchasers move out, the housing is exchanged through a market process rather than the bureaucratic process which would have operated had they remained in the public sector. This opens up the opportunity for a different group of households to move into the neighbourhood. Rather than those who would qualify through bureaucratic allocation processes, it is households which have the resources to buy properties on the market who move in. The British research evidence (Forrest and Murie, 1995; Jones and Murie, 2006) suggests that in some market situations these may not be households very different from those that would qualify through bureaucratic rules, but in high-demand and high-priced markets it is likely to mean that a distinctively higher-income group begins to move in. This is a form of gentrification following explicit policies of the state to privatise the housing stock and, over an extended period of time, could significantly alter the social make up of neighbourhoods.

The consequence of this change of public and social rented housing from a decommodified to a commodified state is that the status of public housing estates have generally been transformed over the last

50 years. In many but not all cases (and less so in Central and Eastern Europe) their reputations have declined as a combination of internal factors (such as obsolescence and poor management) and external factors (social, economic and housing market changes) has altered their position in the hierarchy of choice among households. Together with the increasing commodification of housing in general, the worst estates have been cast adrift in the market. They have moved from being neighbourhoods of choice for the affluent working class to neighbourhoods for those outside the mainstream of the economy and employment. The process of residualisation has generally been speeded by privatisation and these changes represent a continuing erosion of the political gains they originally encapsulated.

The public-sector mass housing estates built in the post-war period are among those most damaged by this pattern of change. They have often become the most residualised and the least valued by households with choice. At risk of oversimplifying we could summarise the different attributes that apply to estates in relation to this. All of them are estates that were built in the post-war period. They have certain superficial things in common: the design and built form associated with towers in the sky, prefabricated construction, mass housing estates constructed by or through the state. All of them have, to a very considerable extent, seen a deterioration in their reputation (least so in Central or Eastern Europe) associated with the declining reputation of social housing in general and of these types of mass housing estates in particular. They have experienced dilapidation and poor maintenance, poor management both of properties and of the estates themselves, including public open spaces. They have also experienced changes in household structures and in incomes, with an increasing pauperisation or residualisation of the population and a role in the housing market that is increasingly residual (again, with the exception of estates in Central and Eastern Europe). At the same time changes in subsidy and housing benefit systems and the advantages associated with homeownership have affected exit from the estates and who has moved into them.

At this stage then we have a modified perspective on the revanchist regeneration theme. This would acknowledge the political and economic pressures on enclaves of state-owned land and housing owned by the state and not-for-profit organisations. But it would argue that the attacks on these enclaves have already taken place, in many cases before regeneration is contemplated. The tenure status has come under attack, ownerships have been fragmented and the neighbourhoods have been absorbed into the market. The interventions that have already taken place have altered the legacy associated with previous political action and the division between the most attractive and least attractive estates has increased. In many cases a reverse gentrification has already taken place, as affluent working-class households have been replaced by those with lower incomes.

This perspective is important, highlighting that we need to recognise that these estates have been exposed to Smith's global pressures for a long time and have, to different degrees, already been reshaped by them. However, rather than being merely wiped away by the market, these estates have all responded in different ways with different outcomes. In analysing this process it is important to differentiate between estates that have already been seriously devalued and those that have been less so. It is also important to identify what is being preserved as the alternative if regeneration is bringing destructive change. It is not some idealised legacy from past political action that is involved but real places that may, in some cases, be improved for existing residents through regeneration and, again, it is the process as much as the outcome of these programmes and projects which is important to note.

Regenerating estates

The estates included in the RESTATE project (See Chapter 1) provide the evidence to take this debate further and explore different approaches to regeneration and to address the forms that gentrification may take, if at all, in the regeneration of large estates. In this chapter we refer to five estates that illustrate the variety of approaches to regeneration. In each case we present an account of the changing social base of the estate and the policies affecting these changes, looking in particular at the process and outcomes of regeneration. In each account we consider the approach to regeneration, the extent of market-orientated intervention and the degree to which gentrification is one of the outcomes.

The Central Estates, Birmingham

The 'Central Estates' in Birmingham are situated on the edge of the city centre just beyond the prime zone for new city centre residential development. They were initially developed between the 1950s and the mid 1970s, providing new accommodation for households displaced through war damage and subsequently to rehouse those affected by slum clearance. New methods of construction and the generous subsidies attached to them resulted in a large range of architectural styles, layouts and densities. Many of the residents of the newly built housing in the 1960s had previously lived in the neighbourhood in dilapidated dwellings. When new dwellings were built they were regarded as state of the art and were highly popular but by the mid 1990s the estates had become increasingly problematic: physically due to the design and building techniques employed; and socially as a result of social and economic processes both locally and more widely. The estates had high turnover and all of the symptoms associated with difficult-to-live-in estates. Seventy-seven per cent of tenants received some state benefits and 64 per cent of these were wholly reliant on state benefits for their income. Despite their proximity to the city centre, the estates formed one of the city's unemployment and deprivation blackspots.

The resulting regeneration initiative was a result of resident pressure and state opportunism. Residents felt that they were being forgotten by the city council, prompting them to embark on high profile protests. This in turn led the city council to apply for government funds through the Estate Renewal Challenge Fund to support a major regeneration programme. The council had previously refused to apply for such funds, as a condition of funding was a transfer of stock from the council to a Registered Social Landlord that would be able to access private finance in addition to the grants provided by government. The application to the Estate Renewal Challenge Fund was successful and the proposals were approved by residents in a ballot. Stock transfer and access to new finance ensued. At the time of transfer, the estates comprised a stock of 2679 units. Most of this stock was flats, with 63 per cent of the stock being flats of over five storeys. Much of the stock had received no modernisation or planned maintenance since its construction: both the exterior and interior of properties required investment. The layout of the estates also presented problems. For example in the Lee Bank area, a series of high rise blocks were set amidst poorly landscaped and managed open space, but the area was regarded as unsafe and few people used it, particularly at night. These conditions, the proximity to the city centre and its attractiveness to private sector developers, and the ownership of land by the city council presented an opportunity for large-scale redevelopment that would involve private developers as well as the public-private sector. The tenant protests, which are often seen as initiating the action, were essentially the key to unlocking this potential.

The process of regeneration has been an inclusive public-private-community partnership. Funding for the programme came through the Estates Renewal Challenge Fund and Social Housing Grant as well as loans from the private sector (made possible by the stock transfer). Importantly the regeneration funding also involved some receipts from land sales for private development. At the time the funding was granted, change on the estate had been slow and fewer than 10 per cent of council properties had been sold under the Right-to-Buy compared with over 30 per cent nationally. Following the transfer of the properties from Birmingham City Council to Optima Housing Association in 1998, the process of regeneration involved the demolition of a large number of the existing properties and refurbishment of the rest. Demolition has facilitated renewal of infrastructure including some relocation of roads and sewers and the construction of new, properly designed public parks. It has also enabled the construction of new housing including private development that tapped into the growing city living market and diversified both the tenure and population in the area. Under the regeneration programme, 1150 social rented properties were refurbished and 1350 were demolished. Some 2500 new homes were to be built in mixed tenure developments; with some 550 of these homes being affordable housing units predominantly social rented housing. The demand from residents was for an improvement in the quality and variety of social rented housing in the area and the inclusion of some 250 houses with gardens to rebalance the nature of the social rented sector in the estates where flats predominated. The plans envisaged a reduction in the number of properties but a reshaping of the neighbourhood to make it one that was more attractive to live in. Mixed tenure was both a means of cross-subsidising the improvement in social rented housing and an explicit mechanism to change the neighbourhood and fund other activities including the new parks. After regeneration, the new estate would undoubtedly be more affluent and in that sense regeneration would have resulted in gentrification, but there would also be more properties than on the older estate and a more attractive social rented sector.

In the regeneration of the Central Estates in Birmingham there was considerable consultation with tenants; indeed the regeneration scheme was triggered by residents' demands for action. Residents agreed in a ballot to stock transfer in 1998. The rate of displacement associated with this regeneration can be expressed in relation to the number of properties that were cleared (34 per cent) but some of these properties were empty; some of the residents were immediately rehoused in vacant units elsewhere on the same estate; and some who moved away and then returned when new properties were completed. Taking these factors into account the level of displacement would be some 15 per cent (households forced to move because of demolition and not returning). This figure implies, however, that all of those affected by demolition would have wished to stay. Some of those who voted for demolition did so because it enabled them to move on from properties they did not wish to stay in, and some of those who did not take up the opportunity to return to newly built housing were also voting to leave. If displacement is to be a measure of the extent to which regeneration forced unwanted relocation on households, then 15 per cent represents the upper maximum; the real displacement would be lower, and because the opportunity to return was available, and everyone who registered an interest in doing so was offered housing back in the area, real displacement could be seen as negligible.

The housing balance sheet for residents living in the area before regeneration involved improvements to their existing homes and, for some, opportunities to transfer to newly built housing. Importantly the development agreement entered into by the city council, the social landlord and the private developer ensured that maximum value was retained from the land for the wider benefit of the community. Rather than the land being sold there was a development agreement that specified essential works, which the developer had to do at the beginning of the project (including infrastructure and parks), and payments would increase if the project generated larger returns than assumed in the agreement. Any such overage as well as any receipts from other sales of council land and property in the area were also – unusually and as a result of resident pressure – ring fenced to be reinvested in the area and so benefit the local community.

This is a picture of managed and regulated regeneration. It involves a calculated 'negotiation' between residents and the city council, using the power that they had to access grants and attract private investment, to achieve a goal designed to benefit the existing community. It involved very little, if any, real displacement and existing residents saw the broadening of the social base, increased density of housing and introduction of new privately owned housing as an acceptable part of the package that would address their primary needs. For the developers and the city council there were other objectives that connect with Neil Smith's perspective, but city centre regeneration and increased competitiveness achieved by transforming existing run down estates is not always revanchist and may, as in this case, reflect a reversal of a long period of neglect experienced by a community.

While there is a form of gentrification emerging in the new opportunities for households to move into new private housing in the area, this is gentrification largely without displacement of existing residents and, indeed, it could be represented as gentrification that enables exiting residents to improve their housing and other circumstances – a far cry from revanchism. There could be a sophistication of this argument that would suggest that the development of housing for middle-income groups crowded out the opportunities for more housing for lower-income groups, but this becomes a circular argument. It involves a different vision for the neighbourhood with less or indeed no attempt to widen the social base, and would have meant that the mechanisms to finance the improvement in social rented housing would have been foregone.

Les Minguettes, Lyon

Les Minguettes in Lyon illustrate a different approach with the major aim being a negative one – the desire to eradicate a particular problem without any clear alternative vision. Les Minguettes comprise seven distinct neighbourhoods on the outskirts of Lyon in Venissieux. Venissieux is a town whose politics are dominated by the local Renault truck factory and as a result has traditionally had a left-of-centre council headed by a communist mayor. In the face of growing housing demand in Greater Lyon in the late 1950s and early 1960s, Les Minguettes was planned as rental housing with the intention of housing mainly working-class households and municipal civil servants. The early years were considered a success in this respect. The majority of households moving in fitted these criteria and the estate received a large number of households returning from Algeria. By the early 1970s, the mayor of Venissieux wanted to attract a growing population to the town to compete with Lyon and Les Minguettes was to play a significant role in this growth (Chignier-Riboulon et al., 2003). However by the end of the 1970s residential mobility had increased. There were high vacancy levels of properties and the French working-class inhabitants were significantly replaced by immigrants, especially from North Africa. Belmessous and Chignier-Riboulon (2006) attribute this change to a new phase of migration associated with family regrouping, increased access to mortgage finance that enabled people to buy houses elsewhere, the displacement of lower-income households from town centres, local economic changes and changes to provision of housing benefit. The council however, largely neglected these factors and focused on the growth of non-European immigrant families living on the estate. They were blamed for the degradation of the social climate on the estates. By 1979 analysis of the vacancy problem on the estates had concluded that it could not be solved through traditional housing management, and that the scarcity of amenities and the form of properties in towers and blocks were the problems. This position was further complicated by rioting and acts of violence especially in 1980 and 1981 (Chignier-Riboulon, 1999). Les Minguettes became *the* symbol of the challenges associated with the integration of young people born of immigrant parents and the transformation of underprivileged *'banlieues'* into towns and was critical in the thinking that informed the new *Politique de la Ville.*

The most recent of a sequence of policy responses in Les Minguettes was the Grand Projet de Ville (GPV), an integrated and holistic, central government-funded scheme. The main focus of the GPV in Les Minguettes was the physical restructuring of the estate to improve accessibility and remake it as the centre of the town (see Belmessous et al., 2004). In addition to the reconfiguration of roads, the main housing intervention was to embark on a programme of demolition to change the estate. During the 1990s all of the ten tower blocks comprising the Democratie sector were demolished and six of the nine in a second sector, Monmousseau, were demolished. In practice this led to a third sector, Darnaise, becoming more heavily stigmatised as tenants relocated to the remaining 'cheap' blocks.

While demolition reshaped the estate, the rebuilding which took place was entirely *habitation à loyer modéré* (HLM), or housing association, and so there is an absence of mixed-tenure or private-sector housing in the demolished areas. Despite the development being rent controlled, the mixed-funding required for the development meant that rents are higher in the new blocks than the old blocks. This has restricted relocation by former residents back into rebuilt areas as a result of the affordability of rents. At the same time there has been no attempt to reduce the stigmatisation and exclusion associated with the rest of the neighbourhood. Indeed discussions about the remaining estate emphasise citizens who are completely excluded or apart from the rest of society. This process has therefore physically squeezed 'undesireable' households to the margins of the estate. At the same time, local residents have been politically marginalised in the process. The policies adopted for Les Minguettes were carried out with very little consultation or communication with local residents, and the demolition of properties arguably added to the sense of separateness and exclusion (Belmessous and Chignier-Riboulon, 2006). This is typical of the French approach to regeneration, based as it is on representative democracy and assumed authority of elected officials.

The actions taken in Les Minguettes could be labelled as regeneration. They were a political response to a particular perception of a problem of urban segregation. The objectives were articulated as a way of reducing segregation and concentration, especially of immigrant communities, by removing the most segregated blocks rather than by attempting to introduce a mixed community. The process has resulted in displacement, which has pushed those households in the demolished blocks further to the periphery of the estate or the wider city housing market and, in so doing, has also exacerbated their socio-economic marginality. One could argue that it is appropriate to include this case within a notion of revanchist regeneration: the displacement of the very poor, together with a lack of consultation, represents a clear disregard for the impact of such regeneration on those living in the neighbourhood. Yet, unlike the revanchist model outlined above, the actions did not include new investment or building in the private sector and, although some new households move in who are relatively more affluent than the extant households, in relation to the wider city the new households still represent some of the lowest income groups. It is hard to believe that this could have led to a reduction of segregation without some other actions, and the lack of involvement of the local community also characterises the approach.

What is clear though is that, unlike the Central Estates, there was no opening up of the area to the market and there was no gentrification, either by the private sector or by individual incoming households. There is limited data about either incomers or the segregation of households because of the limitations of the French census. However, anecdotal evidence from the estate itself suggests that, while there has been population change, the estate remains in a lowly housing market position.

Therefore, the picture which emerges from Les Minguettes is not straight forward. There is regeneration taking place on the estate, orchestrated by the state in a manner which is displacing the old population. Although this may be a form of revanchist regeneration, it lacks some of the ingredients usually identified – it lacks private developer investment and it lacks gentrification in a traditional or in a new sense. The activity is state orchestrated but without the market playing a central role. Through the marketisation of controlled rents in the new blocks, the programme reduces rather than removes the problem.

The Havanna and Josavaros estates, Hungary

Two housing estates in Hungary present a different take on the role of the market in regeneration. Neither estate, Havanna in Budapest and Josavaros in Nyíregyháza, considered here have been subject to explicit regeneration initiatives in an orchestrated and planned way. Rather their increasing exposure to market processes and private finance, through privatisation by sale to sitting tenants and subsequent resale, means that they can be considered within the same framework of previously insulated enclaves to market processes (e.g. the Central Estates example above). The privatisation of state housing in Hungary was a result, as with many other countries post communism, of a radical economic restructuring which introduced a liberal, free market system. This, in combination with a reduced capacity for local government to readily maintain the buildings through a lack of resources and a political imperative to win support through popular actions, led to the introduction of a Right-to-Buy under the 1993 Housing Law (see Szemző and Tosics, 2004). What privatisation has done is to introduce slowly the market into these estates, not through a large scale project involving private sector concerns, but through the atomised privatism of individuals. As a result, regeneration is the result of individual and selective collective action rather than state programmes, befitting of a neo-liberal approach.

Both of these estates were built and owned by the state to provide housing for rent (Erdosi et al., 2003), Havanna was built between 1977 and 1983, while Josavaros was constructed during the 1970s. It is important to understand that these larger estates built in the 1970s and 1980s were never the most prestigious areas to live in, unlike those built in earlier periods, and therefore highlight our previous observation about the different starting point and trajectory of individual estates. The first state housing estates in Budapest were built in the 1950s near the city centre, in green areas, and were often allocated to the 'political elite'. In contrast the later big estates were built of prefabricated components in open spaces far away from the city centre and were allocated more in accordance with social needs.

Josavaros was always considered to be a fairly average estate – it housed neither the lowest nor the highest sections of society and ethnic minorities were never a significant element in the estate. While there was variation between different parts of the estate, its favourable location in the city close to the centre made it more attractive than other estates. For the two decades after 1980, the estate underwent a demographic transition with a significant decline in population, especially in households with children, and a growth in single person households. But the main impact was the narrowing of the social base as a result of privatisation. Before 1989, many of the residents in the estate were co-owners through housing cooperatives or owners of condominium flats. Both of these types of property had been funded by the national savings bank which offered very favourable loans to relatively affluent households.

The impact of the political and economic changes following 1989 was not to trigger gentrification in these neighbourhoods. Those families who found that their income rose after the transformation often moved to family houses or to newly built condominiums. Some poor families also moved away from the estate, often to farms on the outskirts of the city where old houses without amenities and with large gardens are located. At the same time the economic crisis in the late 1990s meant that the demand for housing decreased before it rose again in the early 2000s. However, the structure of demand for the estate has now changed. Students, young couples and lower middle class families moved into the area, replacing more affluent older households.

This picture of the Josavaros estate is very different to the one that applies in Havanna in Budapest. From the outset the Havanna estate had a poor reputation. Its physical design set the tone: its high rise buildings tower above the surrounding areas and its scale and symmetrical layout contrast with the detached and semi-detached family housing surrounding it. The estate was built on the site of what was once called the 'State Estate' built after WWI for the accommodation of low status households, especially refugees. When this was demolished because of health concerns about its conditions, Havanna housed many of the existing households, as well as some from areas undergoing regeneration in the central city. As a consequence there was a concentration of poverty and over-representation of socially underprivileged and gypsy families from the outset.

The significant change in the composition of residents came about as a result of two factors, privatisation and high housing costs. At the time of mass privatisation, from the middle of the 1990s, sitting tenants had the Right-to-Buy their dwellings at a price much below market levels – some 10–15 per cent of market price was an average. Not surprisingly, many households bought their flats for these low prices and sold them on at market rates. This potential gain was a major incentive for households to sell their dwellings on the free market and move on. In this situation the impact of privatisation was very different to that in Josavaros. Havanna had developed the worst reputation of any estate in the city, with high rates of reported crime and huge social problems, poverty and social deprivation. As a result, higher-income households left the estate and there was a considerable fall in the value of property.

Incoming households to the estate bought properties at full market value. They came from the lower middle classes who had sufficient resources to buy at these prices rather than low-income sections of the community who had typically been resident here. An additional motivation for lower-income households to move had been the high heating costs associated with district heating (Erdosi et al., 2003). All of the dwellings on Havanna have district heating. Arrears in relation to housing costs were principally associated with these heating costs and, if they wanted to avoid eviction, many households were forced to sell and buy cheaper homes elsewhere. The consequence of this process was a widening of the social base in a way more compatible with some notions of gentrification. However, there is no evidence of where people who made use of privatisation and sold their flats at market price or were driven out by high heating costs, moved to. It is suggested that they bought houses in other parts of the city or beyond the city boundary where there was inadequate but low priced housing (Tosics, 2005). The Havanna Estate continues to have lower prices than other estates and continues to have a poorer reputation than elsewhere. It has not seen significant regeneration in terms of improvements of the physical infrastructure, maintenance of buildings or other elements, and yet it has seen a change in the social base with an increasing number of middle- and lower-income households moving in.

These two estates in Hungary have much in common, but also some important differences. They have similar origins and designs and have both been affected by political and economic transformation and housing privatisation. However they have different status within different housing markets. Havanna is located in the capital city and, although it carries a stigma, operates in a higher demand housing market. In this context privatisation has set off a different dynamic. It has enabled lower-income households to move away and higher-income households to move in.

If this is defined as gentrification then it is an evolutionary and raw form of gentrification, not one managed and orchestrated by the state. It has involved individual decisions by households both to leave and to move to the estate. To some extent the pattern is counter-intuitive; gentrification has not occurred on the best estates and this is relative to the low status of the estate previously. The process could be regarded as involving displacement: people who have had to move out because of high housing costs, and even those who have chosen to move out because of the opportunities created by privatisation could be seen as having been placed under enormous pressure to move and to change their household financial situation. The people who have moved out have particularly included the lowest income groups and most vulnerable households. In contrast, Josavaros, which intuitively would be more likely to experience gentrification because of its attractiveness compared with other areas, has not experienced the same pattern of change. If anything it has seen a narrowing of the social base more akin to notions of residualisation. The reason for this derives from the market situation and, again, relates to the decisions of numerous individual households, rather than an orchestrated, planned regeneration.

But as a tool for regeneration, the opening of these estates to market processes has failed. In both cases there remain enormous problems related to the buildings, the heating systems, the maintenance and management of estates. There are enormous difficulties in generating funding for effective renovation and renewal of heating systems, or other elements in the structure of buildings. Fragmented ownership underlies these problems and inhibits renovation and renewal. In the long run, this may weaken the market position of these estates and contribute to a narrowing of the social base, as they are seen to be less attractive than new developments. However, the experience of these two estates demonstrates the different kinds of market response to privatisation and to changes in public policy. This is a different pattern of social change in neighbourhoods to that associated with traditional debates about gentrification in cities such as London. It calls into question whether we should see interventions through public policy as necessarily involving gentrification or, indeed, as falling into one type of process.

Implications for market and community

The implications of the previous discussion and the evidence presented above is that we need a more differentiated discussion of regeneration, with more attention given to how the neighbourhood has already changed, and to the characteristics and dynamics of the estate involved, the nature of the regeneration process (including the process of decision making and the extent of demolition and redesign) and to patterns of benefits and loss. There are a number of different types of regeneration that can be identified from the discussion. Our initial analysis leads us to suggest that, far from a dichotomous position of regeneration versus gentrification, the introduction of a mixed-economy approach to renewing large housing estates results in a series of regeneration types. Here we suggest four broad types of regeneration process that are distinct from a no-change situation, or the traditional gentrification associated with nineteenth-century neighbourhoods in cities such as London. These are summarised in Table 10.2 and outlined below, and emphasise the aims and animators of the regeneration process.

Table 10.2   A typology of regeneration affecting large public sector estates

Revanchist Regeneration	Private sector initiated, Supported by the state Designed to displace existing residents Create new exclusive residential areas (e.g. Gated Communities).
Market Regeneration	State co-ordinated Increase private involvement in regeneration Either • unregulated pump-primed intervention (e.g. London Docklands) or • a conscious decision to change ownership of property (e.g. the Right-to-Buy)
Socially-managed Regeneration	Public sector acts as initiator, part funder and regulator Regulation important to ensuring a balance between private/individual gain and collective benefits.
Rhetorical Renewal	Solely public sector initiated and (un)delivered programmes Express aim of arresting decline Often lacks involvement of wider stakeholders At best stabilises the existing situation or at worst manages its decline.

Revanchist Regeneration follows Smith's idea of revanchist gentrification, where projects are initiated by the private sector but supported by the state. It is purposefully designed to displace existing residents in neighbourhoods, both actually and virtually. This takes two forms. The first is associated with wholesale displacement, demolition and rebuilding of neighbourhoods and the creation of new property for occupation and purchase by more affluent individuals; it is a physical demonstration of change designed to bring in new investment. The second is associated with the development of gated communities where displacement may also take a virtual form, highlighted by the exclusion of less affluent households from these exclusive areas.

Market regeneration is, as the name implies, an explicit engagement of the market to bring about change and renewal, where changes in ownership and sources of finance are often fundamental. The process is co-ordinated by the state to increase private involvement in regeneration. The most obvious form in recent years has been where the state facilitates the availability of land and property, but then leaves the market to finance and develop, often favouring large flag-ship schemes such as London Docklands. The attraction of the market into neighbourhoods from where they have previously been excluded may involve areas of derelict land or open space but may also involve some residential areas – but in these cases demolition and redesign is not always evident. The critique of these schemes is well documented and in particular the notion of 'trickle-down' benefits to the 'community' have been questioned. Privatisation through sales to existing residents has been a major mechanism for market regeneration especially in eastern and central Europe.

While private finance and development is a key element of *socially managed regeneration*, under this form, public and not-for-profit organisations are still key players and reflect a concern to achieve wider social and community goals. The public sector plays a role as initiator, part funder and regulator. It is involved in planning and mixed tenure development and the inclusion of affordable housing is a key feature. The regulation of regeneration is important in ensuring a balance is met between private/individual gain and collective benefits. Efforts to capture planning gains through innovative, non-monetary means are an example of how these balances are struck.

The final form of regeneration is what we have termed *rhetorical renewal*. In this approach to regeneration, the public sector dominates the process and private financial or other involvement is limited, if included at all. We term it rhetorical because, while the explicit aim is demonstrate an commitment to arresting decline, it engages strongly neither to harness or utilise market processes for change nor to redesign the estate significantly. Often it is more concerned with stabilising the existing situation or, in some cases, an implicit programme of managing decline. Overall the impact for positive change is minimal and hence rhetorical.

So how do the estates we have studied fit into this typology? We would contend that none of the four estates discussed above – and none of the other estates studied in the RESTATE programme – conform to the revanchist regeneration model as set out by Smith and others. While it is possible to discern some features that conform to either revanchist behaviour, the opening to the market or to gentrifying tendencies, none of them have all of these features. The examples selected in this chapter demonstrate the variety of regeneration processes and the importance of the different contexts that regeneration operates within.

This typology is an improvement on the previous and basic distinction between socially just regeneration on the one hand and revanchist renewal on the other. However, analysing the case studies – and the

RESTATE case studies in general – these four types are not fully reflected in the regeneration of large housing estates. This is not to say that they do not exist in other and wider forms of regeneration, as indicated in the descriptions above. What is clear from the cases presented here is that three elements are important to consider in assessing the role of the market, the extent of gentrification and the charge of revanchism:

- The extent and nature of displacement of existing residents
- The process through which regeneration is delivered, in particular its inclusivity; and
- The extent of the market's role in delivering regeneration and change in the estates.

Key dimensions of differences are summarised in Table 10.3 and outlined more fully below.

Taking the Central Estates first, this is as near as we have in the estates' studies to an example of socially managed regeneration. The programme of intervention and regeneration utilised the market but attempted to insulate the existing population from any adverse impact of market activity. In this case the market has facilitated the reconfiguration and redevelopment of the estate and, furthermore, the development agreement with the private developer has ensured that planning gains have been recycled into tangible infrastructure benefits for the estate. The process has been inclusive throughout. The tenant protests were a signal for change, unlocking the potential of the area for including the market. The planning process leading up to transfer relied on community engagement and planning for real exercises and this has been taken through into the new housing association, which has steered much of the regeneration. Therefore, although the market has been used to deliver regeneration, it has been harnessed to provide inclusive benefits. One stumbling point is that of displacement. The estate has been extensively remodelled involving large scale demolition. This has led to some displacement of households. However, this process too has been managed to ensure that those households who want to return can. In fact the displacement has helped some households realise a better housing offer elsewhere and highlights how displacement is not always negative. Policies in a number of countries involve a significant redesign of neighbourhoods through densification or infill development. Large public sector estates, in many countries, were designed with significant areas of open space or non-residential land uses. In these cases it is possible to build new private-sector housing or

Table 10.3   Regeneration differences

		Central Estates	Les Minguettes	Hungary
Process	Whose Initiative	Residents and then local authority	State	Various actions to increase market exposure
	Consultation	Extensive	Information provided after decisions made	None
	Other Actions	Transfer to HA development agreement to capture planning gain	Crime, education and job creation initiatives co-ordinated through different programmes	Organic as owners improve, sell and move on.
Market Facing	Role of Private Sector	Funding & development partner	None	Market transactions
	Role of the State	Local authority plays key role and national funding	State plays leading role – national programme and funding	Passive facilitator
Displacement	Displacement	Some by choice, some temporary. re-housing locally before returning	Yes – existing tenants cannot afford the rents of new properties	Explicitly none. Implicitly displacement takes place as residents cannot afford housing costs
	Estate Demolition	Extensive	Extensive	None
	New Construction	Yes, both affordable rented housing and new market housing	Yes – social housing	None

mixed-tenure housing without demolishing or changing the properties that are already there. If these new build properties are designed, marketed and priced at levels that mean that different types of household move in then the social composition of the estate changes. In this case there is no displacement, either in the short term or the long term; the gentrification occurs through the addition of new units available to a different segment of the housing market.

The case of Les Minguettes shows an altogether different picture. Here there has been no direct private sector involvement in the regeneration; instead there was an indirect exposure of the estate to the market through the mixed funding of new affordable housing. The result of this process were increases in rents and, in conjunction with the demolition of their previous homes, saw the displacement of a large number of households. The fact that these households were seen by the authorities as the problem for the estate means that such displacement was of benefit for its regeneration. The process lacked inclusivity and openness and the lack of consultation is illustrative of this. We might term this process as a 'reductionist regeneration' which displays signs of revanchism in its displacement and reduction of a problem. However, it cannot be described as gentrification as the incomers to the estate are neither owners nor more affluent. This is further evidence to undermine the claims of Smith and others of revanchist gentrification through state-sponsored regeneration initiatives.

Finally, the Hungarian examples illustrate a form of market regeneration, but one which is neither planned nor pump primed by the state but is reliant on the lottery of the market. In these cases it relied on both the housing market to bring social change and individual property owners and/or condominiums to deliver physical improvements. There was no process per se for the regeneration of the estates and therefore very little to consult around. At the same time, any displacement was the result of households choosing to move from the estates and realise the capital assets that they had gained through the discounted sale under the Right-to-Buy. This created a significant level of uncertainty about the scale and direction of change which may or may not occur on the estates and, as illustrated above, resulted in negative as well as positive change. In the Hungarian estates the level of regeneration at the moment is minimal. This is not unique to Central and Eastern Europe. Other examples from the RESTATE project in Spain (Pareja Eastaway et al., 2003) and Italy (Mezzetti et al., 2004) provide evidence on mass housing estates that have been predominantly owner occupied for a long period of time. They provide a useful history of how 'the market' has both succeeded and failed mass housing estates over time and, importantly, how there has been a need for a renewed role for the state to deliver their recent regeneration. Examples from Central Europe, for example in Warsaw (see Weclawowicz et al., 2003) have seen more regeneration as the result of the sale of vacant land and open space on the estates, as shown above, illustrating the growing influence of the market on these estates.

Different processes of gentrification are associated with different roles adopted by the state and with different purposes or policy objectives. There are differences between actions to achieve change within existing residential areas through demolition and regeneration or densification, and actions to create new residential development in areas that were not previously residential. In these cases there are new opportunities created for middle- and higher-income households in areas that previously were not residential. These new opportunities arise without any displacement of the existing population by building on land available within the area. Where the development involves demolition of existing housing, however, the extent of displacement does not equate with the numbers of dwellings demolished, but is affected by the numbers of empty properties, the preferences of residents (some of whom may escape entrapment rather than be displaced) and the rebuilding and rehousing policies adopted.

While it is crucially important to provide insights into revanchist regeneration, it is also valuable to articulate a process and pattern that promises an alternative both to this and to what, in some cases, would be a protected future as a poverty neighbourhood in decline. Within the RESTATE research there are examples of estates that were built in the same period but have been largely bypassed by regeneration. These areas may have lost reputation and status since they were built and have been subject to more token management and other initiatives. It is important to recognise that these examples of rhetorical renewal do not generally present positive alternatives to some areas affected by more active regeneration. So for example in Birmingham, the Hodge Hill estate, once more attractive than the Central Estates, has not experienced regeneration and bears some adverse comparison as a result. Hodge Hill is part of the planned middle ring development of the city of Birmingham and was built in the 1960s. Today it forms an area of mixed council development with an aging population located in a part of the city affected by the decline in traditional manufacturing employment. While the more desirable parts of the estate have been purchased under the Right-to–Buy, it has been affected by wider processes of residualisation and has largely been by-passed by regeneration initiatives. In practice there has been no demolition and no new build within Hodge Hill and logically little or no gentrification but our research results show this estate as having the highest levels of dissatisfaction (Hall et al., 2005; Musterd and van Kempen, 2005). The fit between this and some form of revanchism appears to us strong and. although it is less about cleansing an area for the market. it is about abandoning place in favour of more productive investment opportunities.

Conclusions

The regeneration of large post-war estates is an important element in the development of cities and emerges both from global and more local pressures. This chapter has argued that the dismissal of regeneration as eroding past political and economic gains has been developed without robust evidence from European cities, and has taken too little account of the patterns of change in estates that have lost value and status or already been absorbed into the market. In our research we found no examples of what could be called revanchist regeneration in the sense espoused by Smith and others. Although some regeneration may have implicit aims of cleansing estates and reutilising space (see market gentrification below), we would conclude that they are not overtly revanchist and that there are mechanisms to mitigate against significant negative impacts on the existing population. The debate has not been informed by robust examples and refers to estates as exemplars of past victories on behalf of the working class. Such stereotypes provide a platform for the launch of critical accounts of regeneration because they allow any change to be presented as eroding working-class gains. However, where social, economic and housing market changes, residualisation and privatisation have already changed estates, we need to revise the discourse. In estates where this applies, defending the status quo and resisting regeneration is not the same as defending what these estates represented when they were first built. They have already been tarnished and no longer represent advantageous situations for those living there. This perspective suggests that we should not be categorical about regeneration of these estates. We can not assume that regeneration necessarily represents revanchist gentrification and there is a need to examine the context, nature, process and outcomes of regeneration.

The debate about whose regeneration needs to take on board changes that have and are occurring in these estates without regeneration. Political gains have been eroded and in some cases gentrification is occurring in any case – through greater market exposure and privatisation rather than regeneration. Against this background regeneration initiatives influenced by thinking about mixed tenure and mixed communities are likely to contribute to gentrification. However the revanchist image is likely to overstate the process and outcome. The process may empower some within local communities; new and refurbished housing available to low-income households is a material gain for others; and the extent and duration of displacement is not consistent with the revanchist image. Moreover it may be argued that some of the housing opportunities created through regeneration for middle income groups may facilitate the reoccupation of neighbourhoods by the affluent working class or new professional classes and others who used to live on council estates. Is this reversing the oppressive action that has turned what were once aspirational, high demand areas into poverty neighbourhoods?

In considering 'whose regeneration?' it is not sufficient to demonstrate that middle class households have benefited. We need also to assess whether there are gains made by lower-income households and the balance between gains made by different groups. Indeed the sensible way forward would be to capture the debate about urban renaissance and regeneration by articulating a process of regeneration that would secure real gains for working-class and lower-income households, and to make this the core issue rather than gentrification or the resistance to any regeneration in neighbourhoods that are difficult to live in. The Hodge Hill (inaction?) or Les Minguettes (oppressive action?) examples are not presented as situations to be defended, although they generate the least gentrification. Instead we would draw upon the experience of other estates to suggest what kinds of patterns of change can be achieved and aimed at that would meet the demands of interests of different groups, and which are compatible with the financial realities associated with these neighbourhoods. Rather than residents being damned if they do and damned if they do not, we suggest that research should address processes and outcomes more directly and seek to identify the circumstances and contingencies that generate different patterns of benefit.

References

Atkinson, R. (2000) Measuring Gentrification and Displacement in Greater London. *Urban Studies*, 37, pp. 149–65.
Atkinson, R. (2002) Does Gentrification Help or Harm Urban Neighbourhoods? An Assessment of the Evidence-Base in the Context of the New Urban Agenda. CNR Paper no. 5. Bristol: ESRC Centre for Neighbourhood Research.

Atkinson, R. (2003) Introduction: Misunderstood Saviour or Vengeful Wrecker? The Many Meanings and Problems of Gentrification. *Urban Studies*, 40, pp. 2343–50.

Belmessous, F. and Chignier-Riboulon, F. (2006) From the Minguettes to the Urban Riots of 2005: Building the Identity Issue. Unpublished Research Paper.

Belmessous, F., Chemin, C., Commerçon, N., Trigueiro, M. and Zepf, M. (2004) *Large Housing Estates in France: Policies and Practices, Report 3a*. Utrecht: Faculty of Geosciences, Utrecht University.

Bourne, L. S. (1993) The Myth and Reality of Gentrification: A Commentary on Emerging Urban Forms. *Urban Studies*, 30 (1), pp. 183–9.

Cameron, S. (2003) Gentrification, Housing Redifferentiation and Urban Regeneration: 'Going for Growth' in Newcastle Upon Tyne. *Urban Studies*, 40, pp. 2367–82.

Chignier-Riboulon, F. (1999) *L'intégration des Franco-Maghrébins*, Paris: L'Harmattan.

Chignier–Riboulon, F., Commerçon, N., Trigueiro, M. and Zepf, M. (2003) *Large Housing Estates in France: Overview of Developments and Problems in Lyon, Report 2a*. Utrecht: Faculty of Geosciences, Utrecht University.

Dekker, K. and Van Kempen, R. (2005) Large Housing Estates in Europe: A Contemporary Overview. In R. Van Kempen, K. Dekker, S. Hall and I. Tosics (Eds) *Restructuring Large Housing Estates in Europe*. Bristol: Policy Press

Erdősi, S., Gerőházi, E., Teller, N. and Tosics, I. (2003) *Large Housing Estates in Hungary: Overview of Developments and Problems in Budapest, Report 2c*. Utrecht: Faculty of Geosciences, Utrecht University.

Forrest, R. and Murie, A. (1995) From Privatisation to Commodification: Tenure Conversion and New Zones of Transition in the City. *International Journal of Urban And Regional Research*, 19 (3), pp. 407–22.

Galster, G., Santiago, A., Tatian, P., Pettit, K. and Smith, R. (2003) *Why Not in My Back Yard? Neighborhood Impacts of Assisted Housing*. New Brunswick: Center for Urban Policy Research Press.

Galster, G. (2007a) Neighbourhood Social Mix as a Goal of Housing Policy: A Theoretical Analysis. *European Journal of Housing Policy*, 7 (1), pp. 19–43.

Galster, G. (2007b) Should Policy Makers Strive for Neighbourhood Social Mix? An Analysis of the Western European Evidence Base. *Housing Studies*, 22 (4), pp. 523–45.

Glass R. (1964) Introduction to London: Aspects of Change (London: Centre For Urban Studies); reprinted in: R. Glass (1989) *Clichés of Urban Doom*, pp 132–58. Oxford: Blackwell.

Hall, S., Murie, A., Rowlands, R. and Sankey, S. (2005) *Large Housing Estates in London and Birmingham, United Kingdom: Opinions of Residents on Recent Developments, Report 4j*. Utrecht: Faculty of Geosciences, Utrecht University.

Hall, S., Murie, A. and Knorr-Siedow, T. (2005) Large Housing Estates in Their Historical Context. In: R. Van Kempen, K. Dekker, S. Hall and I. Tosics (Eds) *Restructuring Large Housing Estates in Europe*. Bristol: Policy Press.

Hamnett, C. (1991) The Blind Men and the Elephant: The Explanation of Gentrification. *Transactions of the Institute of British Geographers*, 16, pp. 259–79.

Harloe, M. (1995) *The People's Home*. Oxford: Blackwell.

Jones, C. and Murie, A. (2006) *The Right to Buy*. Oxford: Blackwell.

Kleinhans, R. (2003) Displaced but Still Moving upwards in the Housing Career? Implications of Forced Residential Relocation in the Netherlands. *Housing Studies*, 18(4), pp. 473–99.

Lambert, C. and Boddy, M. (2002) Transforming the City: Post–Recession Gentrification and Re–Urbanisation. CNR Paper no. 6. Bristol: ESRC Centre for Neighbourhood Research.

Lees, L. (2000) A Reappraisal of Gentrification: Towards a 'Geography of Gentrification'. *Progress In Human Geography*, 24 (3), pp. 389–408.

Mezzetti, P., Mugnano, S. and Zajczyk, F. (2003) *Large Housing Estates in Italy. Overview of Developments and Problems in Milan, RESTATE Report 2d*. Utrecht: Faculty of Geosciences, Utrecht University.

Murie, A., van Kempen, R. and Knorr-Siedow, T. (2003) *Large Housing Estates in Europe: General Developments and Theoretical Backgrounds*. Utrecht: Faculty of Geosciences, Utrecht University.

Musterd, S. and Ostendorf, W. (2005) On Physical Determinism and Displacement Effects. In: R. van Kempen, K. Dekker, S. Hall and I. Tosics (Eds) *Restructuring Large Housing Estates in European Cities*, pp. 149–68. Bristol: The Policy Press.

Musterd, S. and van Kempen, R. (2005) *Large-Scale Housing Estates in European Cities: Opinions of Residents on Recent Developments, RESTATE Report 4k*. Utrecht: Faculty of Geosciences, Utrecht University.

Pareja Eastaway, M., Tapada Berteli, T., Van Boxmeer, B. and Garcia Ferrando, L. (2003) *Large Housing Estates in Spain. Overview of Developments and Problems in Madrid and Barcelona, RESTATE Report 2h*. Utrecht: Faculty of Geosciences, Utrecht University.

Popkin, S., Katz, B., Cunnigham, M., Brown, K., Gustafson, J. and Turner, M. (2006) *A Decade of HOPE VI Research Findings and Policy Challenges*. Washington: Urban Institute (http://www.urban.org/uploadedpdf/411002_HOPEVI.pdf accessed on13 June 2008)

Slater, T., Curran, W. and Lees, L. (2004) Gentrification Research: New Directions and Critical Scholarship. *Environment and Planning*, A 36 (7), pp. 1141–50.

Smith, N. (1996) *The New Urban Frontier: Gentrification and the Revanchist City*. London and New York: Routledge.

Smith, N. and Williams, P. (Eds) (1986). *Gentrification of the City*. Boston: Allen and Unwin.

Szemző, H. and Tosics, I. (2004) *Large Housing Estates in Hugary: Policies and Practices, Report 3c*. Utrecht: Faculty of Geosciences, Utrecht University.

Tosics, I. (2005) Large Housing Estates in the West and in the East: What Can We Learn? Keynote presentation at RESTATE conference, Ljubljana, 21 May 2005.

Uitermark, J., Duyvendak, J. W. and Kleinhans, R. (2007) Gentrification as a Governmental Strategy: Social Control and Social Cohesion in Hoogvliet, Rotterdam. *Environment and Planning*, A39 (1), pp. 125–41.

Urban Task Force (1999) *Towards an Urban Renaissance: Final Report of the Urban Task Force*. London: E and FN Spon.

Weclawowicz, G., Kozlowski, S. and Bajek, R. (2003) *Large Housing Estates in Poland. Overview of Developments and Problems in Warsaw, RESTATE Report 2f*. Utrecht: Faculty of Geosciences, Utrecht University.

11

Deepening Crisis or Homes for the Future? Some Reflections and Implications for Policies in Large Housing Estates

Ronald van Kempen, Sako Musterd and Rob Rowlands

Introduction

Although research has been carried out looking at large post-WWII housing estates since the 1970s, the zenith of activity has been since the second half of the 1990s. At least four reasons can be given for this attention. First, many of these areas have increasingly become the most unattractive places in cities. Second, up until this point, research in these areas has been limited and often narrowly focussed and because much of the research activities has focused on the older parts in the cities. Third, post-WWII high-rise housing has increasingly been seen as a cause of problems in many post-war housing areas, seen most acutely in recent years in the French *banlieues*. Fourth, as the impact of the problems of these areas became more acute and apparent, relatively large sums of both national and European research money became available to study these areas. The rise of the post-WWII as a topic for more and better research has been linked to the need to develop improved policies for addressing the decline and improvement of these areas.

Earlier work focused on post-WWII housing estates, notably that by Niels Prak and Hugo Priemus (1984; 1985) and Anne Power (1993; 1997), can now be seen as pioneering in focusing the initial lens on these estates. These have been followed by numerous books (see, e.g., recent publications such as Turkington et al., 2004, on high-rise estates; and Van Kempen et al., 2005, on the restructuring of large post-WWII housing estates) and an increasingly numerous set of local, national and European research reports including those of the RESTATE project (Restructuring Large Housing Estates in Europe), in which the editors of this book were also involved.

In this book we have attempted to issue a warning against over simplifying the problems of large housing estates, their causes and their prospective solutions. In particular we highlighted the notion of differentiation and the importance of its recognition when researching these areas. In many of the articles, books and reports about large post-WWII housing estates a negative attitude prevails and with this book we wanted to make clear that these are not telling the whole story. The remainder of this conclusion chapter will highlight this differentiated view. The chapters in this book have focused on a number of different issues, such as resident satisfaction, the role of public space, social cohesion, spatial segregation, policy interventions, local participation and urban governance. We will not summarise here all the conclusions of all chapters. We want to focus on a few but, at the same time in our opinion, rather crucial issues that came to the fore in this book. Together these issues provide some clues for the future development of large housing estates.

Satisfaction and dissatisfaction in large housing estates

Although to some it may seem an obvious finding, it is important to underline that not everybody is dissatisfied living in a large post-WWII housing estate. Although a significant number of people do express negative attitudes, many people in many different types of household are satisfied or even very satisfied with their home, their neighbourhood or both. Many of these households have lived in such a satisfactory state for years or even decades. Definitely not everybody wants to move as soon as possible. From the research on resident satisfaction in large housing estates (see Chapters 3 and 4) our idea of differentiation is clearly supported. Differences between housing estates do exist, but differences between household types seem to be as important. This means that policies aimed at improving housing estates should not only focus on the characteristics of the estates, but also on the households living there.

Although research into resident satisfaction is not very new, it is an important topic. Creating satisfied residents can be a main goal of urban policy. Moreover, a large number of dissatisfied residents on an estate can be detrimental for the development of an estate. They can set in motion a negative spiral of decline: they might show less responsibility for the environment, resulting in more dirt on the streets, more graffiti, less social control, more criminal activities, more feelings of insecurity. For the atmosphere in an estate such a development can have very negative effects. It can also lead to out-migration of those who can afford to move elsewhere, leaving dwellings behind that are often allocated to households who cannot afford a home in another part of the city or urban region.

Satisfaction thus seems to be a key topic and probably it should be a key topic in urban policies. Without satisfied residents the future of large housing estates does not look very bright. A practical question then becomes: how to create satisfied residents? In the sections below we will come back to this question.

Physical aspects of large housing estates

In Chapter 2 it was stated that, on first sight, many post-WWII large housing estates look the same (see also Turkington et al., 2004). Indeed, because they were almost all built according to the same philosophy (agreed upon during several International Congress of Modern Architecture (CIAM) conferences) and many of them were built in the same period, they do look similar in many respects. The earlier estates generally comprise open, low-rise apartment blocks, often with some single-family housing and definitely also a lot of green open space. The later estates (from about the second half of the 1960s) are also characterised by green open spaces, but in addition to that, in many cases functions are separated and high-rise blocks have entered the scene. The green spaces are still seen as a major asset of the estates by many inhabitants (as shown in Chapter 6).

Some previous explanations of problems have focussed on the importance of the physical character of an estate for the quality of life of the residents of that estate. A number of them focused on the negative characteristics of the estates, such as: the physical monotony of the place and, on a smaller scale, the existence of unsafe places (see Newman, 1972). We do not want to completely discount the importance of the physical aspects of these estates and clearly there are some estates in European cities where poor design, layout and structure mean that they would be better off demolished and remodelled. However, in many cases the physical issues are not the primary factor in determining residents' quality of life nor the main driver of their satisfaction or dissatisfaction.

This means that radical strategies involving restructuring and large-scale demolition are not always necessary to improve the liveability of large housing estates. While they may form part of the solution, the imperative to implement such significant and capital intensive changes may lie elsewhere in other objectives. We will return to this issues below.

The importance of the dwelling

Dwelling satisfaction seems to be crucial for the overall satisfaction of residents of large housing estates. If they are not satisfied with the dwelling, there is a big chance that they are not satisfied at all. Good housing thus seems to be a *sine qua non* for neighbourhood satisfaction. This finding of Chapter 4 underlines the importance for individuals of private living space over neighbourhood characteristics. On the other hand, satisfaction with the dwelling is not a sufficient condition: not everyone who is satisfied with his or her dwelling is satisfied with other aspects of living in a large housing estate. Efforts to increase liveability in a neighbourhood should pay attention to this. It basically means that investments in the neighbourhood only seem to work when there is a large degree of satisfaction with the dwelling. Investments in districts in which the degree of satisfaction with the dwelling is low might be considered an ineffective use of resources.

Yet this does not mean that large-scale demolition of dwellings is the solution. Dissatisfied inhabitants are in many cases not concentrated in specific blocks of houses. Moreover, dissatisfaction with the dwelling is in many cases not related to the quality of the dwelling itself, but often to a combination of dwelling and household circumstances. The dwelling may, for example, be too small for the number of household members, located too far from work or some crucial services, or people live in a rented dwelling, while they would like to move to an owner-occupied dwelling, or they want to move from a flat to a single-family house. In other words, dissatisfaction is definitely not always related to the physical characteristics of a dwelling and more often related to the housing career aspects of households.

Social aspects in large housing estates

The growing consensus that social relations and community life positively affect resident satisfaction is highlighted in Chapter 4. Van Kempen and Musterd (1991) have previously indicated that identical blocks of flats in similar locations performed very differently due to other residential compositions. Their explanation was that the social functioning of a neighbourhood seems to depend largely on the residents, and thus on social mechanisms, and not on design and management.

In the past few years, numerous papers have been written on the aspect of social cohesion, also in post-WWII large housing estates. Social cohesion is a difficult concept. In its most general meaning it refers to a kind of glue holding society together (Dekker, 2006). In a lot of research projects, the clear operationalisation by Kearns and Forrest has been employed. They distinguish five domains of social cohesion: common values and a civic culture; social order and social control; social solidarity and reduction in wealth disparities; social networks and social capital; and place attachment and identity (Kearns and Forrest, 2000). In a number of cases, researchers have reduced these dimensions to only three: common values, social networks and neighbourhood attachment (see also Chapter 7). This selection has been carried out, because these dimensions especially can be influenced on the neighbourhood level.

There are some advantages to social cohesion. First and foremost, people might like to live in socially cohesive communities, basically because it is convenient to live among others with more or less the same values and norms, because it is nice to have social contacts in the neighbourhood, and it gives a good feeling to be attached to the neighbourhood. Next to that, social cohesion is found to be a strong determinant of neighbourhood confidence (Chapter 2). It also plays a key role in explaining mobility decisions: the more attachment to the neighbourhood and the more social contact, the less mobile the population. And this also works the other way around: when there is less mobility, there is a bigger chance for a more cohesive neighbourhood. More social cohesion may thus be related to positive evaluations of the neighbourhood and may prevent neighbourhoods from social decline.

Striving for more social cohesion in large housing estates can be accompanied by some question marks, however. First it should be recognised that not everybody living in those estates will feel the need for more cohesion. Some people just want to be left alone and this is probably quite a normal attitude for at least part of the urban population. This means that striving for a situation in which all people have exactly the same values and norms, in which every inhabitant of an estate has contacts with every other inhabitant, and in which all people feel positively attached to the same degree to the neighbourhood is impossible. This seems to be trivial but in fact it is a warning to those policymakers who uncritically write down in their memorandums that social cohesion should be a main goal of urban policy.

Secondly, the possibility for social cohesion may vary between groups. If an estate comprises mainly of households who have a spatially diversified activity pattern and use their dwelling only as a place to sleep, creating social cohesion is an impossible task. At least the estate should have a certain mass of people who are willing to do something with each other. In Chapter 7 it was concluded that ethnic minorities had a higher level of social cohesion within the neighbourhood than native inhabitants. This does not always have to be the case, but it at least indicates that social cohesion differs between groups.

The presence of socially cohesive groups can also have its disadvantages. When ethnic minorities show a large degree of social cohesion and when they live in the estate in large and even increasing numbers, the original – native – inhabitants may feel threatened or jealous. This may then lead to negative attitudes or even racism. In the Dutch estates it was indeed discovered that ethnic minorities feel comfortable with the presence of people of their own minority ethnic group, whereas the native Dutch found these concentrations too high and complain about the large proportion of ethnic minorities in their neighbourhood (Chapter 7).

Thirdly, social cohesion is not and should not always be regarded as a positive thing. A large body of literature focuses on the different kinds of bonding people can have. The most basic distinction is between the so-called bonding and bridging ties (Granovetter, 1973; Cochran, 1990). *Bonding ties* refer to strong ties between people that deliver not much new information. *Bridging ties* are about relations that produce information on the wider world, such as the availability of jobs (Granovetter, 1973). Especially for those on lower incomes, the neighbourhood functions more often as a place for bonding ties than as a source for bridging ties (Burns et al., 2001). In other words: the neighbourhood offers contacts with people who are about the same. The question then becomes whether contacts between those equals are enough for creating sufficient competence to participate in the larger society. The clearest example of areas in which bridging ties are almost totally absent and bonding ties are prevalent can be found in the slightly older literature on ghettos (see, e.g., Wilson, 1987), and we also might refer to the work on cultures of poverty (Lewis, 1966). However, Wacquant (2008) recently noticed that the current black ghetto has actually become a disorganised place.

Towards socially mixed housing estates?

A recurrent issue for an increasing number of large post-WWII housing estates is the discussion about the social mix (see, e.g., Musterd, 2008; Van Kempen, 2008). Especially in Western European cities this discussion is quite prominent on the urban policy agenda (Friedrichs et al., 2005; Musterd and Andersson, 2005). In countries such as the Netherlands, and partly in France and the UK, the idea is to demolish social rented dwellings and replace them with more expensive rented and mainly owner-occupied dwellings. In our opinion there are at least five arguments underlying the desire of policymakers to create mixed districts (see also Van Kempen, 2008). They are:

- *Providing opportunities for a housing career in the district.* Some urban districts are highly homogeneous with respect to their housing stock, which makes a housing career within the neighbourhood impossible. When households want to improve their housing situation, they have to move to another district.
- *More social contacts and social cohesion.* Mixed districts are said to improve contacts between different groups of people; the formation of social networks becomes possible.
- *Increasing social capital.* The concept of social capital refers to the means that persons or households have as a consequence of social networks and to reciprocity, norms, and trust (Kleinhans et al., 2007). Mixed districts should lead to more social capital because there are simply more opportunities for contacts between different kinds of people and, in particular, to bridging capital (see above). More middle class households would also result in a stronger organising capacity of the district involved.
- *Providing role models.* Even without having real contact with each other, mixed districts can be advantageous. This is because they can provide positive role models. Despite the fact that in these times many role models are probably found on television and the internet, it is still possible that they can be found in the neighbourhood or district.
- *A reduction of the stigma of an area.* An area's stigma is often related to the population composition. Authorities often think that they can remove the negative stigma by changing the population composition.

Mixed districts have further possible advantages, but they are not often used as motivations for creating such districts. These advantages include: better services, especially when new inhabitants have higher incomes (Arthurson, 2002), although we should also consider that more affluent people imply more expensive services as well – this may be seen as a negative side-effect. There may also be positive effects from new developments in one area on other areas: more stability, with less mobility of households (Tunstall, 2003), and more social mobility (Andersson et al., 2007; Galster et al., 2008; Musterd et al., 2008). A final argument for creating mixed districts is the avoidance of concentrations of low-income households because they foster problems, such as high crime levels, vandalism, feelings of insecurity, and so forth. De-concentration then leads to the idea of spreading the burden of problems over a large number of districts (Van Kempen, 2008).

The problem with the arguments mentioned above is that the relationship with mixed housing is not always sufficiently underpinned and that positive and negative effects should be considered simultaneously. Mixing almost always has negative impact on local social interaction. Social contacts between existing and new residents, between old and young inhabitants, between rich and poor, between tenants and owner-occupiers is almost always much more limited than between people belonging to the same category (see, e.g., Jupp, 1999; Hiscock, 2001; Van Beckhoven and Van Kempen, 2003; Arthurson, 2007). Also in the US it has been found that there is almost no interaction between different income groups in mixed neighbourhoods (see, e.g., Rosenbaum et al., 1998; Popkin et al., 2002; De Souza Briggs, 2005). So this means that a mixing policy that aims at increasing social cohesion and social capital runs a big risk of failure. However, a reduction of social cohesion and social capital may be taken for granted if more social mobility can be realised through a mix policy (Galster et al., 2008). More research on the relationship between residential mix and social mobility is however needed. On the other hand, we should not neglect recent research outcomes in which clear negative effects of peer group role models could be shown (Pinkster, 2007).

Yet, in some cases problems might diminish when households are displaced to other areas. Indeed, crime levels and feelings of insecurity may go down in an area in which some of the older, low-income households have been forced to leave and where other types of households have entered. But this is only a partial solution. A so-called waterbed effect might have been created: problems (such as crime) diminish in one area, but emerge in other areas (see, e.g., Van Kempen et al., 2008). Displacing problems is definitely not the same as solving problems. However, here too the sum of effects (including the waterbed effects) may be regarded as having a positive sum outcome because of non-linearities in the relationship between problem concentrations and effects on individuals.

The policy conclusion of this more or less theoretical exercise must be that policymakers should be cautious with their expectations of positive outcomes of policies towards socially mixed neighbourhoods. Creating mixed districts is a very expensive policy and it remains to be seen what the exact results are.

Participation

Participation is not only a way to ensure that residents have a say in the (regeneration) plans for their neighbourhood, but it may also strengthen the social cohesion in the neighbourhood (Dekker, 2006), which in its turn engenders more stability. The problematic issue of involving participation by all relevant groups in an area should however not be overlooked. Getting sufficiently representative participation seems to be the most problematic issue of resident participation in the whole of Europe. As has been set out in this book, selective participation of local residents implies legitimacy problems and may even be regarded undemocratic. On top of that some restructuring plans in specific areas should not just be influenced by local residents as participants, but should also address potential newcomers. This obviously is not an easy thing to realise.

Explaining the changing positions of large housing estates

A lot of theories and models have been formulated that explain or can be used to explain the development and decline of large post-WWII housing estates (see Chapter 2). We argue that it is not sufficient to look only at physical issues. We also argue that it would not be sufficient to focus only on better or new management as a solution for declining estates. Even so we argue that only looking at external drivers of decline (such as globalisation, changing labour markets, migration) is not enough.

When explaining the development of an estate, there should at least be attention paid to the following aspects and their inter-relations:

- The physical situation of the dwellings on an estate
- The (semi) public space in and around the estate
- The changing supply of housing in an urban or regional housing market, for example as a consequence of the creation of new districts
- The (changing) preferences of households in an urban or regional housing market
- The pressure on the housing markets, for example as a consequence of changing patterns of immigration and out-migration
- The role of government, exemplified in official memorandums, allocation rules, subsidies
- The decisions of gatekeepers, such as directors of housing associations, aldermen, building companies, as well as the influence on decisions by local representatives and inhabitants

- The changing economy, resulting in changing income divisions and changing possibilities of households on the housing markets
- And the changing social composition of the estate

This list can probably be extended and has to be seen as highly correlated as well. Thus we argue that physical, social, managerial and housing market issues should be taken into account simultaneously. Moreover, the roles of various stakeholders should be considered, because interests may not be the same to all of them.

The new social configuration of many of the post-WWII housing estates (more low-income households, some with many non-western minorities) induced many other inhabitants to leave. As a consequence, the estates became even better known as housing areas for the poor. When such a concentration goes hand in hand with a declining number of services, growing dissatisfaction with the neighbourhood and with the dwelling, racism, growing unemployment, declining physical quality of the housing stock, increasing numbers of drug addicts and drug dealers, more graffiti and dirt on the streets, vacancies and broken windows, then we truly have problematic urban areas. Fortunately we do not have many of such extremely deprived post-WWII areas in European cities.

Deepening crisis or homes for the future?

A lot of post-WWII large housing estates in European cities can be seen as sustainable. They do not show any problems or only minor ones. They are inhabited by people who are satisfied with their dwellings and with the surroundings of their dwellings, their block, their street, their neighbourhood, their district. They report that services are sufficient, that they get along very well with at least a number of other residents of the neighbourhoods, they do not feel unsafe on the streets and in their house, and they see the future for the estate positively. Despite the large and still growing literature on negative developments of the post-WWII housing estates we should not forget that many of these areas function well. In these areas there is no crisis and there is a future.

But definitely some estates are in need of improvement. These estates often show an intricate combination of physical, social, managerial and economic problems and face serious competition problems in their respective housing markets. We have already indicated that a radical programme of demolition and repositioning might have some advantages (better quality dwellings and environment), but that often such measures are used for totally different goals, such as creating more socio-economic diversity and more social cohesion.

A large number of post-WWII housing estates in Europe have undergone a fairly radical transformation process. They have moved down in the urban hierarchy. From very attractive areas for a lot of different household types, they have become areas that solely attract those who cannot afford to live elsewhere. They have changed from areas with quite a stable population to areas with a highly mobile population. This, however, is not necessarily a bad thing. Most estates can still have a very relevant function in the wider housing market and many households may experience living in the estates as a reasonably good – perhaps temporary – step in their housing careers. Some will be satisfied and stay there for a longer period of time; others may be satisfied but still search for another place for other reasons; others may be unsatisfied and leave the areas; and a few may be trapped (see Musterd and Van Kempen, 2007).

What does seem to be important is that we should, from time to time, think back to the time when there was no social housing, when private owners created unacceptable conditions where people had to live in. Social housing was 'invented' to get rid of these situations and in most places with success. This in itself implies that we should be reluctant to blame the tenure or the housing type.

However, what is true, is the fact that many housing estates were constructed in similar types of relatively affordable housing, and this resulted in similarly large concentrations of households with a relatively weak social position. This happened more rapidly in contexts where the volume of social housing was reduced over time. The remaining, smaller share of social housing was intended to house those who were most in need. But if this is done in big concentrations, then these areas, and with them the social housing, start to become seen and stigmatised as 'problematic'. In contexts in which social housing is still amply available, the residualisation of the social housing stock and the estates involved will be much less extreme, so it might help to maintain a relatively large social housing stock. However, over a longer period of time the larger stock may also become sorted towards weaker social households (as we see in Sweden, the Netherlands and France). This actually implies that, in these countries, society is so affluent that it can afford good housing for all, but that the small differences will, in the end, become visible in segregated patterns.

A possible response to this type of sorting and concentration of the relatively poor, may be to develop much smaller areas with social housing, embedded in other types of areas that are slightly better positioned in terms of a housing hierarchy. New housing projects, therefore, should refrain from the classic large-scale programmes, but be characterised by incremental policies instead. The smaller concentrations of social housing will result in smaller concentrations of socially weaker households and if the neighbourhood effect exists, which we tend to believe, these effects will be smaller due to the smaller size of concentrations, since this implies that plenty of other role models, peer groups, and success stories would be nearby. At the same time, the available social housing may fulfil its task: to offer good housing for those who cannot afford to spend more on housing. This will shed new light on the function of post-WWII large housing estates.

References

Andersson, R., Musterd, S., Galster, G. and Kauppinen, T. (2007) What Mix Matters? Exploring the Relationships between Individual's Incomes and Different Measures of their Neighbourhood Context. *Housing Studies*, 22 (5), pp. 637–60.

Arthurson, K. (2002) Creating Inclusive Communities through Balancing Social Mix: A Critical Relationship or Tenuous Link? *Urban Policy and Research*, 20 (3), pp. 1–29.

Arthurson, K. (2007) Social Mix and Social Interaction: Do Residents Living in Different Housing Tenures Mix? Paper for the Conference of the European Network for Housing Research, Rotterdam, 25–28 June 2007.

Briggs, X. De Souza (2005) *Who Bridges and How? Race, Friendships, and Segregation in American Communities*. Cambridge (MA): MIT.

Burns, D., Forrest, R., Flint, J. and Kearns, A. (2001) *Empowering Communities: The Impact of Registered Social Landlords on Social Capital*. Edinburgh: Scottish Homes.

Cochran, M. (1990) *Extending Families: The Social Networks of Parents and Their Children*. London: Cambridge University Press.

Dekker (2006) *Governance as Glue: Urban Governance and Social Cohesion in Post-WWII Neighbourhoods in the Netherlands*. Utrecht: Faculty of Geosciences, Utrecht University.

Friedrichs, J., Galster, G. and Musterd, M. (Eds) (2005) *Life in Poverty Neighbourhoods: European and American Perspectives*. London, New York: Routledge.

Galster, G., Kauppinen, T., Musterd, S. and Andersson, R. (2008) Does Neighborhood Income Mix Affect Earnings of Adults? A New Approach Using Evidence from Sweden. *Journal of Urban Economics*, 63, pp. 858–70.

Granovetter, M. S. (1973) The Strength of Weak Ties. *American Journal of Sociology*, 78 (6), pp. 1360–80.

Hiscock, R. (2001) Are Mixed Tenure Estates Likely to Enhance the Social Capital of the Residents? Paper for the HAS-conference, Cardiff, 3–4 September 2001.

Jupp, B. (1999) *Living Together: Community Life on Mixed Housing Estates*. London: Demos.

Kearns, A. and Forrest, R. (2000) Social Cohesion and Multilevel Urban Governance. *Urban Studies*, 37 (5–6), pp. 995–1017.

Kleinhans, R., Priemus, H. and Engbersen, G. (2007) Understanding Social Capital in Recently Restructured Urban Neighbourhoods: Two Case Studies in Rotterdam. *Urban Studies*, 44 (5–6), pp. 1069–91.

Lewis, O. (1966) The Culture of Poverty. In: R. T. LeGates and F. Stout (Eds) (1996), *The City Reader*, pp. 217–24. London and New York: Routledge.

Musterd, S. and Van Kempen, R. (2007) Trapped or on the Springboard? Housing Careers in Large Housing Estates in European Cities. *Journal of Urban Affairs*, 29 (3), pp. 311–29.

Musterd, S. (2008) Residents Views on Social Mix: Social Mix, Social Networks and Stigmatisation in Post-War Housing Estates. *Urban Studies*, 45 (4), pp. 897–915.

Musterd, S. and Andersson, R. (2005) Housing Mix, Social Mix and Social Opportunities. *Urban Affairs Review*, 40 (6), pp. 761–90.

Musterd, S. and Van Kempen, R. (2005) *Large-Scale Housing Estates in European Cities. Opinions of Residents on Recent Developments.* Utrecht: Faculty of Geosciences, Utrecht University.

Musterd, S., Andersson, R., Galster, G. and Kauppinen, T. (2008) Are Immigrants' Earnings Influenced by the Characteristics of Their Neighbours? *Environment and Planning A*, 40, pp. 785–805.

Newman, O. (1972) *Defensible Space. Crime Prevention through Urban Design.* New York: Macmillan.

Pinkster, F. M. (2007) Localized Social Networks, Socialization and Social Mobility in a Low Income Neighborhood in the Netherlands. *Urban Studies*, 44 (13), pp. 2587–604.

Popkin, S., Harris, J. and Cunningham, M. (2002) *Families in Transition: A Qualitative Analysis of the MTO Experience, Final Report.* Washington DC: US Department of Housing and Urban Development.

Power, A. (1993) *Hovels to High-Rise: State Housing in Europe since 1850.* London: Routledge.

Power, A. (1997) *Estates on the Edge. The Social Consequences of Mass Housing in Northern Europe.* London: Macmillan.

Prak, N. L. and Priemus, H. (1984) *Post-War Public Housing in Trouble.* Delft: DUP.

Prak, N.L. and Priemus, H. (1985) A Model for the Analysis of the Decline of Postwar Housing. *The International Journal of Urban and Regional Research*, 10, pp. 1–7.

Rosenbaum, J., Stroh, L. and Flynn, C. (1998) Lake Parc Place: A Study of Mixed-Income Housing. *Housing Policy Debate*, 9 (4), pp. 703–72.

Tunstall, R. (2003) 'Mixed Tenure' Policy in the UK: Privatisation, Pluralism or Euphemism? *Housing, Theory and Society*, 20, pp. 153–9.

Turkington, R., Van Kempen, R. and Wassenberg, F. (Eds) (2004) *High-Rise Housing in Europe. Current Trends and Future Prospects.* Delft: DUP Science.

Van Beckhoven, E. and Van Kempen, R. (2003) Social Effects of Urban Restructuring: A Case Study in Amsterdam and Utrecht, the Netherlands. *Housing Studies*, 18 (6), pp. 853–75.

Van Kempen, E. and Musterd, S. (1991) High-Rise Housing: Some Research and Policy Implications. *Housing Studies*, 6, pp. 83–95.

Van Kempen, R. (2008) Social Cohesion, Social Mix, and Urban Policies in the Netherlands. Paper for the Housing Studies Spring Conference in York, 2–4 April 2008.

Van Kempen, R., Bolt, G. and Slob, A. (2008) Displacement Effects of Urban Restructuring: A Case Study of Three Dutch Cities. Paper for the UAA-Conference in Baltimore (MA), 23–26 April 2008.

Van Kempen, R., Dekker, K., Hall, S. and Tosics, I. (Eds) (2005) *Restructuring Large Housing Estates in European Cities*. Bristol: The Policy Press.

Wacquant, L. (2008) *A Comparative Sociology of Advanced Marginality*. Cambridge: Polity Press.

Wilson, W. J. (1987) *The Truly Disadvantaged: The Inner City, the Underclass, and Public Policy*. Chicago: Chicago University Press.

Index